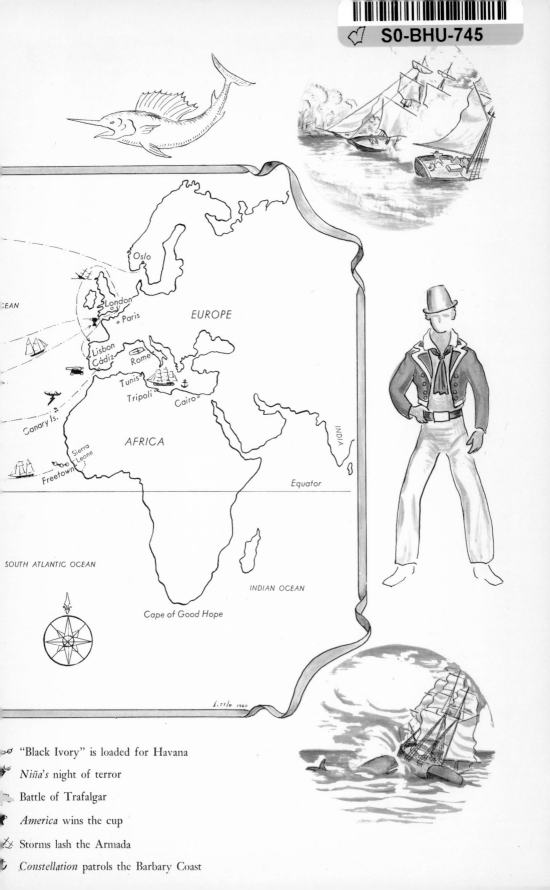

Oslo

London
Paris

EUROPE

Lisbon
Cádiz
Rome

Tunis

Tripoli
Cairo

Canary Is.

AFRICA

Sierra
Leone
Freetown

Equator

OCEAN

INDIA

SOUTH ATLANTIC OCEAN

INDIAN OCEAN

Cape of Good Hope

Little 1960

"Black Ivory" is loaded for Havana

Niña's night of terror

Battle of Trafalgar

America wins the cup

Storms lash the Armada

Constellation patrols the Barbary Coast

TALL SHIPS AND GREAT CAPTAINS

TALL SHIPS AND

by A. B. C. WHIPPLE

Illustrations by G. A. LITTLE

GREAT CAPTAINS

A narrative of famous sailing ships through the ages and the courageous men who sailed, fought or raced them across the seas

HARPER & BROTHERS · PUBLISHERS · NEW YORK

CONTENTS

The author wishes to thank *Life* Magazine for permission to use the chapter on the *America*, which first appeared in *Life* under the title "$20 Million for Revenge"; and *American Heritage* for permission to use the chapter on the *Constellation*, which first appeared in *American Heritage* under the title "The Hard Luck Frigate."

I

From the Vikings to the FLYING CLOUD

The first sailing vessels . . . Marauders from Scotland to Rome . . . Rolling down to the Crusades . . . The full-rigged ship is born . . . A floating tennis court . . . England's "wooden walls" . . . The glorious clippers . . . End of a great age

In a little port town on England's Dorset coast one day in the latter part of the eighth century, every inhabitant was alerted at the sight of three weird vessels ghosting into the harbor and up to the beach. Never had the villagers seen such vessels before. They were long and narrow. Their sharp sterns rose high in the air like tails. Their bows rose even higher, ending in elaborate carved heads of serpents. Along the vessels' sides were multicolored shields. But the outstanding characteristic of each craft was its tall mast, which carried a huge, bellying, brilliantly colored square sail. The strange vessels swarmed with men.

The merchants of the village happily prepared for some trading. The women and children flocked to the waterfront to gawk at the odd spectacle. The port reeve, as was his custom, made ready to collect his dues. He was the first to approach the strangers.

It was over before the villagers realized what had happened. The invaders killed the port reeve, rushed through the streets nearest the waterfront killing and looting, loaded booty and captives aboard their vessels, backed into the water with their long oars and loosed their big square sails to the breeze. So fast did the strange ships move away that the villagers could not have caught them if they had set out. Before nightfall the last brilliant sail had disappeared below the horizon, and the English village was left to count its losses, bury its dead and mourn the fate of those kidnaped across the waters.

This incident, a Viking raid on England's Dorset coast, marks one of the earliest voyages in the history of sail.

To be sure, there had been earlier ships. Many of them carried sails. But not until the incredibly tough and daring Vikings did ships go on open ocean voyages depending primarily upon their sails. The earliest known vessels, even including Ulysses' craft, carried sails. In 4700 B.C., sixty-six centuries ago, Egyptian boats made of reeds carried small sails to aid the slaves, who paddled the vessels like canoes. The later Egyptian galleys also carried sails, as did the heavy warships of the Phoenicians and the Greeks, with their rows of galley slaves at the oars and battering rams at the bows. Even the biremes and triremes, their double- and triple-banked rows of oarsmen straining to the beat of a drum, carried sails. But always the sail was an aid; never was it as important as the oarsmen. These were still the days when the art of using a sail in any direction other than directly downwind had not been mastered, when oarsmen were more manageable than the elements, and when slave power was nearly as cheap as the wind. There were a few exceptions to this course of ship development—the Greeks had a clumsy, round-bottomed merchantman with very few oarports, and the Romans had an even cruder copy of this vessel. But neither was as efficient as the galley, and for centuries manpower was more important to a ship than wind power. The sailing vessel had not really been born—until the eighth century and the Vikings.

The Viking ships also had oarsmen. But the difference now was that while the Mediterranean oarsmen propelled the vessel, the Viking oarsmen served as crew, rowing only when the ship could not sail. And rarely was this the case. The Viking ship was a completely new naval design. It bore scarcely any resemblance to its flat-bottomed, bluff-bowed, oar-propelled predecessors. The Viking ship was a sailing ship, molded to the run of the sea and shaped to cut through the water. With shallow draft, upswept bow and stern and low center of gravity, the Viking ship rode the waves like a gull, high and dry. It had a beam one-fifth its length; it had smooth, clean lines and, for the first time, a keel. Its element was the sea.

The thirty examples that have been discovered or dug up indicate that these vessels were generally seventy-five to a hundred feet long, with one giant perhaps running to three hundred feet. The hulls, weathered dark by centuries of burial, once were brilliantly colored. They were clinker built (with overlapping construction) and sometimes each strake was a different color. The famous Bayeux Tapestry shows these many-hued Viking vessels, including one that was all gold. At their bows were the great serpents' heads. In fact, there is evidence that the Vikings called their vessels serpents. Some of the ships were so named: *Long Snake; Long Worm.* Others carried more majestic and romantic names: *Lion of the Waves; Deer of the Surf.*

But the vital part of the Viking ship was its sail. Raised on a tall mast just forward of amidships, rigged with blocks and halyards, the Viking sail filled before the strong North Sea winds and took the long, sharp vessels racing across the water. The Vikings put much emphasis on their sails, even giving them separate names: *Cloth of the Wind; Tapestry of the Masthead; The Fine Shirt of the Tree.* More important, the Viking mast had shrouds, ropes at the sides which could only have been there to support the mast when the sail was canted about and the wind came from abeam. That meant that the Vikings, first of all mariners, actually sailed their vessels, using the wind from abeam instead of coasting before it when it blew from directly astern. This was the difference between using the wind as an aid to oar power and using the wind to sail.

And as the Viking ship sailed, heeling over in the howling winds, the Vikings raised their low gunwales by stacking their shields along the rack built at the rail. Like the striped hulls and the colored sails, the shields bore vivid heraldic designs. The outsides, red and black or yellow and black, were turned to the sea to denote warlike intentions; the white insides were turned to the sea if the voyage was a peaceful one.

There were not many peaceful voyages. From the time of their first visit to England in the eighth century, described above, the Norsemen ranged farther and farther from home. They had no compass nor any charts except perhaps the crudest maps. Yet for two centuries they traveled up around Scotland, down the western shores of England, along the coast of Europe, into the Mediterranean and even out across the stormy Atlantic to Iceland and what was later to be North America. And nearly everywhere they went, they went as marauders.

Striking at Scotland, the Vikings sacked a monastery at Lindisfarne, then rounded the island and swept down the west coast, looting another monastery at Iona and killing all the monks. By the ninth century they were working over the coast of Europe. Sailing and rowing all the way up the Seine, they reached the Frankish capital that is now Paris. But Paris then was confined to the island (Ile de la Cité) and was heavily walled and fortified; the Norse attackers were evidently driven off.

Spain was next. Scarcely any large coastal town was spared. Against the Spanish Army, then one of the world's best, the Vikings fought their way up the Seville. When they finally retreated, the Spaniards built ships to fight them off if they should return. They did return, and a series of early naval battles were fought off the Spanish coast.

Swinging south, the Vikings sailed through the Pillars of Hercules and into the Mediterranean. They raided the coast of North Africa, then turned north to attack Spain and France again. Here they took some Moorish prisoners, whom they called "blue men" and whom they later put ashore at Ireland. But first the expedition paused for rest and recuperation in the marshes of the Rhone Delta. Then the Vikings launched their most ambitious campaign—against Rome.

One of the leaders of the Norsemen was named Hastings, and it was he who devised a Trojan horse style of attack. Messengers went overland to the city, carrying the news that a mariner was dying and wanted the last rites. The priests found Hastings himself playing the part so well that when he "died" the next day, they agreed to bury him in the city and allowed the small army of Vikings to accompany their leader's "body" to the church for the ceremony. So the Vikings penetrated the city's walls. In the cathedral Hastings leaped from his coffin—the signal for the rest of the Vikings to throw off their black robes and draw their swords. The defenders, taken by surprise, were overwhelmed, and the Norsemen looted the city before making their escape. It was only later that Hastings and his men found they had captured the wrong city. It was not Rome, but the nearby city of Luna.

While some Viking fleets were sailing through the sunlit seas of the Mediterranean, others were driving before the wild winds of the North Atlantic. In 861 one fleet of Viking ships discovered Iceland. Eric the Red, searching for land farther west, found Greenland in 982. His sons pushed on to the continent. Here too, wherever they found habitation, the Vikings attacked, killed, plundered and took prisoners. The treasure was brought back to the Norse chiefs; the captives, called thralls, were put to work on Norse farms.

But gradually, as if responding to some cycle, ship design began to tend away from the sharp, clean vessels of the Vikings and toward the fatter tubs that would follow. The last real link with the Viking ships was William the Conqueror's *Mora*. She had the same serpent-like bow, the same high, sharp-ended stern, the same single mast and huge square sail. Rows of shields lined her sides, and a lantern burned at her masthead at night for the rest of the fleet to follow her course across the Channel. But the long, slim lines of the Viking ship had undergone a transformation. The *Mora* was wide, capacious and a great deal slower. The day of the seaworthy Viking vessel had passed. Bigger ships would be built, but not for centuries would the maritime world see the like of the Viking ships again.

The next three centuries, in fact, were spent learning to sail. The full-rigged sailing ship as we know it was not developed until early in the fifteenth century. From the time of William the Conqueror's *Mora* until the three-masted carrack there was an expanding commerce and innumerable battles were fought on the sea. But the merchantmen were little better than barges, and the warships were floating forts. Vessels increased in size, usually more in breadth than length. Shrouds became more numerous, permitting a larger sail area. Drawings, tapestries and seals of medieval times show the first reef points for shortening sail and the first bonnets for increasing sail area. The Vikings' starboard steering oar was replaced by the stern rudder, permitting a ship to heel over farther and sail closer to the wind in rough weather. Probably the best-known characteristic of these times was the castle that rose on bow and stern as the bulk of the ship increased. But more important was the bowsprit, which stretched the sail area forward and aided the ship to point up more efficiently than ever before. Slowly man was learning the principle of the sailing ship.

With the rudder now directly abaft, a vessel no longer had to be double-ended, but could have a wide stern. And as all these developments helped a vessel to sail instead of simply riding before the wind, the hull could be made deeper. So developed the capacious vessels that sailed down the European coast and across the Mediterranean to the Holy Land and the Crusades.

A typical style of this time was the French nef. Like other medieval vessels, it was still a long way from being a real ship; it had only one stubby mast and carried only one sail of any importance. It could scarcely tack into the wind, and often it was unable to reach its destination at all unless the wind changed or the crew got out the sweeps. But while the nef was no sailing ship, it was a comfortable floating castle.

Some nefs were nearly a hundred feet long, with more than forty feet at the beam. They carried as many as a thousand passengers, a selected few of them in medieval luxury. Along both sides were private cabins, and at the stern were the choice apartments reserved for royalty. Their windows looked out on the sea, their cabin doors fronting on a rectangular deck that served as a courtyard. Bulkheads were painted in gay colors and hung with the shields and bucklers of the traveling nobility. In the manner of the times, the noble passengers promenaded in this courtyard, shielded from the sun by sails slung over the deck. As dinner was served in this gently rolling plaza, with the king and his court enthroned at the stern and the one huge sail emblazoned with its red cross filling above them, it must have been a pleasant voyage when the sun was high and the breeze held fair. But when the wind blew foul and the nef pitched and rolled and boarding seas filled the central deck, the Crusaders must have wished they had made the journey overland. And their horses, in their stables below, must have suffered far more. Such a voyage could take months; one wonders how the Crusaders retained enough strength to smite the infidel.

Despite such voyages the sailing ship remained a crude and cumbersome tub for more than three centuries. At the turn of the fifteenth century the rigging suddenly became more complicated as more sails were added. And the sailing ship went from one mast to three with no transition period of two masts. Evidently this was because shipbuilders, declining to move the single mast in order to add another, left it there and placed one at the bow and one at the stern to balance each other. With the extra masts came more than two extra sails—a

forerunner of the jib, a tiny topsail and others to add to the new main-
sails fore and aft. Now at last the full-rigged ship had arrived. It
changed little in basic design for four more centuries. A sailor aboard
the fifteenth-century *Niña* would have had to learn little more to step
aboard the nineteenth-century *Victory* and acquit himself well.

The *Niña*, the first real sailing ship to become famous, was a caravel.
Unlike many vessels of the time, including many caravels, which were
square-rigged, the *Niña* carried lateen fore-and-aft sails (triangular
sails whose yards extended forward of the masts). But they were
quickly altered, as we shall see in the next chapter. Larger than many
of the earlier types, the caravel was still small in relation to today's
ships; the *Niña*, for example, was a great deal shorter than the *Queen
Elizabeth* is wide. Soon after Columbus' time the caravel and the
carrack had been superseded by the galleon, the eminently seaworthy
vessels that led the Spanish Armada against England (Chapter III),
carried the settlers to the New World and brought the wealth of the
New World home. Designed lower to the water than the carrack
and caravel, the galleon was more maneuverable and sometimes faster.
Still, the galleon could be fairly easy prey for the quick little fighting
sloops favored by the pirates along the Spanish Main, as will be demonstrated in Chapter IV.

The galleon carried forward the trend toward combining capacity
and sailing qualities. It also carried on the trend toward grandeur. This
trend reached its culmination in a curious competition between an
English and French ship in the sixteenth century—the *Great Harry* and
Le Grand François.

The *Great Harry* was actually a nickname; she was *Henri Grâce à
Dieu*. She was well over two hundred feet long; she carried four
masts (fore, main, mizzen and bonaventure) and spread a cloud of
canvas. For perhaps the first time, a ship had masts that were not single
poles but lengths locked together to gain height. She had eight decks,
and along her sides and at bow and stern she carried, in two rows, a
total of 184 guns. Virtually every inch of her was carved, tooled,
decorated, crenelated or otherwise embellished. At her bow, on her
poop and even amidships she had stout wooden castles complete with

towers. She was the first and greatest pride of the British Navy, and she carried the royal flag from the time of Henry VII to Elizabeth. What she added in grandeur, however, she evidently lost in sailing qualities. She was an extremely uncomfortable ship in a heavy wind, and when Henry VIII sailed in her across the Channel to the Field of the Cloth of Gold, he chose another ship for the return voyage.

Nevertheless the *Great Harry* was the envy of the other navies. Attempts to outdo her were made by Sweden, Portugal and the Knights of Malta. But the most ambitious copy was ordered by Francis I of France.

Francis asked for a ship twice the size of the *Great Harry*. What the designers came up with was a vessel of two thousand tons' burden and about three hundred feet, only one-third larger. In 1532, a little more than a decade after the *Great Harry*'s launching, the keel of *Le Grand François* was laid down in a creek which is now a yacht basin at Le Havre. When she was finished, in only a year, she was the largest vessel afloat. Of her four masts, the mainmast was twenty-five feet in circumference. She had fore and after castles, and a windmill at her bow to power a grindstone so she would not have to carry perishable flour in her hold. She also had a baker's oven, a forge and a private chapel done all in gilt. Between her castles was a tennis court, protected by an awning to keep the balls from flying into the sea.

On September 22, 1533, riding the equinoctial tide, *Le Grand François* was triumphantly towed across the harbor toward the sea. But the triumph was short-lived. On a bar halfway across the harbor she ground to a halt. Nothing would move her. Vessels crowded around her trying to pull her loose. A girdle of barrels and hogsheads at her sides did not raise her enough to help. Finally she was hauled off backward and returned to her berth. Two months later a hurricane caught her unprepared, pounded against her high sides and capsized her. She lay there for years, until she was eventually broken up, without ever getting to sea.

Similar expressions of naval exhibitionism followed, notably England's *Sovereign of the Seas*, one-fifth of whose cost was for decoration. A special tax had to be levied to pay for her, and she was thus a major contributing factor to the downfall of Charles I. Cromwell kept her, however, and she proved to be a formidable battleship. After the Restoration she was stripped of much of her gold and red decoration. The time was gradually approaching when designers of British ships-of-the-line would place less emphasis on a ship's embellishments and more on her sailing and fighting qualities.

But, unfortunately, not enough. During this same period the French ships were as lavishly decorated as the British (one French three-decker, the *Monarque*, carried twenty-seven wooden statues, all larger than life size, on her stern). The French vessels made better warships, though, and by the late seventeenth century British designers were copying the lines of French ships.

For centuries the British merchant marine had enjoyed a huge monopoly (largely through the British East India Company) and had had no incentive for improving the sailing characteristics or the speed of their ships. The superiority of the French warships was another matter. The time was long since gone when war at sea consisted of ramming the enemy or propelling a floating fort alongside for boarding. Heavier guns made the difference; by 1513 the first ship had been sunk by cannon fire from another ship, and now the speed and maneuverability of a warship was important.

Invulnerability remained equally important, and so developed the huge, stately ship-of-the-line, of which Nelson's *Victory* was the greatest example. Even the *Victory* bore a close resemblance to warships nearly two hundred years before her time. But she was a better sailer, and her sides were so stout that she became famous as the "wooden walls of England." Nothing, it was thought, could subdue the British Navy with great impregnable ships like these, particularly after the *Victory*'s performance at Trafalgar, as related in Chapter V. But stout walls were not enough, as history was about to demonstrate.

For the world was at the threshold of a revolution in ship design. Just as the Vikings launched the age of sail with the first real sailing vessel, just as the age of maturity came with the first full-rigged ships like the *Niña*, so the sailing ship reached its perfection in the nineteenth century. If the centuries-long period from the Vikings to the

Victory embraced most of the history of sail, the nineteenth century was the great age of sail.

Its beginnings were in America. Until the late eighteenth century ship design in the colonies was largely a copy of ship design in Europe. American merchantmen varied little from such sturdy vessels as the *Mayflower*, the *Goodspeed* or the *Arke* which had brought the settlers to the New World. But gradually Americans began to break away from tradition in shipbuilding as in other ways. While naval design in England, complacently protected by the "wooden walls" of its navy and the monopoly of its "John Company," subsided into a period of stagnation, while ship development in the rest of Europe progressed little more, the Americans launched their revolution in the age of sail.

They had the wherewithal. Shipyards from Maine to Maryland were managed by salty characters who knew the sea as a farmer does his fields, and who had been brought up in the spirit of adventure and experiment. America was rich in forests that provided hardwood timbers and tall masts, and as the American South developed excellent cotton her ship designers converted it into the lightest, strongest sails the world had ever seen. But most of all America had the incentive. Not only were there no monopolies or restrictive trade patterns to hobble her shipbuilding and trading, but the European monopolies forced her to compete in the only way she could: with better and faster ships. The Yankee character was taking shape; if there was money to be made in swift ships, swift ships would be built.

As in commerce, so in war. The Revolution and the War of 1812 had an enormous effect on warship design. It did not seem so at first. Of the thirty-five vessels put to sea by the American Continental Navy, exactly one remained in American hands at the Revolution's end; meanwhile the British lost only five warships, two of which were shortly recaptured. The legendary John Paul Jones was the only American captain to make a glorious name for himself. But the paradox was that while the rest of the American Navy was making a fool of itself, the American privateers were making fools of the British. In the separate American states and in some cities Americans, disgusted by the Navy's performance—and attracted by the promise of financial gain—were subscribing to build their own ships and sail them against the enemy, keeping the prizes and cargoes for themselves. The privateers were small, maneuverable and extremely fast. They concentrated on British merchantmen, fleeing like the wind before Britain's big, lumbering naval vessels. By choking off the enemy's supply lines they played a vital part in winning the Revolution.

This also was incentive at work, since the rich prospects of the privateers lured most of America's best shipbuilding and ship-handling talent away from America's naval vessels. But even though the captains and seamen of the Continental Navy were no match for the British officers and men of Nelson's era, American naval vessels were proving themselves spry and fast. Since they were not stout enough to withstand the traditional broadside-to-broadside naval battles fought by the British, those that were caught were quickly battered into submission. But catching many of them was sufficiently difficult so that often an American prize was sailed home to England to have its lines taken off for British study and emulation, before the ship was sent off to sea under British command. American sailors did poorly against the British in the Revolution; but American ship designers, of naval craft and privateers as well, were already pointing the way.

By the War of 1812 the pattern was clear to all. From the start, the new American frigates were smashing British warships to hulks. One American frigate, the *Constellation,* had an odder story, as described in Chapter VI. But in general the American naval vessels of this war were better designed, better sailed and even better armed than the enemy. Within a few months of the outbreak of the war everyone knew that Britain was no longer the greatest naval power in the world. And if there had been any doubt, it was removed by the harassing activities of the American privateers, which were even better than those of the Revolution, as related in Chapter VII.

The steady trend toward the sharp, fast, light ship culminated in the famous Baltimore clipper model. This was at once the perfection of small-ship design and the precursor of the big clipper ships of the mid-century. The Baltimore clippers, and others that varied the pattern slightly, were the glamour ships of the War of 1812. But many of them shortly went to the opposite extreme; after the War of 1812 hundreds of successful privateers became successful slavers. And so fast were they that they could be run down only by other vessels on the sharp Baltimore model. We shall see more about the slave trade in Chapter VIII.

The Americans pressed their advantage, developing speed for legal as well as illicit commerce, for passenger packets and for combined trade and exploration with their own East Indiamen. Then came an important milestone. In 1836 the Baltimore clipper model was enlarged and refined into a full-fledged clipper ship, the three-masted *Ann McKim*. In a time when large, world-girdling cargo carriers were still apple-bowed, the sharp-bowed, sleek, low-freeboard *Ann McKim* was a breakthrough in ship design. She was the fastest thing afloat. She could carry nearly full sail in a gale, and she could ghost along in a near calm. She raced down around Cape Horn and out across the Pacific in the China trade and astonished all the skippers who watched her sweep by. But the *Ann McKim* was not quite the clipper ship in its full glory. She sacrificed too much cargo area for her speed. That problem was shortly to be surmounted, and the revolution in ship design would be complete.

It came with the glorious clipper ships of the mid-nineteenth century. Here was the final triumph of the sailing ship. Such clippers as the *Sea Witch*, the *Challenge* and the *Flying Cloud*, whose story is told in Chapter XI, were as different from their merchantmen predecessors as the jet is from the propeller-driven airplane. Nearly everything about the clippers, from the lighter but stronger masts and spars spreading forty thousand square feet of sail to the long, lean hulls, represented advances greater than in previous centuries of ship design. The clipper ships were freighters; but they sailed faster than anything else on the sea, and they set speed records that have not been matched to this day by anything under sail. In fact, some of their records were not exceeded by steamers until comparatively recent times. Some of the clippers ran up average speeds that are still not matched by steamers today. The clipper ships were not only the fastest ever built, but also the most beautiful. The fastest and most beautiful of them all was the *Flying Cloud*.

Spurred by incentive again, this time the Gold Rush, the clippers sped down around Cape Horn and up the west coast, setting records that were not believed when they were first reported. Some of them ran out to China and the Indies, where they took cargoes off the dock alongside the slower British vessels, which were forced to take what was left and accept lower rates. The British, who had had to copy the lines of American ships in earlier days, were now reduced to the further humiliation of ordering their clippers built in the U.S.

The clipper ship was at once the finest expression and the end of the great age of sail. In America the clipper was so successful that it blinded most shippers to the inevitable. Now, finally, the British were more foresighted. They turned to steam, while the Americans kept on banking on their clippers. The Americans had their reasons, for a time. The early steamships were slow, expensive and almost as unpredictable as the wind; nearly all of them had to carry auxiliary sails. On many long ocean runs the fastest clippers continued to beat the steamships. The packet ship *Dreadnaught*, for example, nicknamed "The Wild Boat of the Atlantic," competed successfully against steam on the Atlantic's "Railroad Route to Europe" for thirty years. And in the year 1853 occurred an event which was significant both for its echoes and its forecast: the clipper ship *Sovereign of the Seas*, like the seventeenth-century *Sovereign* a beauty but a beauty in her basic lines rather than her decorations, beat the Cunard steamer *Canada* on a run from New York to Liverpool. The history of the sailing ship had come full circle; for this was one of the last times that the clippers showed complete superiority over the steamships. The plodding but steady tortoise had beaten the fleet but flighty hare.

And the tortoise slowly improved its speed. Meanwhile the Civil War, the diminishing priorities on fast delivery, and the opening of the American West rendered the clipper impractical. America turned away from the sea. A few examples of her maritime successes carried on. The fat, slow, wonderfully utilitarian whalers—such ships as the one whose story is told in Chapter X—continued to sail to the ends of the earth until well into the twentieth century. The famous Gloucester schooners, as fine a combination of speed and utility on a smaller scale as the clippers had been, sailed out to the Grand Banks and raced each other back until only a couple of generations ago. American pilot boats carried on and developed the Baltimore model, and one of America's first pleasure yachts, built along these lines, started the long tradition of the America's Cup—for a curious reason explained in Chapter IX. Today's American yachts have defended that tradition by beating off seventeen concerted attempts to win the Cup away from the U.S. But these few examples stand virtually alone. America's maritime supremacy disappeared even more rapidly than it had developed. The best clippers of the end of the nineteenth century were built in England and Germany, and the ocean-long races now made famous such names as the *Cutty Sark* and the *Thermopylae* and the *Taeping;* the *Sea Witch* and the *Challenge* and the *Flying Cloud* were fading memories. The new clippers were designed for economical runs at great distances that were still impractical under steam —to China for tea and Australia for wool and hides. But they were fast, and they staged some thrilling races; the *Taeping* and the *Ariel* raced each other halfway around the world in four months, and finished in the Thames within a few minutes of each other. Races like this went on for nearly another century, before steam finally drove sail from the commerce of the sea. But these sailing ships were only refinements of the American clippers. They carried on somewhat longer, after American shippers defaulted. They were, however, only the knell of an age that had already died.

The intense progress and activity of this last period in America was of course in the mainstream of ship design. In the tributaries were many vessels that remained unchanged, and many remain so even today. Throughout the entire history of sail, from the time of the *Niña* to the *Flying Cloud,* many specialized types of vessels in many parts of the world went on virtually unaltered. Probably the best-known example is the Chinese junk; her high sides, flat bottom, watertight compartments and many-battened sails are the same as they were centuries ago. Like other specialized craft, she was developed for her own type of work; and her odd sails, combining some of the advantages of both square and fore-and-aft rigs, permit her to sail closer-hauled than nearly any other ship—a particularly useful aid in the innumerable bays and coves along the Asian coastlines. So well designed was the Chinese junk many centuries ago that even today no more efficient craft has been found for her kind of work, and in fact many junks are now appearing in American waters as pleasure craft.

Similar special types range from the Javanese proa to the Portuguese moleta, from Siam's balon to Italy's tartan. The Persian Gulf still has dhows, garukhas and sambuks. The fishermen of Saint-Malo still sail three-masted, lug-sailed chasse-marées. The Dutch sail botters and boyers, tjalks and hoogarts, schokkers and schuyts. The most picturesque example of a specialist's survival was the great Venetian galley—rowed by a hundred or more oarsmen, brilliantly decorated, her lines swooping into a towering stern and her mast carrying one enormous lateen sail. Well into the eighteenth century her long, narrow shape could be seen gliding across the Mediterranean, a spectacularly beautiful anachronism.

For even in the eighteenth century she was of an era long gone by. The great age of sail that was then dawning was exemplified in the clipper *Flying Cloud*, her thirty white cotton sails ballooning before the trades, her bow slicing through the sea and shaking off the spray as she took a thousand tons of cargo flying down the Atlantic to the Horn. Hers was an age of beauty and much more. Like the entire span of the sailing ship's history, it was an age of bravery and adventure, of commerce and war, of discovery and progress. The great ships whose stories you are about to read were selected because they epitomize the history of sail—a period in which man explored, conquered and settled this planet, over the broad and turbulent highways of the sea

II

Caravel: The NIÑA

Departure at dawn . . . The menacing Sargasso Sea . . .
"All night the sound of birds" . . . "Tierra!" . . . The
Niña *becomes flagship . . . Night of terror . . . Home to*
Palos

Her origin is unknown. But she happened to be lying at anchor in the river Tagus in Spain on a fateful day in 1492 and so became famous for all time. And she proved, in a desperate battle for her life, that she was one of the great ships of history.

She was the little caravel *Niña*, and she came on history's scene when a young sailor named Christopher Columbus traveled to the Spanish seaport town of Palos with a curious message. He presented the letter to the town's mayor and councilors. The letter reminded them that "for certain things done and committed by you to our disservice you were condemned and obligated by our Council to provide us for a twelvemonth with two equipped caravels at your own proper charge and expense. . . ." The letter now claimed the forfeit, the caravels to be put at the disposal of the bearer of the letter, Christopher Columbus. The letter was signed: "Given in our city of Granada on the 30th day of April, year of Our Lord Jesus Christ 1492.

I the Queen

I the King"

At this order from Ferdinand and Isabella, the mayor and councilors of Palos had no choice. So the *Niña* and the *Pinta*, which were anchored in the harbor, were delivered over to Columbus. While they were being outfitted, at the expense of the local ship chandlers to whom Columbus also brought royal decrees, the young captain-to-be went looking for a third vessel. In the Rio Tinto nearby, he found her. She was the *Santa Maria*, a ship, larger than the two caravels and a likely-appearing choice for his flagship.

It took ten weeks for the three vessels to be readied for the voyage Columbus planned. He estimated that they would be gone about a year. Where? Out across the unknown ocean. It is a sign of sailors' courage in those days—and perhaps of the hard times—that he had no trouble enlisting his crews. It seemed a short time before the morning of Friday, August 3, when Columbus and his officers and crew trooped into Palos' Church of St. George. There they made their confessions, received absolution and took communion. In the near-darkness they knelt at their prayers. The church was lit only by flickering tapers. Dawn had not yet broken. Columbus wanted all on board before sunrise, to catch the morning tide.

It was still dark when the men made their last farewells on Palos' wharves and climbed down into their boats. They were rowed out to vessels that were only looming hulls in the black water. It was the time of faint, cold light in the sky, half an hour before sunrise. The families watching on the shore could hear the soft call of the chantey, the creak of the anchor windlass and the splashing as the anchors were cleaned of the harbor mud. Then, slowly, the three ships got under way, bound down the river Saltés to the uncharted sea.

From the *Niña*, as from the *Pinta* and the *Santa Maria*, only the rough outlines of roofs against the sky could be discerned. There was scarcely a breath of wind. As the sun finally rose, it was hidden by clouds. Men heaved at the long sweeps to move the *Niña* enough so she could be pointed toward the river. Almost imperceptibly the little fleet moved downriver with the ebbing tide. Now some of the sailors' kin could be seen walking along the water's edge, easily keeping pace with the creeping vessels and accompanied by most of the small boys of Palos. But by the time the fleet had gone a mile or more, most of the landsmen had been left behind. The vessels inched past the monastery at a Robida, and on the *Niña*'s deck the men could hear, as if in farewell, the voices of the friars as they chanted their liturgical hymn. Slowly the sounds died as the *Niña*, the *Pinta* and the *Santa Maria* dropped down the remaining stretch of river and across the bar into the open Atlantic.

A breeze was waiting for them. But it blew straight in from the sea. Caught aback, the three vessels could not make any headway. So they were swung about parallel to the shore and worked down along the coast. All day, at a speed of about four knots, the *Niña*, the *Pinta* and the *Santa Maria* followed the coastline, until just at sunset the wind hauled into the north. Now they could swing about from south to southwest and run off from the land. When night fell the lanterns aboard the *Santa Maria*, Columbus' flagship, could be seen from the *Niña* and the *Pinta*, following in her train. All that night, under a clear, starlit sky, the fleet left land astern, bound on a course south and by west. And already the men aboard the *Niña* had to shorten sail in order to keep from running up on the *Santa Maria*.

By morning the crews of all three vessels had settled down to a fairly well-organized routine. Crews were apportioned in their watches. The same course they had followed through the night, south and by west, was leading them to the Canary Islands, where they could pause after this "shakedown" leg before plunging out across the Atlantic. The voyage to the Canaries should take about a week. Meanwhile the crews of the expedition could settle back and learn the ways of their vessels.

The *Santa Maria* was the flagship only because she was the largest; even on this first short leg of the voyage Columbus could see that she had few of the sailing qualities of the *Niña* and the *Pinta*. A ship instead of a caravel like them, the *Santa Maria* was roughly 130 tons; her exact measurements are not known. She was less than a hundred feet in length, with a draught of about six and a half feet. On her deck, at bow and stern, were castles, survivors of earlier days when battles were fought from floating forts. The *Santa Maria*'s most striking feature was a towering mainmast, all in one piece, rising from amidships and taller than the ship was long. The main yard, which held the principal sail on this huge mast, was itself longer than the *Santa Maria*'s keel. It was made from two regular spars, tapered and joined together, and was hauled aloft on one halyard, by nearly the entire crew. Her foremast and mizzenmast were much shorter than her mainmast. The *Santa Maria* carried square sails on her main and foremasts and a lateen sail on the mizzen, plus small square sails on the bowsprit and above the main. On one particularly good sailing day, according to Columbus' journal, he supplemented these sails with one from the ship's boat, rigging it on the poop just aft of the mizzen.

Still she could not keep up with either the *Niña* or the *Pinta*. The latter was square-rigged like the *Santa Maria*, but apparently built at Palos instead of Galicia. She was about half the tonnage of the *Santa*

Maria, and approximately seventy-five feet long, with a twenty-five-foot beam. Her owner was Cristobal Quintero, who sailed aboard her on this voyage as a seaman. Evidently he had no choice when the town fathers commandeered his ship to fill the royal order. And when, three days out, her rudder broke loose, her captain, Martín Alonzo Pinzón, told Columbus that it had been broken by Quintero, in hopes that the *Pinta* would be sent home. She was not sent home, even though she started to leak badly before reaching the Canaries. Already Columbus may have sensed that the *Pinta* would be a trouble ship.

Perhaps he also sensed this early that the *Niña* would be the queen of the fleet. Her real name was not *Niña* at all. It was *Santa Clara*. But she became better known, and has come down through history, by her nickname, which in the current fashion was coined from that of her owner. He was Juan Niño, of Moguer, a town near Palos, where the little caravel was built. Juan Niño was her captain as well, and when she was commandeered for the expedition he elected to come along as master.

The *Niña* was of sixty tons' burden by the old measurement (used for ships until the mid-nineteenth century) which meant that she could carry sixty tuns of wine in her hold. Her length was about seventy feet, her breadth about twenty-three feet, her draught about six feet. She had one deck where the *Santa Maria* had a second deck forward. But the *Niña* probably had a raised quarter deck with quarters for the captain's cabin. Her rig was fore-and-aft, with long tapering spars jutting ahead of each mast. This was the lateen rig, one of the first designs and one that is still seen today in the Mediterranean and the Far East.

As a "fore-and-after" the *Niña* could work better to windward than the square-rigged *Santa Maria* and *Pinta*. But she did not sail as conveniently before the wind as the square-rigged vessels, fast as she was. And the prevailing winds from Palos to the Canaries were mostly from astern. On such a course, with such winds, a fore-and-after would spend most of her time yawing and threatening to jibe. The *Niña's* helmsmen no doubt complained to her captain, and no doubt the complaints went on up to Columbus himself—because at the Canaries the *Niña's* rig was altered from fore-and-aft to square sails. Thus she became a *caravela redonda* instead of a *caravela latina;* but the square rig did not change her designation as a caravel.

Other alterations and repairs were needed too. The shakedown leg of the voyage turned out to be a very good idea, because it uncovered a number of difficulties that would have plagued the expedition if they had not been corrected at the Canaries. The *Pinta's* rudder not only worked loose but threatened to wrench free again after it had been repaired at sea. Her leaks increased until the water was gaining on the pumps. The men in her crew were happy to see the outline of Grand Canary Island against the early morning horizon on August 9. But with dawn the wind disappeared and for three days the fleet drifted in the frustrating calm while the men of the *Pinta* sweated at the pumps and the rest of the fleet's ninety men and boys panted at the long sweeps.

Finally Columbus decided to split up the fleet. He had decided to get rid of the *Pinta* and find a better ship to replace her. So as soon as the wind picked up a bit on the twelfth, he sent orders to Pinzón, the *Pinta's* captain, to take her into Las Palmas, Grand Canary's harbor, while he took the *Niña* and the *Santa María* farther west to Gomera, where he hoped he could find another caravel or ship. That same evening he reached Gomera's harbor of San Sebastián and dropped anchor.

But he could not find the kind of vessel he wanted, so the *Pinta* had to be repaired. Fixing the leaks must have been a messy business because this was before the day of copper plates or antifouling paints; ships' bottoms were impregnated with tallow, pitch and similar substances designed to speed the hull through the water and ward off barnacles and teredo, a warm-water, wood-boring organism. Repairing the rudder meant dismounting a huge slab of wood which projected astern of the vessel and was controlled by a long, heavy tiller. But both of these repairs were made to the *Pinta* while the *Niña* was being rerigged. The *Santa María* evidently did not need such drastic alterations. She had developed a habit of plunging so badly in a heavy sea that she took water over the bow. But a simple shifting of the cargo seemed to correct this. There was plenty of work to do, though, just to make the three vessels shipshape for the long voyage out across the Atlantic.

While the repairs and alterations went on, Columbus was having everything checked: the heavy tarred standing rigging; the hempen running rigging; the crude blocks, which were made by boring holes in chunks of wood; the ballast of sand and cobblestones; the heavy guns, which fired stone cannon balls; the lighter swivel guns designed to repel boarders with showers of twisted iron; the long ashen sweeps which had already been tested in the calm off the Canaries. Each vessel also carried as many as seven anchors. Two working anchors were lashed at each bow, their cables pulled taut through hawseholes to a windlass; these were the bower anchors, and two extras were carried because one or two could be expected to go if the ships were anchored during a storm. Each vessel in the fleet also carried a stream anchor, to keep her headed into the swells which could "roll the sticks out" of such chunky craft; a kedge anchor which could be carried ahead in the boat and dropped, to haul the ship forward in calms in shallow waters; and a huge sheet anchor to be used along with both bowers only in the worst storms. The *Niña* in particular would have use for them all before her voyage was done.

While all the gear was being checked, all the repairs made and the alterations tested, Columbus meanwhile made his last-minute calculations for the course he would lay off across the unknown ocean.

The course he set lay due west from the Canaries. Beyond these islands he knew nothing; nor did any other man. Still, it is surprising how much he had already deduced. He apparently knew from Portuguese and Spanish fishermen that prevailing westerlies would strike him head on and make the voyage extremely difficult in vessels which could not point any closer to the eye of the wind than fifty-six degrees. He no doubt knew as well, from voyages of his own down along the African coast, that smooth northeast trade winds seemed to take over in the latitudes of the north twenties. His plan, then, evidently was to set out from the Canaries (28 degrees North Latitude) and head straight out across the great ocean—to where?

To Asia. A great many schoolbooks still convey the impression that

Christopher Columbus was alone in believing that he could get to
Asia by going west. This is untrue. Virtually no geographer or cartog-
rapher of Columbus' time still believed that the world was flat. All
agreed that it should be possible to reach "the Indies" by sailing west
instead of down around the Cape of Good Hope and east across
the Indian Ocean, the only route then used. In fact, there is no evidence
that Columbus had any difficulty enlisting officers and crews for his
fleet because of any "superstitions" or fears of sailing off the edge of
the world. Even the common sailors of the time regarded this as
nonsense. The main concern of those who were reluctant to sign
on—and those who began to worry later during the voyage—was over
the practicality of the venture. Nearly all of them agreed that it was
possible to get to Asia by sailing west, but most of them felt that this
was the hard way. It might take considerably longer than Columbus
estimated, and the winds might be unfavorable farther out on the
Atlantic. The vessels could not carry stores for an indefinite voyage.
And how was it possible, without being sure of prevailing winds, to
calculate the point of no return? Nevertheless, despite these reserva-
tions, ninety men signed on for the expedition. And Columbus did not
have to go far afield to find them. All but eleven of the men came from
Palos and environs, and none came from farther north than Venice.
Even more impressive, evidently not a crewman of the entire fleet
deserted when opportunity presented itself at the Canaries.

The myth that most of Columbus' men were released prisoners is
simply myth. In all three crews there apparently were only four men
in trouble with the law, and their case was a questionable one. All four
returned safely from the voyage and all four were granted royal
pardons. Far from being outlaws and wharf rats, the men of Columbus'
crews were virtually the pick of the local coastal towns, all experienced
and dependable men.

So much for the legend that Columbus alone believed the world
to be round and that he set off to prove it with a band of superstitious
jailbirds who had been forced aboard. However, Columbus did disagree with the general opinion of the time; the fact is that he did *not*
believe that the world was round. His personal theory was that the
earth was pear-shaped, and thus he planned his course, from the

Canaries to Japan, along what he believed to be the latitudes of favorable winds and around the narrower circumference of the pear. His
prescience was dramatically confirmed only recently; the first significant calculations based on the orbiting of the space satellite Vanguard
I indicated that the earth indeed is roughly pear-shaped, with the narrower circumference at the top (north).

The course-charting, repairing and altering took nearly a month,
with Columbus sailing from Gomera to Grand Canary to check on
the *Pinta*'s progress. Finally all three vessels were convened at Gomera.
And then the day came when Columbus and his officers and men
marched into San Sebastián's Church of the Assumption for a final mass.

It was September 6, nearly dawn, as it had been when the fleet had
left Palos. There were no relatives for lingering good-bys this time,
though a few temporary attachments had no doubt been formed;
Columbus himself is reported to have become infatuated with the
beautiful Doña Beatriz de Peraza y Bobadilla, not yet thirty and the
official governor of the island. The farewells were made quickly. It
was still very early when the anchors were hauled free. The three
vessels gathered way toward the mouth of San Sebastián's harbor.

It was an inauspicious beginning for so historic a voyage. In light
and baffling airs the three vessels worked their way out of the harbor
and off toward the west. All that day, that night and the next day
they drifted and floundered about, waiting for a substantial breeze.
It came in the predawn hours of Saturday, September 8—a fine, strong
northeast wind. But then the caravels had to beat back and forth
waiting for the *Santa Maria*. She was shipping water over her bows
again, and the rest of Saturday was consumed by the efforts to correct
this condition. If it could not be corrected now, there would be no
point in taking the *Santa Maria* farther. So the *Niña* and the *Pinta*
waited while crewmen worked over the flagship, evidently moving
some cargo which had been stowed in the bow just before her
departure.

It was Sunday morning before the fleet could make its getaway.
Now the wind blew steadily out of the northeast. All three vessels were
sailing well. The course was set: due west for the Far East. By sundown on Sunday the men aboard the *Niña* could look astern and watch

the top of the twelve-thousand-foot-high peak of Tenerife disappear
below the horizon. Ahead lay the darkness of the coming night—
and the boundless, watery wastes of the New World.

The first day on the open ocean, with nothing but empty horizon
on every side, was a good one. The wind held steady and the fleet
ran more than a hundred miles, due west. Aboard the *Niña* the crew
had already settled into its daily routine. Watches had been set, to
change at three, seven and eleven instead of the standard four, eight
and twelve known today. Why Columbus chose the odd hours is still
not known. Every half-hour one of the ship's boys chanted a prayer
as he turned the glass. Shaped like the hourglasses of later years, these
took half an hour to drain the sand from top to bottom, and are the
reason why even today ship's time is measured by eight bells for
every four hours, one bell for every half-hour. Other crew members
did their daily stint at the pumps, heaving at the long handles until
a sucking sound told them that the *Niña* was dry except for the bilges
where no pump could reach. Others trimmed the lamps for the coming
night. Others scrubbed the decks with salt water and brushes made
from branches. Others served as lookouts, one of them swaying from
side to side in the little basket perched high on the mainmast. Others
were kept busy trimming sail. Partly so she could be steered more
easily before the wind and partly because she had to be held back to
keep from passing the *Santa Maria*, the *Niña*'s fore-and-aft mizzen and
fore courses were furled and she sailed under her square sails alone.
At the midday change of the watch, 11 A.M., everyone was served
the only hot meal of the day; it was cooked in an open firebox with
a sand bottom and a shield to keep the wind from blowing the burning
coals onto the deck. The type of food they were served was described
by Columbus in his journal: ". . . good biscuit . . . salt flour . . .
wheat . . . wine, salt meat, oil, vinegar, cheese, chickpeas, lentils,
beans, salt fish . . . honey, rice, almonds and raisins." The other
meals amounted to little more than a piece of bread and cheese, washed
down with some water or wine. Tea and coffee were unknown to
Columbus' crew, and in these days Spaniards did not like beer.
The crew of the *Niña*, as of the other two vessels, prayed regularly

during each day. The entire crew assembled for prayers on deck at 7 P.M., at sunset and just before the early evening watch. That first evening on the open ocean they all had reason to praise God. It had been a fine run after the frustrating start. Now the day was fair, the wind steady and almost dead aft, and the little caravel lifted and rolled gently in a following sea while a million stars spangled the dark sky from horizon to horizon. A nearly full moon climbed out of the sea. The Niña's off-watch men found places to sleep on deck. They had no bunks and knew nothing of hammocks; in fact, it would be the Indians of the New World who would introduce the hammock to them. The men did not undress, but simply pulled their hooded smocks up about them and lay down wherever they could. The main hatch was generally preferred because it was flat; the Niña's deck tilted toward the scuppers.

The galley fire was extinguished. Through the dark night the Niña followed the stern lanterns of the Santa Maria, running before the fair trade wind. Aboard the flagship, in his cabin Columbus studied his big sheepskin charts and wrote in his journal. He realized that this was the best part of the voyage and that trying times would come before he would return with the wealth of the East Indies. He could not know, or perhaps even guess, how difficult and in fact desperate the days ahead would be and how close he would come to death. But even at the outset he was preparing for trouble. On Sunday night, September 9, 1492, he noted in his journal that the fleet had "sailed this day 19 leagues." He also noted that he had decided "to count less than the true number, that the crew might not be dismayed." As it turned out, his estimates would provide plenty of margin for error, since mileage at that time was figured only by watching the sea or objects floating past the ship.

The expedition's troubles were indeed soon to start. Little by little the doubts, the suspense and the close quarters of shipboard life began to have their effect. The steady wind that pleased Columbus instead worried many of his crew. If the trade winds out here always blew from this quarter, how were they ever to return home? By September 13, the seventh day out, Columbus and his pilots noticed that their compass needle did not seem to be holding true. When sighted against the North Star it varied as much as a full point on either side. They knew that the North Star itself could vary east of true north. But since they had never sailed in this part of the earth before, they did not know that the North Star has a westerly variation too. All they knew was that on one sighting the compass needle seemed to be "off" to the northwest as much as a whole degree, even after it had been re-magnetized with the lodestone. Further sightings finally convinced Columbus and his pilots that these were indeed variations of the North Star and not the compass. But the "scuttlebutt," which no doubt ran through Columbus' fleet as fast and as loose as it does on shipboard today, must have spread apprehension among most of the men, especially by the time it had passed through countless distortions until it reached the crew of the *Niña*.

On the eighth day out, there was what at first appeared to be a good omen; it turned out to be unfortunate. The men spotted a large bird, and hopes rose that they were already near land. No one thought that they could have crossed to the Indies in so short a time, but this was a sign that there were islands along the way. There were, however, no islands. And as the days passed, with more and more sea birds appearing, the constant expectation of finding land only aggravated the suspense.

Then, on the tenth day out, the fleet encountered the Sargasso Sea.

The Sargasso Sea is a vast body of floating weed, stretching across more than half the width of the North Atlantic and from the Gulf Stream down to below the Bahamas. At first it appeared as a few patches of floating seaweed, further increasing the expectancy of sighting an island. But day by day, and then hour by hour, it increased until on the fifteenth day out all three vessels were sailing through a great pasture of green and brown, stretching from horizon to horizon. Although the sargassum weed does little to hinder a ship's way, the officers and crew began to worry about becoming trapped in an unyielding tangle of weed, there to sit and die and rot. Scooping up buckets of the stuff, they found that it was yellowish brown, stringy and covered with small pods which popped when squeezed. Some of the weed had new green shoots at one end, and some carried tiny green crabs. These could be further signs of land nearby. Columbus ordered soundings with the dipsey lead, but no bottom was found. So the weed could also mean that from here on westward the ocean was an impassable, eerie mass, neither water nor land, a graveyard for all who did not turn back.

In near-panic the officers changed course a number of times, searching for a way out of the floating mass. There appeared to be none. But meanwhile the weed appeared not to slow the vessels' progress. So it was decided to keep on course at least until the mass thickened. Nevertheless there must have been some worried head-shaking and even some outspoken criticism over this decision as the men of the *Santa Maria*, *Pinta* and *Niña* gathered for their midday meal that September 21.

Those who were worried could point to plenty of cause for it. Here they were, more than a month at sea, tantalized by countless signs of land—birds, crabs, branches—but with nothing in sight day after day but a boundless, watery horizon, and now a vast meadow of evil-looking green and yellow weed. Where was the land they had expected since the first bird had been sighted a week ago? Where was there any sign that they would not go on to death and eternity floundering in this yellow mass? Where, indeed, was there even some hope of being able to turn back, against winds that had driven them westward almost without change? No wonder then that the grumbling rapidly grew.

At this crucial point the wind changed. The fleet was forced to alter course. Columbus recorded this in his journal and added a cheerful note: "This head wind was very necessary to me, for my crew had grown much alarmed, dreading that they never should meet in these seas with a fair wind to return to Spain." This was important. Now the men aboard the *Niña*, the *Pinta* and the *Santa Maria* knew that the wind did not always blow them westward. If worst came to worst, there *was* a chance of a fair wind to Spain.

The tension eased. When the wind dropped the men worked willingly at the sweeps, still pulling westward. The masses of weed were giving way to open water. Between turns at the heavy oars the sailors went over the side and cooled off in the quiet sea. Across the calmly rolling ocean messages could be shouted from ship to ship. And on Monday, September 24, at sunset, there came a call from the *Pinta* which electrified the entire fleet.

"*Tierra! Tierra!*"

The *Niña*'s rigging was instantly dotted with the figures of men swarming aloft. Most of them shouted that they could see it too: land, about twenty-five leagues to the southwest.

On the *Santa Maria*'s deck Columbus knelt and offered his prayer of thanksgiving. Others knelt around him. At his order the new course was set: southwest. Few men aboard the *Niña*, the *Pinta* or the *Santa Maria* slept that night.

Next morning everyone was straining his eyes as the pale light of dawn lightened the sky. The sun rose and the morning haze dissipated. They could see nothing—nothing but the endless circle of sea around the horizon. There was no land. It had been a figment of an over-excited imagination.

The reaction throughout the fleet can be imagined. But Columbus recorded no disappointment in his journal. Instead he pointed out that by his calculations they must still be a considerable distance short of Japan, so he was not surprised by the false sighting. Then the weather turned so beautiful that the crews seemed for a while to forget their gloom. On the day after the fruitless search for land, the breeze was so gentle and the seas so smooth, clear and inviting that many of the men went over the side to swim. For most of the day they paddled about or floated on their backs as the vessels above them lifted to the swells and rolled their masts against the fleecy clouds. It was another world, hundreds of miles beyond any world they knew. And on a day like this, with a soft breeze on deck and the sun sparkling on the light blue waters, it was a pleasant world indeed.

Still the gnawing question was never far from anyone's mind. How much longer before they would sight something—the coast of Japan, an island, any clear evidence of land? How much longer could they continue westward before they reached the point of no return? Indeed, how much *were* they lengthening their return voyage with each day they kept on this course? The mild weather gave the men more time than usual to ponder such questions, to let their imaginations run on, and to excite each other's fears in the grumbling nocturnal conversations around the main hatch.

A few of the officers finally approached Columbus with the proposal that they turn back. In refusing he made it clear that he recognized the situation. The men could kill him, he told the officers. He had a few followers who would never desert him; but there were not enough of them, and any real mutiny would easily succeed. He was well aware of all this. But, he warned them, no mutiny in this fleet could succeed in the long run. No matter what alibis they fabricated King Ferdinand and Queen Isabella would never believe them. If any of the officers and men returned to Spain without Columbus, they would probably find themselves at the end of a rope. For the time being revolt was suppressed.

On the little fleet rolled. The atmosphere improved a bit in the first week of October. The breezes freshened and the vessels came to life, the *Niña* forging ahead of her slower companions. This was against Columbus' orders, but it was difficult to hold the swift little caravel back, and after a while Columbus decided to ignore the fact so long as the *Niña* kept in sight of the others. All of them now made fast, exhilarating time—averaging 142 miles every day from October 2 to October 6. In fact, the best day's run of the voyage came during this spell of fine wind: 182 miles in twenty-four hours, an average of nearly eight knots an hour. And as they raced along, flights of petrels appeared, seeming to come out to meet them. From nearby land? Everyone hoped so, and everyone began to feel a little better.

They were in fact very near land. On October 6, they stood at 65 degrees North Longitude, just north of Puerto Rico. It was at this point that Martín Alonzo Pinzón urged Columbus to turn southwest by west. Pinzón was now certain that they had missed Japan, and he wanted to set a course for the coast of China. But Columbus decided to stay on a course nearly due west. He was sure that this would soon bring them to China. As for Japan, he figured that they could visit that country on the return voyage.

But it was only the next day when the *Niña*, still forging ahead, fired a gun. A flag rippled to her masthead. This was the prearranged signal, to be given when someone had sighted land.

The *Niña*'s signal was given shortly after sunrise. All that morning and afternoon everyone watched for a clearer sign. None came. At sunset there was no indication of land. By the morning of the eighth, everyone knew that their eyes had fooled them again.

It was, of course, possible that someone had glimpsed a tiny islet and that they were now nearing some substantial land. The bottom was still beyond soundings, but there were other signs that they were at last approaching land. One was the huge flocks of birds. The crew members had long since learned not to rely on the sight of birds; they had appeared off and on during most of the voyage. But now came whole flocks of them, so many that Columbus ordered the course changed to west southwest to follow them. And the men, as they lay on the deck the night of the ninth, could look up and see and hear the great hordes of them flying overhead. All night they went by, their throaty cries echoing down from the sky and their soaring shapes outlined against the moon. As Columbus wrote, "*Toda la noche oyeron pasar pajaros*"—"All night we could hear birds passing." Surely all these birds were heading somewhere, somewhere that must be land.

They were. This was the annual migration of North American birds to the West Indies by way of Bermuda. And now the *Niña*, the *Pinta* and the *Santa Maria* were following them straight toward the Bahama Islands.

Yet this was when the expedition nearly did turn back. On the same night that the men lay about on the deck of the *Niña* listening to the flocks of birds fluttering by overhead, a far different scene was taking place aboard the flagship. There Columbus and two of his captains were arguing over whether to put about and head for home. It was evidently a long and bitter argument, and so strongly did the captains make their case that apparently Columbus was forced into a strange agreement: if land were not sighted within three days, he promised, they would turn back.

When Columbus made this promise, the fleet was a full two hundred miles from the nearest land. And the breeze, blowing gently from the south, was pushing them forward at only two knots—far too slow a rate to reach land in three days. But the situation changed next day. A fresh trade wind sprang up again and the vessels picked up their lumbering speed. Then, suddenly real mutiny did flare.

It is not too difficult to understand. This was October 10, 1492. The men aboard the *Niña*, the *Pinta* and the *Santa Maria* had already sailed twice as far as anyone they had even known. They had long since passed the point where Columbus had assured them they would find Japan. Not once but twice their hopes had been dashed when they had apparently sighted land. Visits by a few birds had deluded them into thinking a landfall was near, and now for nearly two days they had followed great flocks of birds without sighting the tiniest island. Some crew members estimated that even now they stood little chance of making it home, especially against the easterly trades. There was no time to lose, they argued. This mad captain would lead them on to death because of his foolish obsession. Aboard the *Santa Maria* the men marched before Columbus. Aboard the *Niña* and the *Pinta* the rest of the crew stood ready for open revolt.

How did Columbus staunch this mutiny at its critical point? We can only guess. But perhaps the most idealistic conjecture is the most practical: Columbus' very stubbornness was convincing. He was so much in the grip of his idea that he could even persuade these ship-weary, frightened, rebellious men to wait just a little longer. We do not know today what arguments he used to wheedle another day or two out of his men. What we do know is that this little time was all he needed.

Throughout the eleventh day the winds increased, and the fleet surged forward until it was making seven knots. Someone aboard the *Niña* managed to scoop up a branch. It was green, and it bore a flower resembling the roses of Castile. Still there was no sign of land itself, and at sundown everyone searched in vain. The winds increased still more, and the vessels raced forward at nine knots.

It was 10 P.M. when Columbus himself thought he saw a spot of light. It flickered again. Standing high on the plunging sterncastle of the ship he watched for another glimpse of it. There it was again. He later wrote that it was "like a little wax candle rising and falling." Then the moon rose and the tiny light disappeared.

Still he watched. He pointed out the direction of the light and the crewmen watched. Midnight came and went, as the vessels plunged and plowed through the roaring seas, the tossing spray flashing silver in the moonlight. One A.M. Two A.M. And aboard the *Pinta* the lookout, Rodrigo de Triana spotted a flash of moonlight reflecting off some solid surface. Could it be a sandy cliff? Or was it yet another disappointment? Then he saw it again. There were two of them. They looked like sand cliffs bathed in the light of the moon. Below them was a dark line, steady in contrast to the tossing waves. Perhaps it was a shoreline connecting the two cliffs. Rodrigo de Triana saw it more clearly, gasped and let out a bellow.

It was land.

Watlings Island is one of the smallest of the Bahamas. It is a dozen miles long and half a dozen miles wide, with hills that are high by Bahamian standards. These were the cliffs that were sighted that night by Rodrigo de Triana. The island gets its Bahamian name in honor of a locally famous pirate of the eighteenth century. But two centuries earlier the natives who lived on the island called it Guanahani.

The natives were gathered on the western side of the island when the *Niña*, *Pinta* and *Santa Maria* came edging along the reef to the opening and into the bay. The anchors went down for the first time since they had been hauled from the bottom in the Azores. Columbus climbed into a small boat. As he was rowed toward the beach, other boats came away from the *Niña* and the *Pinta*. The royal standard rippled from Columbus' boat, and the white and green banners of the expedition were hoisted in the other two. When the boats crunched onto the coral sand Columbus and his captains jumped out and strode up the beach above the high-water line. There they kneeled and offered prayers of thanksgiving. Columbus rose and claimed the island for King Ferdinand and Queen Isabella. Then he gave the island the official name it bears today: San Salvador.

Farther up the beach the naked natives watched in awe. Columbus walked toward them, holding out some gifts of glass beads and red caps. The natives happily accepted them. Thus on a dazzling coral beach, amid a weirdly contrasting group of bearded, buckled sailors and painted savages, the first contact was made between the Old World and the New.

The natives promptly responded to Columbus' gifts in kind. Even as he and his captains returned to the vessels, the West Indians came swimming out to the boats, holding above the water their offerings of skeins of thread, darts and even a few parrots. All that day and the next they came out to the ship and the caravels, some in boats which were hollowed out of the trunks of trees. For both days Columbus' sailors and the natives swapped beads and other trinkets for birds and fish-tooth darts. Soon all three vessels echoed to the squawking of dozens of pet parrots. The long voyage, the agonies of suspense, the fears of being lost, the thoughts of mutiny were forgotten in the celebration of reaching the Indies at last.

For they had found Asia—of that they were certain, Columbus most of all. And now he set out on a search, island by island, for the gold, jewels and other wealth with which he knew the Indies abounded.

The search took him from San Salvador down through the Bahamas to Cuba, the Windward Passage and Hispaniola. Everywhere he went the tantalizing evidences of gold led him on. At one Bahama island the natives conveyed to him in their sign language that on the next island, as he noted in his journal, "there is a lot of gold and they wear it in the form of bracelets on the arm, legs, ears, nose and neck." On Long Island (which Columbus named Ferdinand) he found an old man with a gold nose plug. The native would not part with it and Columbus refused to force it from him. Here some other natives indicated that there was a king who had a great deal of gold. But Columbus could not locate him. At the island he named Isabella (now known as Crooked Island) natives told Columbus of the larger island of Cuba; in his journal on October 23, Columbus wrote: "It is now my determination to depart for the island of Cuba, which I believe to be Cipango [Japan], from the accounts I have received here, of the multitude of riches of the people."

But Cuba provided only the same will-o'-the-wisp. In the Bay of Nipe the natives claimed, so Columbus wrote, "there were mines of gold here and pearls." There were none. In a nearby harbor Columbus even had the crew diving for oysters in hopes of finding some pearls. None were found. And so it went. Always there was the promise of gold on the next island, in the next bay, up this river, on the other side of that mountain. On November 22 the *Pinta* disappeared, her master, Martín Alonzo Pinzón, veering off to follow his own hunch, searching for gold. The *Niña* and the *Santa Maria* kept on their own course, searching for gold. The course took them in and out of every promising bay along the coast of Cuba, across the Windward Passage to Hispaniola and along that coast. All through November and into December the quest went on. And then came catastrophe.

It was Christmas Eve, December 24, 1492. All day the *Niña* and the *Santa Maria* had been beating against a head wind along the Haitian coast, and near sunset the men could see the promontory now known as Cap-Haïtien. With dusk the wind dropped, and the vessels ghosted along under full canvas. It was a soft, gentle night, the only sounds being the creak and groan of the ship and, far away, the rumble of surf on a reef. Drowsiness crept through the crews. Perhaps someone aboard the *Niña* was alert enough to notice as he looked across the dark sea at the lights of the *Santa Maria* that she seemed too near land for safety; no one knows. But it is known what happened just after midnight.

The cry that rang through the *Niña* waked everyone. And everyone who came on deck could see that the *Santa Maria*'s lights were surging up and down in weird arcs and that the flagship was not making way. It was clear that she had run aground.

The *Niña* was brought about. But she did not venture in any closer. Who knew the length of the reef on which the *Santa Maria* had crashed? A boat was readied and sailors were being selected to row it over to the flagship when out of the night came a hail from an approaching boat.

It was from the *Santa Maria*. As everyone aboard the *Niña* watched, the boat came alongside. In the feeble gleam of the *Niña*'s stern lanterns the crew could make out the *Santa Maria*'s sailors and Juan de la Cosa, one of the flagship's officers. But where was Columbus? The answer from de la Cosa was frank and shameless: the *Santa Maria* was going down with all hands, including Columbus, and they had got out as fast as they could.

Vincente Yáñez, the *Niña*'s officer of the deck, was outraged. He refused to allow them aboard and ordered them to return to the ship. Reluctantly the men rowed back, followed by the boat from the *Niña*.

The *Santa Maria* was still above water, but it was obviously a matter of minutes. The swells rolling across the reef were lifting and pounding her and the sharp coral heads were punching holes in her bottom.

She had swung around and the waves were hitting her broadside. Columbus had already had the masts cut away to lighten her, but it was too late. They would never be able to pull her off the reef. Her seams were opened. The sea could be heard rushing into her hull. With each wave she thumped and wallowed, and the water sloshed back and forth in her hold.

Columbus took a last look around and climbed into the *Niña*'s boat. Slowly they left the broken flagship astern and rowed across to the *Niña*. For the rest of the dark, dreary Christmas Eve, Columbus could do nothing but stand on the *Niña*'s deck and wait for dawn to reveal what was left of the *Santa Maria*.

Daylight showed that she was a derelict. All that Christmas Day was spent in the tedious labor of salvaging what they could of her stores. Out from the shore came the canoes of Guacanagari, the local chieftain, and the natives helped with the loading and ferrying to the shore. Guacanagari placed a guard over the salvaged material and, Columbus later recorded, not a board or nail was stolen by the natives.

While his subjects were helping in the salvage operation, the chieftain came out to the *Niña*, which now flew the admiral's flag. Trying to console Columbus, Guacanagari said, according to Columbus' journal, "that he must not show grief, that he would give him all he had, and that he had given the Christians who were ashore two very big houses and would give more if necessary." But the chieftain had even more to offer, a gift that must have done much to revive Columbus' spirits; it was gold.

Some of the natives, paddling alongside in their boats, held up "pieces of gold as big as the hand." As soon as Guacanagari saw Columbus' reaction, he promised the admiral that there was a lot more where this came from, in fact that "there was such a lot of it that they held it for naught." As if to confirm this, one of Columbus' seamen came out to the caravel with some gold, saying that it was amazing how many pieces of it the natives would barter for almost nothing. It looked as if, in a very well-disguised blessing, Columbus had finally discovered the treasures which he had set out among the islands to find two months earlier.

Little wonder that he now indulged his almost Pollyanna-like optimism. "So many things came to hand," he reportedly said, "that in truth it was no disaster but great luck; for it is certain that if I had not run aground I should have kept to sea without anchoring in this place. . . ." And the more he thought about it, the more he realized that he never had liked the *Santa Maria* as much as the *Niña*. The flagship may have been bigger, but she was "very heavy and not suitable for the business of discovery." More important was the prospect of at long last finding the gold, and perhaps the spices, that had brought him across the ocean. He was now even more convinced that he had indeed found his way to the Asian coast, or at least to some islands off the coast.

Nevertheless, he faced a dilemma. He was convinced that he had achieved the purpose of his expedition, but here he was on the coast of Japan with more men than the *Niña* could comfortably or safely carry. Where was the *Pinta?* No one knew; and in the back of Columbus' mind was the suspicion that Pinzón, the *Pinta*'s master, might be speeding home to take the credit for the success of the voyage. Columbus felt that he had no choice but to establish a shore station, leave some of the men there to carry on the explorations for gold and spices, and sail home. As soon as possible he would outfit the *Niña* with fresh supplies and come back. In the meantime his men would consolidate their discoveries.

Along a narrow, twelve-mile-long beach on the north coast of what is now Haiti, Columbus built the first Old World settlement in the New. Back of the settlement was a mangrove swamp. Before it was the little bay and the reef on which could still be seen the ribs of the wrecked *Santa Maria*. The rest of her—masts, planks and timbers—were brought ashore to be used in the construction of a fort. Columbus called the settlement La Navidad, in recognition of the Christmas Day on which he had finally, through seeming misfortune, made his and his sovereigns' fortune.

The forty men who stayed behind were all volunteers. In fact, more than enough volunteered at the thought of the gold waiting to be dug up. Here was the opportunity of a lifetime, to prospect among all the riches of Asia before everyone else in the Old World came flocking across the ocean. Settlers and seamen alike worked to construct the "tower and fortress." Then the *Niña* was provisioned with fruit, vegetables and water, and Columbus prepared for the long voyage home.

Then word came through some natives that the *Pinta*, exploring the coast, was only two days' sail away. Columbus sent a message, by some natives in a canoe lent by Guacanagari, requesting Pinzón to rejoin him. The canoe turned back without delivering the message. So at dawn on Friday, January 4, the *Niña*'s sails were hoisted and she glided slowly out of the bay, her boat leading the way to make sure she did not strike the reef. Out in the open sea the boat was hauled aboard, Columbus took a farewell look at the little settlement on the beach, and the *Niña*'s course was set: east for Spain.

But he could not sail east. The winds blew against him for two days. Tack and tack, he tried to beat his way along the coast of Hispaniola; even with the nimble *Niña* he could not make much headway. Had Columbus not been such an optimist, he might have pondered on the voyage home with foreboding. But he did not. Perhaps one reason was that at this point he was rejoined by the *Pinta*.

She came sailing over the horizon on the second day after Columbus had left La Navidad. In company the two caravels worked their way into a little bay east of La Navidad (the bay is now called Monte Cristi). Martín Alonzo Pinzón came aboard the *Niña* and proffered his excuse: he had been driven off course by contrary winds. Columbus was coldly polite, but he wrote in his journal that Pinzón's alibis were "totally false." Martín Alonzo, Columbus was certain, had left him to go searching for gold on his own. Together the two masters made ready for the voyage home, calking ship and loading wood and water while they waited for the wind to stand fair.

Still it blew from the wrong quarter. Finally, at midnight on January 8, Columbus ordered sail hoisted. The two caravels went rolling out of the harbor on a slant to east northeast. Swinging away from the island and back toward it in long tacks, the *Niña* and *Pinta* made their way toward the end of the island. There Columbus sailed into Samaná Bay and anchored. Both caravels were leaking, and he decided to careen them. In his journal he blamed this on the shipyards back in Palos; but both vessels had sailed many thousands of miles since then.

Here, for the first time, the natives were not only unfriendly but savage. To stay in the area looked too dangerous. Despite the leaky condition of the vessels, Columbus decided to head out on the long voyage home. Had he known what lay in wait for him, he certainly would not have taken this chance.

Finally the wind turned fair. Three hours before dawn on the ninth, the caravels stood out from Samaná Bay in a westerly wind, the course east by north. A few hours later Columbus changed the course slightly: to northeast by east. The next landfall, he hoped, would be Spain.

He could not know it, but he was on the wrong course. He might have missed not only Spain but the Continent altogether, had not the contrary winds headed him off his direct line until he was in the latitude of Bermuda. Then the prevailing westerlies took over. Thereupon the two caravels were able to run east before the trades, almost directly for Spain.

The slower *Pinta* held them back, but the vessels rolled along smoothly. In one day, January 19, they logged 138 knots. Columbus wrote in his journal that "the air [was] very soft and sweet as in Seville during April and May." At this rate Seville, and fame and fortune, were not very far away. Even in the "horse latitudes" (later so named because the prevalent calms were the death of hundreds of horses) the caravels dipped along, slowly enough for the men to catch some fish including "a tremendous shark," but fast enough to keep on course. By February 3, they were running free before a fresh breeze, sloshing through the weed of the Sargasso Sea while the full moon above made the nights soft and glowing, as if to mask the tempests that lay ahead.

That night, in fact, the weather changed. Columbus noted that "the sky was very overcast and rainy, and it was rather cold." Sweeping on them from astern was a wild winter gale. Even after it hit, Columbus kept his fore and main courses set, and for a time the two caravels plunged ahead. For four days they sailed faster than they had at any time during the voyage, in either direction. At times their speed, even that of the *Pinta*, came close to eleven knots. This is faster than most modern racing yachts go, and in 1492 it was faster than most of the

Niña's and the *Pinta*'s men had ever gone before, on land or sea. No one knew for certain where they were, whether on the proper latitude for the Azores or many miles to north or south. But they knew that they were racing faster than ever before, and straight for the Old World once again.

Just over the horizon, however, lay the worst series of winter storms that Southern Europe had seen in years. The harbor at Genoa was locked in ice by Christmastime, and ships were trapped in Lisbon Harbor for months by contrary winds. A whole series of cold masses from the Arctic were thundering down the European coast to come crashing up against the warm fronts of the south, causing devastating storms. Winds were up to full gale force, and seas towered as high as the yards of most ships. And at this point at least three of the storms were converging right at the area for which the *Niña* and the *Pinta* were headed.

The first omens of the storm came on Monday, February 12, in the form of huge seas and near-gale-force winds. All sails had to be lowered, those that had not been blown out, and the *Niña* ran before the storm under what the Spaniards called "dry tree"—not a sail on her. Columbus noted in the journal that "the wind began to blow furiously with a heavy sea," and added that "if the caravel had not been a good vessel and well prepared, they would have been in danger of perishing." It was a rough night, lit by lightning and howling with wind and wave. By next morning the storm had moderated slightly, and Columbus ordered a small sail set. But by the night of the thirteenth the winds were back up to near-gale force, out of the southwest. Again the one small sail had to be lowered, and again the *Niña* ran off to the northeast, at the wind's will.

Now the converging storm patterns were setting up huge crisscrossing waves which staggered the *Niña* and pounded over her decks with each plunge. All night, while the helmsman stood in foam sometimes sloshing as high as his waist, the watch officer peered ahead at the towering waves and yelled the course changes to save the caravel from being swamped or batted onto her beam ends. With the wind against her tall stern, the *Niña* ran before the storm at nearly eight knots despite the fact that she carried not a sail.

Columbus had no aids to weather forecasting, so he could only hope that the storm would blow over. But it did not. Instead, by next day it was worse. In an attempt to work back near his course, he ordered a tiny sail set again, this time low on the mast; the wind was so strong that if the sail did not blow out, it might split the mast. It threatened to tear and had to be lowered. And now the *Pinta*, which had been visible for the past two days at ever-widening distance, disappeared over the horizon astern.

Watching the seas smash his little caravel, Columbus might well have wondered if he and his men had been forsaken. He decided that they should make some expression more significant than normal prayers, to show that they still had faith. At his order, one of the sailors counted out as many peas as there were men aboard the *Niña*. One of the peas was marked with a cross. They were shaken up in a cap. Columbus called together all the men who were not struggling with the helm or the yards. They would draw lots, he explained, shouting above the din. The one who drew the pea with the cross would make a special pilgrimage to St. Mary of Guadeloupe, to express the crew's thanks for deliverance from this storm, if they did get through safely. Then he reached into the cap first—and drew the pea with the cross. He gave his oath that he would make the pilgrimage if they reached shore alive.

The storm showed no sign of tempering. Columbus decided to appeal to heaven again. Once more the peas, one of them marked with a cross, were shaken in a cap. This time the pea with the cross went to a sailor named Pedro de Villa. He swore that he would make a pilgrimage to St. Mary of Loretto, in Ancona. Columbus promised to pay the cost of the pilgrimage. Everyone withdrew to his own private hopes and prayers.

Still the storm mounted. Columbus called for the cap again. This time, he shouted over the storm, the one who drew the lot would spend a night on watch and pay for a mass at St. Clara de Moguer, near Palos. What followed was either astonishing coincidence or evidence that the drawing was well planned, because it was Columbus who again drew the pea with the cross. He made his vow to carry out the pledge, and the men of the *Niña* waited for the divine help they devoutly expected to follow.

Instead, the wind seemed to increase. Everyone wondered how long it would take before the *Niña* simply disintegrated. She had been pounding across the Atlantic and plowing through the Caribbean for four months. The *Pinta* had unshipped her rudder and now had apparently disappeared. The *Santa Maria* had gone aground and broken up. The *Niña*'s leak kept her men at the pumps. But she had survived storm and escaped shipwreck and was now standing up gallantly in the battle of her life. She did indeed seem to be fighting like a live animal in the grip of the gale.

The seas kept hitting her head on—in fact, worse than head on as one sea pounded across her from starboard to be followed immediately by another from port. It was this combination of crossing seas that made the storm so vicious. The caravel rolled until she seemed to dip her yards under, only to right and roll over as far on the other side. Her tall forecastle and towering stern seemed about to pull her over each time, but each time she hung there momentarily and then righted herself. In her hold, below the water line, there was a crashing and thumping as dozens of water casks lurched within their restraining ropes. Columbus had hoped to ballast the *Niña* with stone but had been unable to. With most of the provisions and water gone, the *Niña* was too buoyant. The crew had filled the empty casks with sea water, but the weight was not enough, and the caravel rolled far over.

With every roll the water broke across the high bulwarks onto the deck. The tallest waves came at them from astern as they ran before the gale. Each mountain of water rose high above them and came crashing down, the great white breakers dashing about as the wind batted the tops off the waves. As each watery wall rose toward them, the *Niña* rose under it at the last moment, her high stern saving them from being overwhelmed. Then the wind would catch her sterncastle and send her racing ahead, but not before a torrent had poured through the open rudder port. The helmsman, lashed to his post, could only hold his breath as the icy water engulfed him and hang on to the tiller, hoping it would not be wrenched out of control.

The sounds alone were enough to demoralize the whole crew. Nothing but the loudest shout could be heard above the tumult. Each time the single sail was raised, the thundering canvas sounded as if it would blow out with every gust. Every roaring, towering wave rolled away to be followed by the next, and the next, hour after hour, all through the day, the night, the next day, the next night until all count was lost. Columbus had not slept since the storm had first struck them, nor had any of the crew. Time blurred. They were lost in a nightmare of smashing water and shrieking wind that seemed to go on forever.

It was particularly frustrating to Columbus to have achieved his goal (so he thought) and then die before he could return to report it. As he recalled the scene later, he concluded that God, for His own reasons, apparently did not intend the *Niña* to make it to her home port. So Columbus steadied himself against the jostling of his cabin and scrawled out a brief account of the voyage, of the landfall, of the explorations among the islands, and of his conviction that he had finally found the westward route to the Indies. He was certain that he would not be spared to return and prove that there was gold in the islands. But somehow he had to get word of his discovery to the rest of the world, before the *Niña* and he and all his men went down.

The scene can be imagined—the lamp flickering as gusts of wind seeped in at every crack, the thundering of the water against the sides, the scratching of the quill pen on parchment heard only in the sudden still moments between gusts as the caravel slid to the bottom of a wave. With the account written, Columbus added a request for the finder to take it to the King and Queen of Spain. He rolled the parchment in waxed cloth and tied it firmly. Then he called for a wooden cask, put the parchment in it and pounded the lid in place. He did this himself because he did not want any of his men to guess that he had virtually given up hope. No doubt most of them were nearly resigned to their fate, but any obvious resignation on the part of the captain would be disastrous. Carrying the cask on deck, Columbus took it to the rail and tossed it into the sea. In his journal he later noted that none of the crew realized what it was, "all taking it for some kind of devotion."

Well the religious sailors might, for within a few hours the storm actually did seem to calm, very slightly but enough to provide a hope of relief. All the night of the fourteenth the *Niña* was thrown from one surging wave onto another. But the wind was not so violent. And she survived. With dawn, finally, came a shout from Seaman Ruy

Gard García. It was a shrill, wavering cry that rose above the thunder of the storm, sounding as if it came from miles across the heaving water. García had seen land.

This landfall was just as welcome as the one at San Salvador in the New World. Yet this one nearly proved a delusion. It took the *Niña* seventy-two hours, fighting headwinds, to reach the island. It turned out to be Santa Maria, in the Azores. And what should have been a welcome home instead became a series of misadventures. Anchor cables chafed and parted twice, forcing the exhausted men to haul up sail and put back to sea. Columbus had just had his first sleep in three days and nights. Wearily he guided the caravel around the island, searching for a safe anchorage. When he finally found one, he sent some of his crew ashore to find the nearest church, to make the promised penitential pilgrimage. They were set upon by islanders, led by an officious young Portuguese army captain who claimed that Portugal's King had ordered all Spaniards captured wherever they landed on Portuguese soil, including the Azores. The officer, one João de Castanheira, evidently did not for a moment believe Columbus' tale of finding a new route to the Indies. He was finally persuaded to release the *Niña*'s men, however, and once more the caravel plunged off into the open Atlantic, this time running before a blustery southwest wind. A large bird, which looked to Columbus "like an eagle," flew overhead. Columbus set his course: east to Palos, eight hundred miles away. Everyone settled back to fight out this last leg of the voyage.

The *Niña* ran about 250 miles, racing before strong southwest to west winds, before the next storm struck. It was a cyclone, with even stronger winds than the *Niña* had withstood earlier. In this passage between the Azores and the mainland winter winds have been clocked at one hundred miles an hour. It was February 27 when the first effects of the cyclone were felt. Within a few hours Columbus noted in his journal, in a masterly understatement, that he was "much afflicted at meeting with such a storm so near home."

Again the violent winds batted the *Niña* about. Again her struggles were illumined by lightning flashes as she labored through more vicious cross seas. Reeling, plunging and shuddering, she fought them for four days and nights. On March 3, just after sunset, came a squall that split her one sail to tatters. Even the sails that were furled and tied down were ripped off the yards. In a few moments, as the *Niña* heeled far over, plunging her bow into the seas and shaking each one off as she rose, nothing was left of her sails but ragged ribbons streaming straight out in the wind.

All day on March 3 the winds kept up to hurricane and near-hurricane force. Once more the seaman's cap was filled with peas. Once more the officers and men gathered on deck, as much in the lee of the tall quarterdeck as they could. Once more Columbus drew first, and drew the pea marked with the cross; evidently it was planned that way. Columbus vowed to make a pilgrimage to the church of St. Mary de la Cinta, near Huelva, up the coast from Cádiz. His vow seemed to have no effect on the storm, so the crew made a mass vow: to fast on bread and water the first night ashore. Even this drastic resort seemed to have no effect.

March 3 ended in a night of terror. The cross seas were now coming aboard on both sides, engulfing most of the ship. The wind seemed at times to lift her bodily off the tops of the huge waves. The lightning was all around them. Columbus confessed in his journal later that they "were near meeting destruction." Despite the storm, it was a bright night, lit by a full moon behind the storm clouds. Then, on the first night watch, a sailor bellowed faintly above the wind: "Land! Land!" It was the rock-girt coast of Portugal, and they were being driven straight for it at top speed.

In the *Niña*'s depleted sail locker there was still one small forecourse —their only hope. Columbus ordered it set. The men wormed their way up the swaying rigging and set it, and everyone prayed it would not blow out. This was the only way the *Niña* could veer away from the coast and keep from driving onto the rocks. Slowly she eased about on a starboard tack, her pace changing from a rolling to a bucking motion. As the seas loomed higher over her bow and poured the length of her deck, she appeared to be going under each time she plunged. For the rest of the night, while everyone crossed himself and prayed that the one sail would hold, the *Niña* fought for her life within sight of the rocky, storm-lashed shore. Columbus and his crew, exhausted by the long battle, weak from not enough to eat, sick of heart at what seemed to them certain death, could only put their last faith in God and the *Niña*.

God, and the *Niña*, brought them through. And next morning, in the little fishing village of Cascais, where every ship had been storm-bound for more than a week, the residents were astonished to see a battered little caravel, her topsails in ribbons, come dusting into the Tagus estuary and settle in the quiet waters of the harbor like a duck lighting on a pond. The *Niña* was home.

She was, of course, not home in Spain but in the Old World. The Tagus led into Lisbon, Portugal, and after his experience at the Azores Columbus no doubt would have preferred to avoid this port. But with the storm sweeping the coast he had no choice. By March 13 the *Niña*, patched and repaired, dropped down the Tagus and out to sea again, her course set this time for Cape Saint Vincent, Faro, Saltés, and finally the Rio Tinto, off the town of Palos, Spain. This was the harbor the *Niña*, the *Pinta* and the *Santa Maria* had left only thirty-two weeks earlier. In less than a year Columbus, and the *Niña*, had completed the most famous voyage in history.

So Columbus' astonishment can be imagined when, only a few hours later, what should come riding into the harbor but the *Pinta*. After crossing with her to the New World, losing her and finding her in the Caribbean, losing her again off the Azores, Columbus now watched the *Pinta* come into the harbor on the same tide that had just ridden the *Niña* to her anchorage.

What had happened to the *Pinta*? Driven north of the *Niña* in the storm off the Azores, she had missed the islands entirely and had also missed the cyclone that had nearly finished off the *Niña*. The *Pinta* made her landfall at Bayona, Portugal, and Skipper Pinzón sent the news racing to Ferdinand and Isabella in hopes of beating Columbus to it and copping the credit. He was taken aback when the reply came that the King and Queen preferred to wait for the official report from Columbus, the commander of the expedition. After the storm had swept by, Pinzón took the *Pinta* out of the harbor and down the coast to Palos, hoping that the storm had sunk the *Niña* and that he, Pinzón, would still become the hero of the historic voyage. He was standing on deck relishing the familiar sight of the entrance to his home harbor when the lookout announced that the *Niña* was in the harbor, sails furled and riding at her anchor. She might have been there for weeks.

Pinzón did not even report to the *Niña*. As soon as the *Pinta*'s anchor was down, he had himself rowed ashore. He walked to his house and went to bed. He never got up again. Weakened by exposure and the hardships of the voyage, demoralized by his failure to take the credit away from Columbus—the victim of an ambition as deadly as a disease—Martín Alonzo Pinzón died within a few days.

But if Columbus remained the hero of the voyage, the *Niña* remained the heroine. To the *Pinta* went the honor of the first sighting of land in the New World. But to the *Niña* went the fame of becoming Columbus' flagship for the explorations of the New World and the return home, not to mention Columbus'—and the world's—gratitude for bringing him safely through a storm that would have sent most other caravels to the bottom.

Nothing more is known of the *Pinta*. But the *Niña*, under her old name of *Santa Clara*, was in the fleet of seventeen sails that took off from Cádiz on September 25, 1493, on Columbus' second voyage to the New World. Although Columbus selected a larger vessel for his flagship to cross the Atlantic, he transferred his flag to the *Niña* as soon as they arrived among the islands which he still believed to be the East Indies. During this voyage the *Niña* went aground once but worked free without serious damage. When the fleet was hit by a hurricane, she rode it out while every other vessel in the fleet went down or aground. When Columbus returned home, the *Niña* was still his flagship; she carried 125 officers and men, in safety if not comfort, through more Atlantic storms.

She then virtually vanishes from history. It is known that she sailed on the third voyage with Columbus, and a caravel of her name and description is recorded as being on a trading voyage to the Pearl Coast in 1501. All else is silence—all else except her near-final known adventure, which is completely in character.

Between the second and third voyages of Columbus, the *Niña* was chartered out on a trading voyage to Rome. As she was leaving the harbor of Cagliari, Sardinia, a pirate swept down on her and captured her. She was taken to a smaller Sardinian harbor and looted. The crew was forced aboard the pirate ship. But in the night's darkness her captain, Alonso Medel, and three of his crew slipped their chains, got over the side into one of the pirates' boats and silently rowed across to the *Niña*.

Since all her men were aboard the pirate, no one had been left as ship watcher aboard the *Niña*. So Captain Medel and his men were able to hoist sail, cut her cable and glide away. All depended upon the little caravel's response, maneuverability and speed, and the *Niña* had all three at the time they were needed most. Once she had got the lead, there was no catching her.

It would have been an ignominious end for Columbus' favorite caravel to end her days in the hands of a pirate. But, almost as if she could order her own fate, the *Niña* escaped to sail again, on another voyage of exploration with Columbus. How and when she finally came to the end of her days no one knows. But it is a good guess that she had an honorable retirement. Certainly she deserved it. She had proved that a little caravel could sail out across the uncharted seas to unknown lands. She had proved herself a match for the Atlantic's winter gales, for cyclones and for hurricanes. As with few men—one of them Columbus—so with very few ships: the *Niña* had the quality of greatness.

III

Galleon: The SAN MARTÍN

The Armada forms up . . . "To kill the Drake" . . . The formidable crescent . . . Where are the landing forces? . . . Floating fire . . . "We are steering for Spain."

The greatest fleet the world had ever seen crowded the harbor of Lisbon in the spring of 1588. There was every kind of ship from the loftiest merchantmen to the lowliest *urcas*. But the first line of the fleet was made up of the galleons, and one of the galleons, the *San Martín*, was the flagship. All would meet their test shortly, when the Spanish Armada set sail for England.

The galleons would meet the sternest test of all. For it was the galleon that was at once the workhorse and battle wagon of the sixteenth century. Not a very great step forward in ship design, the galleon was basically little different from its predecessors, the caravel and the carrack. The galleon seemed to sit lower in the water because it had far less freeboard. It might be called a cross between a ship and a galley, that longer, lower vessel which carried a sail but relied principally on its oars. Though designed along the slimmer lines of the smaller galley, the galleon used no oars for propulsion, depending on sails alone. Sometimes the galleon has been confused with another similar vessel, the galleass; this ship was larger than the galley but still supplemented its sail power with oar power. Not the galleon, which was a full-fledged sailing ship.

The *San Martín* had a sharper bow as well as leaner lines than the *Niña* (previous chapter). She was larger and although she still carried a towering stern, her waist and bow were built far closer to the water than the caravel. The *San Martín* was designed on the same principle as vessels more than a hundred years older than she. But she was a considerable refinement of the basic design. Other galleons had already proved themselves; they had taken Drake on his exploits in the New World; they had taken Magellan across the Atlantic and the Pacific. But never had so many galleons participated in an enterprise as enormous as the Armada's.

There were nineteen galleons besides the flagship *San Martín* in the Armada. Besides this first line there were galleasses, heavily armed merchantmen, smaller ships, freighters and even some galleys, to a total of 130 vessels of all sizes and shapes. And as this huge flotilla gathered around the *San Martín*, the apostolic fervor of the Roman Catholic world went with them.

They were there because the world was split by a war as great for the sixteenth century as any in our time. The issue, Catholicism against Protestantism, seemed as wide a schism as that between democracy and Communism today; perhaps in some hearts it was an even more passionately felt cause. And when on February 18, 1587 (all dates in this chapter are New Style, although the English had not yet adopted it), the Catholic Mary Stuart was beheaded at the orders of the Protestant Elizabeth Tudor, the final conflict was inevitable.

It had to come by sea. Foremost guardian of the Faith and adversary of England's Elizabeth was Philip II of Spain. It was the Spanish New World that Elizabeth's fleets looted under Drake. It was Spain itself that so often suffered the maraudings of Drake in his galleons in the 1580's. To Philip II and the other protectors of Catholicism there could be no alternative to the subjugation and final humbling of Lutheran England; otherwise, they were convinced, the disease of Protestantism would spread throughout the Christian world. And so the great plan was formed.

Since England could be assaulted only from the sea, the key to the plan was the huge fleet. Nothing was spared in its formation; the galleons and galleasses, merchantmen and *fregatas* were borrowed, begged and appropriated from Spain and Portugal, Naples and Venice and every port along the European and Mediterranean coast that could spare them, plus many that could not. The plan called for this massive Armada to sail up through the English Channel and join forces with an invasion army under Alexander, Duke of Parma. Convoyed by the Armada, Parma's army would cross the Channel in landing barges and swarm onto the beaches of England. A similar maneuver would be attempted unsuccessfully centuries later by Napoleon, and another by Hitler. It also had been attempted before—by William the Conqueror.

The strategy was simplicity itself. In fact, not enough staff work went into it, and many vital details were left unplanned. But what the Armada and Parma's forces lacked in planning they made up in the fervor of their Holy Crusade. Every Catholic knew that if England fell, what remained of Protestant Europe could not long hold out. In the words of Garrett Mattingly, "the shadow of Spain, of the banners of the unending crusade, of the unitary state which was the armed aspect of the Church, lay long across Europe." The spirit of this sail-borne crusade echoed in a Spanish girl's song by Lope de Vega:

> My brother Don John
> To England is gone,
> To kill the Drake,
> And the Queen to take,
> And the heretics all to destroy;
> And he will give me,
> When he comes back,
> A Lutheran boy
> With a chain on his neck;
> And our Lady-Grandmama shall have
> To wait upon her a Lutheran slave.

The Armada's leader bore the fine Spanish name and title of Alonso Pérez de Guzmán el Bueno, Duke of Medina-Sidonia. He was a small, spry, sensitive man, and he had been second choice for the command. The Marquis of Santa Cruz had died just as the final preparations were being made, and Philip II had immediately appointed Medina-Sidonia in his place. The duke's most important previous function for the king had been diplomatic, and Medina-Sidonia himself was far from convinced that he was the proper man to be appointed Spain's Captain General of the Ocean Sea. In an overly modest letter he wrote to the king's secretary: "My health is not equal to such a voyage, for I know by experience of the little I have been at sea that I am always seasick and always catch cold. . . . Since I have had no experience either of the sea, or of war, I cannot feel that I ought to command so important an enterprise." Since Philip was firm, Medina-Sidonia faithfully accepted the post and offered a prayer that God would make up for his shortcomings. This was somewhat the spirit throughout the fleet. One of the Armada's officers told a questioner that "we are sailing against England in the confident hope of a miracle."

What the Duke of Medina-Sidonia found when he took over at Lisbon could only have confirmed his reluctance and saddened him the more over his inability to escape his fate. Some of the vessels he found were among the best in the world, particularly the great galleons of Castile and Portugal, including the flagship *San Martín*. But even some of the galleons—the ships of the first line—were badly in need of repair, and one was too rotten to sail at all. Many of the armed merchantmen and smaller vessels making up the fleet also had to be reconstructed or junked. Armor, supplies and men were in a total state of confusion. Some ships had more guns than they could safely carry; others were virtually unarmed. Many vessels had the wrong ammunition for their guns, when they had any ammunition at all. Some entire ships' companies had not enough small arms or clothing. Some had no food. And what provisions there were turned out to be spoiling fast. While stores went rotten after months in the casks, more and more food had to be procured from the countryside, where the farmers did not always sell the fleet provisioners fresh merchandise.

While coping with all these shortcomings, the new commander even had to take time out for a special plea to Philip II to keep his predecessor's secretary from decamping with the fleet's entire file of intelligence reports and battle plans. Somehow, though, Medina-Sidonia began to bring order out of the chaos. An organized drive collected more foodstuffs, and the duke could only hope that the new barrels were not made of green wood. The men were properly paid and clothed. Farm hands were supplemented by some more seasoned seamen. Guns were distributed more evenly, the supply of powder was almost doubled, and the supply of cannon balls was increased to fifty rounds per gun. The vessels were hauled over on their sides, scraped and calked and covered with tallow. Enough wood was rounded up to supplant rotten timbers, and cracked spars were sent down to be patched or replaced. Many of the galleons had low-slung bows and sterns, which allowed them to sail closer to the wind. But

most of the Spanish captains preferred higher castles at bow and stern.
Their way of fighting was to swing alongside and board the enemy,
and high castles were best for this. So castles were built on most of
the galleons. Medina-Sidonia would regret this decision later.

For an entirely different type of preparation was going on across
the water. In England John Hawkins, Elizabeth's foremost ship designer, had concentrated on galleons with lower lines and heavier
guns; his galleons were built not to grapple the enemy but to outsail
him and blow him out of the water. Hawkins' galleons were longer
than usual, and the bulwarks were so low that the waist had to be
decked over to protect the gunners. The longer English galleon could
mount more guns, and as many of these as possible were the big ship-
smashing culverins and demiculverins, long cannon which could throw
an eighteen-pound (nine-pound for a demiculverin) shot one thousand yards accurately, a considerable distance in those days. The re-
sults of these weatherly, punishing qualities of the English galleons
would be seen when battle was joined.

The preparations at Lisbon took more than a year. It was March
of 1587 when Philip II set the project in motion. It was April 25,
1588, when the Duke of Medina-Sidonia went to the Cathedral of
Lisbon to be given the standard of the Armada. The Archbishop of
Lisbon said mass and pronounced a benediction. The standard was
carried between lines of the men of the Armada to its place of honor
aboard the galleon *San Martín*. All knelt and listened to the friars reading the papal absolution and indulgence. The banner carried the arms
of Spain, the image of Christ crucified, His Holy Mother, and a scroll
reading, "Arise, O Lord, and Vindicate Thy Cause." The Holy
Crusade was ready to sail.

Then, as if their prayers had gone unheard, came the first of many
harassments that would plague the Armada. Expected supplies were
delayed. Manpower was still too short. It was not until May 9 that
all supplies, armament and sailors and soldiers were aboard. Finally, to
the cheers of the crowds and the ringing of church bells, the *San
Martín*, with nearly 130 in her train, started dropping down the har-

bor to the sea. But at the bar all had to anchor again. The wind was blowing strong and straight into the harbor mouth.

Astrologers had predicted that it would be a violent May, and they were right. In fact, for three bruising weeks the Armada was tied down, pitching and rolling at anchor while wild storms raged along the coast. It was not until May 28 that the *San Martín* weighed anchor again and led the galleons, merchantmen, galleasses, *fregatas* and *urcas* down the mouth of the Lisbon River and out onto the Atlantic.

The distance from Lisbon to Finisterre is about 160 sea miles. The Spanish Armada, struggling against winds from every point of the compass, hobbled by the limping leeway of the least seaworthy freighters, was nearly two weeks making this distance. Time and again the *San Martín* had to come about and retrace her course while waiting for the slower vessels to catch up. And while the Armada struggled to keep together in the shifting, often contrary winds, it became obvious that the entire fleet would have to put back into port.

Medina-Sidonia had taken his ships out before all the necessary provisions had arrived, leaving orders for supply ships to meet the Armada off Finisterre. They did not appear. Then the captains began to report that the water supply was already low. Many of the tubs had been made of green wood, and the water was slimy and undrinkable when they were opened. Medina-Sidonia called a council. In the great cabin of the *San Martín*, swaying high over the water, the squadron commanders all agreed that the Armada should put into the nearest big port, Coruña.

The sun was setting on June 19 when the *San Martín* dropped anchor in Coruña Harbor. Many of the slower ships in the fleet were still outside the harbor when dark came; they put out farther to sea, to cruise off and on until morning. That night a raging storm came down on them. Some thirty vessels and six thousand men were caught in the open and scattered all over the Bay of Biscay and the Atlantic. It took a full month for the farthest to find their way back and for the fleet to repair damage, stow provisions and regroup. And when the Armada finally set sail, this time for England, Medina-Sidonia could profit by intelligence reports from two of his captains who had been blown all the way to the Channel. One had sighted what he took to be part of the English fleet. But another had sailed along part of the English coast and had even captured a couple of enemy merchantmen, without sighting an English warship. Evidently the enemy was unprepared.

Medina-Sidonia's intelligence could not have been more wrong. The English fleet had been tied down in Plymouth by the gale which had scattered the Armada. But, far from being unprepared, it had put out in search of the Armada, hoping to trap it in its harbor. Strong head winds had forced it back, and now on July 22, the same day that the Spanish Armada weighed anchor for the Channel, the English Armada was gathering its forces in Plymouth Sound. More than a hundred vessels, at least fourteen of them big first-line galleons, were ready to defend England's shores. The fleet was under the command of England's Lord Admiral, Charles Lord Howard of Effingham; his second in command was Sir Francis Drake. It is Drake who is reported to have replied, when a captain interrupted his game of bowls on the afternoon of July 29 with word that the Armada had been sighted: "We have time enough to finish the game." There was indeed time, for it was not until the tide turned that evening that the great English fleet rode the ebb down the sound and out to sea to meet the Spaniards.

Five days earlier, as the Armada pushed northward before a welcome favorable breeze, the duke had sent his first messenger on ahead in a fast pinnace to give the news to Parma, waiting with his assault troops at Dunkirk, that the Armada was approaching the Channel. Then, as the Lizard, England's southernmost promontory, drew nearer, the *San Martín* was surrounded by boats as the squadron commanders gathered in the flagship's great cabin for another council of war.

There was a discussion over whether or not to attack Plymouth, if indeed the English were as unprepared as it seemed. But some further intelligence suggested that the English fleet might be organizing right outside Plymouth. The duke reminded his officers that the Armada's main mission was to join forces with Parma and convey his landing barges across the Channel from Dunkirk. Following custom, each officer presented his opinion, in order of precedence from the lowest rank to the highest. The unanimous agreement was to proceed up the Channel to their rendezvous with Parma. The captains returned to their ships. The Armada sailed on toward England.

And that evening as they drew within sight of the coastline, the night was lit with the signal fires the English had placed along the shore and inland to alert the entire countryside. Had the wind been from the north, the men of the Armada might have heard some of the hundreds of church bells also sounding the alarm through the land. But the wind was not from the north; it was west southwest. After all its mishaps, the Armada finally had a favorable slant of wind, just as it went into battle.

Next morning, Saturday, July 30, Medina-Sidonia was pacing the high poop deck of the *San Martín* when dawn uncovered what he was watching for: an English squadron of eleven ships was working its way along the coast, obviously trying to get upwind of the Armada. The duke quickly swung his ships in pursuit, and shortly the first, long-range volleys were being fired. Then someone reported an ominous discovery. Astern of the *San Martín* was the rest of the English fleet. It was far larger than the group of ships near the coast, and this one had somehow maneuvered upwind. The main body of the enemy had already gained the weather gauge.

Aboard the *San Martín* Medina-Sidonia had only begun to recover from this development when he saw, all too clearly, what the Armada was up against. Despite the best the *San Martín* and the other Spanish galleons could do, even the squadron trapped downwind was working away from them and across their bows to sail upwind. Slowly the eleven English ships tacked across the wind and swung around the Spanish pursuers. Here plainly, before the battle had even started, was a vital factor in favor of the English; while the *San Martín* and the other galleons from Portugal and Castile were huge, well armed and well able to handle any English ship in close encounter, the lower-slung English galleons were more maneuverable. It could be an even battle if the Spanish galleons could close with those of England. But it was already apparent that the English were not going to let that happen if they could help it. The Spaniards had never seen anything like this. The keeper of the journal aboard the *San Martín* was inclined at first to credit the English performance to excellent seamanship. "Their ships were very fast-sailers," he recorded, "and so well managed that they did with them what they pleased."

The Spaniards, however, could demonstrate some impressive seamanship themselves. Watching the English vessels escape him, Medina-Sidonia fired a signal gun and, smoothly and gracefully, the Armada swung into a prearranged formation—a huge crescent. Its ends, composed of the biggest galleons, pointed toward the enemy, and the main body of the Armada formed the thick center of the crescent. This formation was of no use on the attack, but the English would find it an awesome and frustrating defensive tactic, before the last gun was fired in the murderous battles to come.

The first of these battles did come next day. The wind held at about the same point of the compass, and the English kept the advantage. This first battle was a feeling-out process. It started more like a tournament on land than a battle at sea, as an English pinnace sailed over, hailed the *San Martín* and formally delivered England's challenge, and as the holy banner of the Armada rippled to the maintop of the Spanish flagship. The encounter itself accomplished little. An English attack proved the efficacy of the Spanish crescent formation. It could only be assaulted at its ends; an approach on the center would bring the two wings closing in on the attacker from both sides. So the English tried both ends ineffectually, except when one galleon, the *San Juan de Portugal*, came out to fight, evidently in hopes of creating a melee that might permit some of the Spanish ships to grapple. This skirmish ended inconclusively; when the *San Juan* tried to close, the English galleons held their distance and pounded her with their long-range guns, and the Spaniard was finally herded back into the crescent by a few of her sister ships. The two fleets disengaged early in the afternoon, with nothing accomplished but with the important first blood drawn.

Grief came to the Armada in another form that afternoon. From the poop of the *San Martín* the duke was watching his fleet close formation and proceed on its course, when there was a shattering explosion.

The *San Salvador*, flagship of one of the squadrons, sent a shower of wood and debris skyward as her sterncastle blew up; evidently her powder magazine had somehow been ignited. Medina-Sidonia quickly took the *San Martín* down alongside and from the flagship's rail he directed the salvage operations as the *San Salvador*'s crew fought the blaze and smaller vessels darted about taking off wounded and adding reinforcements to the firefighters. But the damage was too great. The crew had to go over the side too quickly even to scuttle her, and what was left of the *San Salvador* was later captured by the enemy. To the loss of the ship and men the *San Martín*'s journal added a poignant note on the *San Salvador*'s demolished sterncastle: "The Paymaster-General of the Armada was in this part of the ship, and also a part of His Majesty's money."

Scarcely had the *San Salvador* been given up as a loss when ill fortune struck at another squadron flagship. The *Nuestra Señora del Rosario*, which earlier had struck another vessel and lost her bowsprit, now suddenly staggered before a gust of wind; unable to answer her helm because of her lacking headsails, she lost her weakened foremast. The *San Martín* raced to the scene and Medina-Sidonia ordered a line thrown to the crippled ship. The freshening wind that had caught the *Rosario* aback now made towing her impossible. The cable broke. Smaller vessels came to her assistance but could do little. As darkness obscured the scene Medina-Sidonia reluctantly ordered the *San Martín* back on course and the crescent reformed. He had not eaten since the battle lines had formed ten hours earlier. Now he stood alone on the *San Martín*'s lofty deck, rolling heavily in the tossing sea and trying to eat the bread and cheese that had been brought to him. His thoughts may not, however, have been as gloomy as presumed. The losses had weakened the Armada's strength considerably. And this first engagement, while not damaging in itself, had foreboding indications; there was no longer any doubt that the English galleons could outsail the Spanish galleons at will, particularly upwind. But the duke could remind himself of the Armada's chief mission: to run the gantlet up the Channel, meet Parma's landing barges and shepherd them across the narrow gap between Dunkirk and England. Today the enemy had attacked his defensive crescent with no success whatever. Only ill luck had cost him any ships. The Armada, reformed and unbroken, was resuming its march up the Channel to its rendezvous. Judging by today's action the English were unable to cope with the Spanish crescent, and at this point Medina-Sidonia did not see how they could. He could not, of course, foretell the terrible way they would.

By next morning, Monday, August 1, the Spanish crescent was maintaining its steady procession, and the duke did not even permit one of his captains to make a dash after three English vessels that almost sailed into the formation. Already Medina-Sidonia realized that in such a chase the English galleons could outdistance the Spanish. The duke evidently knew that one of these intruders was in fact the enemy's flagship *Ark Royal;* but he probably did not know how it had happened: the English commander, Lord Howard, had lost sight of Drake's lantern, which had been leading the fleet, and had followed the lantern of the *San Martín.* Thus the Spanish had very nearly, though innocently, lured the enemy's flagship into a trap. But Howard recovered from his blunder just in time, and the *Ark* and her two escorts raced back to rejoin the English fleet.

The rest of the day was consumed by the enemy fleet's reforming, and there were no battles that afternoon. Near evening, as the wind died, another council of war was held in the *San Martín's* cabin.

It was obvious by now that the Spaniards were confronted with tactics of naval warfare they had never faced before. More important, they found themselves fighting against what amounted to a new type of warship. The Holy Crusade had set sail from Lisbon confident of its ability to catch, close with, grapple, board and subdue any enemy. There was nothing about the sheer size of the English force to frustrate these tactics. What did frustrate the Armada was the combination of English tactics and English galleons. John Hawkins' longer, leaner vessels carried more guns and could sail closer to the wind than anything in the Armada, including the *San Martín.* These galleons were perfectly adapted to—in fact dictated—the new type of warfare. The English obviously had no intention of fighting the Spaniards' kind of battle—grapplings and boardings. Instead their more maneuverable, heavier-gunned galleons kept out of reach of the Spanish galleons and blasted them with their long-range culverins and demiculverins. The Spaniards' high castles would give them the advantage if only they could close; but in this kind of wheeling, darting battle the castles made the Spanish galleons harder to sail and put them at a crucial disadvantage. The Duke of Medina-Sidonia must have seen how drastically the rules of battle were being changed before his eyes. But he probably did not realize that here in the English Channel a few refinements of a basic ship design were altering the history of naval warfare. What he did know was that the galleons of the Armada had to get within grappling range of the galleons of the English defenders if the Spaniards were to carry out their mission. And as the captains met around the big table in the *San Martín*'s cabin, all agreed that time was working against them. Everyone had seen, during the day, the steady stream of reinforcements coming out from England to join the fleet. If this kept up, the enemy would soon have a vastly superior force, in quantity as well as quality.

If any doubt had remained on the score of English tactics on Monday, it was removed on Tuesday. With dawn the wind hauled east. The English, keeping between the Armada and the shore to forestall a landing, now lost the weather gauge. As they tried to work their way out of the trap, the two fleets came within close range and the first full-fledged battle ensued; with it came the first full-fledged test of the *San Martín*. Running down to intercept an attack on a Spanish contingent, Medina-Sidonia found himself crossing course with the English flagship, the big galleon *Ark Royal*.

The duke sent the *San Martín* rushing at her, then rounded to and backed topsails, in the confident assumption that the English commander would not duck this bold a challenge to grapple and board. But the *Ark Royal* sailed on past, loosing a thunderous broadside as she went. In her train came galleon after galleon, each one pounding the Spaniard in its turn. Then the English line wheeled about and came back on the other tack, each galleon lambasting the *San Martín* again.

The *San Martín* took it. She not only took it but she returned the fire so strongly that the attackers had begun to veer off by the time more Spaniards came up to their flagship's rescue. So far to leeward had the *San Martín* gone from the main body of the Armada that she fought off more than a score of attackers for a full hour before the other Spanish galleons could reach her. As the Spanish line came down onto the scene, the English broke off. The Armada swung into its crescent formation again and proceeded up the Channel.

Thus the assumptions of the previous day were confirmed beyond doubt. Evidently Medina-Sidonia did not call another council aboard the *San Martín* that evening, but he probably had no reason to. It was painfully clear that nothing would make the English fight in the manner all Spaniards expected them to fight. Not only were the enemy's guns more effective at long range, but their gunners were better; they fired at least twice to every Spanish broadside; and only the stoutness of the *San Martín* saved her from being hulled and sent to the bottom in that one-sided exchange. Now everyone in the Armada, and particularly the lonely man on the poop deck of the flagship, knew that their estimate of yesterday was a certainty today. The question no longer was whether the Armada could destroy the English fleet; it was whether the Armada could fight its way through.

So far, however, it was accomplishing this lesser objective in an impressive manner. All Tuesday afternoon and night the massive floating crescent moved up the Channel, the English fleet dogging its course. It appeared that the English had begun to recognize their inability so far to halt the Armada, because they seemed to move in closer on the attack next morning. This battle took about two hours, until the wind dropped off. The calm lasted through the night and into Thursday, when a weird but ineffectual battle was fought in the breathless air, with oarsmen heaving away in ships' boats to tug the heavy galleons into firing range One of the leaders of the English line in this battle was the *Victory;* her namesake would achieve greater fame two centuries later and some seven hundred miles south, off Trafalgar (Chapter V). A breeze came up in the afternoon and, in an engagement with all the slow-motion grace of a huge quadrille, the English almost succeeded in luring the Armada onto the Owers, a tangle of rocks off the Isle of Wight. But Medina-Sidonia's pilot, standing beside the duke on the *San Martín*'s towering poop, spotted the shoals in time and Medina-Sidonia expertly led the entire fleet out of danger. Again the crescent formed up, and again the Armada resumed its march up the Channel.

By Friday, August 5, when Medina-Sidonia called another council, the Spaniards were confronted with a dilemma. If the Armada sailed on very much farther, it would come out into the stormy North Sea. If the fleet anchored, it might find itself at a defensive disadvantage. But the duke had no choice. During the past week he had sent messenger after messenger to the mainland to alert Parma and ask him to prepare for their meeting. He had received no answer. Was Parma ready? How long could the Armada wait? The constant traffic of reinforcements continued to come out to the enemy, obviously bringing men, provisions, powder and—most important—cannon balls. The Armada's stock of cannon balls was almost gone. Now the Duke sent a more urgent message to Parma, asking for six-, eight- and ten-pounders and urging him to ready his assault forces. The invasion army's time was at hand; and the Armada's time was running out.

So was its seaway. Earlier, when the plans had been formed, the Duke of Parma had advocated the seizure of the port of Flushing, so the Armada could anchor safely to await the joining of forces. This proposal had been overruled, and now, on Saturday afternoon, the Duke of Medina-Sidonia had no choice but to drop anchor near Calais Roads. The English quickly followed suit and the two huge fleets came to rest opposite each other, at impasse for the moment but not for long.

There were councils of war aboard the English flagship too. As the captains met with Lord Howard, they must have conversed in worried tones. Whatever the obvious superiority of the English galleons' sailing qualities, it was equally obvious that the Spanish galleons could take tremendous punishment. The new design of the English galleons, the new longer-range guns and the new tactics were beating the Spaniard whenever he showed fight. But they were not stopping his steady advance. The Spanish crescent had continued to move inexorably forward to its present anchorage. And who knew but what this was the rendezvous? How would the Armada and the assault group join forces? Would the English then be able to penetrate that formidable crescent when it shielded thousands of soldiers on their way to England's beaches? No one knew the answer. But clearly something had to be done to break up the Armada before it was too late. A complete change of tactics was called for. By the time the conference aboard the *Ark Royal* adjourned, the Lord Admiral had determined what the new tactic would be.

Aboard the *San Martín*, at anchor and rolling with the swells, the Duke of Medina-Sidonia was preoccupied with his concern over the lack of news from Parma. Another messenger headed for shore. The Armada could not sit here for long. A storm from the west would drive them onto the beach. And there was an even graver danger, of which his advisers had warned him. The next night it came.

All evening an increasing southwind made the galleons pitch and surge at their anchors. Then, at midnight, Medina-Sidonia could spot from his high vantage point the first signs of what he had dreaded. Within minutes there were eight of them lighting up the night sky— fireships, fiercely ablaze and roaring straight downwind into the anchored Armada.

The duke had made what preparations he could. The Armada's pinnaces swept into action at his signal, ducking under the guns of the enemy and attempting to grapple and tow the fireships away from the main fleet. But they could not catch all eight. On the rest came, their sails roaring in flame and their double-shotted guns exploding in all directions as they drove before the strong wind.

For the first time the Spanish captains panicked. Cables were slipped, sails were shaken out and the galleons rushed helter-skelter out toward the open Channnel. Vessels of all sizes charged about like whales in a flurry. After more than a week of unmarred seamanship and discipline, the Armada finally went to pieces.

Medina-Sidonia took the *San Martín* out a short way and then returned to anchor near her original spot. The last of the fireships could be seen burning near the shore. But most of the Armada had scattered. The duke spent a painful night pacing the *San Martín*'s poop waiting for light. At dawn he could see only four other galleons. But the entire English fleet stood a short distance away. And as Medina-Sidonia watched, the English sails rippled out, anchors splashed and the great fleet moved in for the kill.

The duke fired a signal and the remaining Spanish galleons weighed anchor. As they stood out to sea, while their pinnaces dashed off to round up the rest of the scattered fleet, the duke took the *San Martín* forward to face the entire oncoming line of the enemy.

First to come up to her was the *Revenge,* commanded by Sir Francis Drake. The English galleon fired her bow guns first, and as she swung past the Spanish flagship she let go a full broadside. The *San Martín* replied with her own; the *Revenge* came away shot full of holes. The next English galleon, and the next and the next, swept down on the *San Martín,* almost lost in the smoke from their thundering broadsides. The *San Martín* took them all and answered them. One line wore off from the battle, but another came up to take its place. Still the *San Martín* withstood them. By now even her thick inner layers of Spanish oak were holed and leaking. Her masts were splintered and her sails in shreds. Still she stood her ground. And now reinforcements came up—both English and the returning Spaniards. The naval battle that followed was the biggest and most violent that the world had ever seen. From his deck Medina-Sidonia could watch the chaotic swirls of warfare, with each galleon fighting for its life, sometimes in battle line and sometimes on its own. But again it was obvious that the English galleons were the better sailers and the English guns the more powerful. Time after time a Spanish galleon almost caught an enemy and grappled, only to have the Englishman dart away and fire a parting broadside. But it was not alone the superiority of the English ships that dictated the outcome. What finally beat the Armada was a crueler, more frustrating fact: the galleons ran out of ammunition. The English had been able to send ashore for more cannon balls; the Spanish had not. Now, as the battle entered its eighth hour, the duke had to watch each of his galleons, one after another, go silent.

But still they fought. The duke watched one big carrack, her cannon dead, her spars shattered and blood spilling from her scuppers as she heeled over, sail back into the melee with every man firing a musket. A Spanish galleon nearby began to settle in the water, but when the duke took the *San Martín* alongside to rescue the survivors, now only half of the complement, her captain refused to abandon ship. When an English galleon came up to the crippled vessel and an English sailor asked for surrender, a Spanish crewman shot him. It was now a matter of an hour or so before the entire Armada would be reduced to smoldering hulks; but they refused to break off. Then suddenly a squall came screaming down upon them.

Driven before the wind, the remnants of the Armada flew off, its captains trying to keep together in the blinding sheets of rain. By the time visibility returned, they had accomplished the impossible. Answering signals from the *San Martín*, the battered, crippled Armada was forming a smaller, ragged crescent. And now it stood down toward the English, ready to take up the battle again.

But what had beaten the Spaniards saved those who remained. The English too had run out of cannon balls. Darkness came down on the two fleets before the conflict was renewed. In fact the battle would not be joined again. Through a stormy night the remaining ships of the Armada ran on up the Channel, while stragglers and sinking casualties veered off and ran aground. By morning the *San Martín* was leading only a part of the huge Armada that had left Lisbon three months before. And as the English pressed the pursuit, the duke found himself being driven onto the Zeeland sands. Even without their battle damage the *San Martín* and the other Spanish galleons could not sail close enough to the wind to weather the shoals; so the duke had to order the wounded fleet about and back into battle, to fight its way out of the trap. Then, miraculously, the wind hauled about. The *San Martín*'s journal noted that "in only six and a half fathoms of water, God was pleased to change the wind to west-south-west, which enabled the Armada to stand to the north." No wonder the sailors aboard the flagship believed they had been saved by the hand of God, as the *San Martín* led the Armada away from the sands and off into the North Sea.

The next three days were a running impasse. In another council held aboard the *San Martín* the captains gamely elected to return to the battle if they could. But they could not; the wind drove them on northward. On Friday, August 12, the last English pursuers turned away and sailed off in the direction of the Firth of Forth. The Duke of Medina-Sidonia was at his taffrail watching them go, shivering in the increasing cold and tasting the full bitterness of defeat.

More than defeat, it was near-destruction. Not a ship among those remaining was undamaged. The *San Martín*, holed dozens of times, leaked steadily; her pumps could barely keep up. Not only ammunition but also most of the food was gone. The men had only summer uniforms, and already they were suffering as the galleons rolled steadily northward. In some ways the Armada's worst was still to come.

The duke prepared for the long, harsh voyage up around Scotland by putting everyone on reduced rations. The horses were thrown overboard, squealing, splashing and swimming alongside, their eyes white with terror as they were left astern. But even as the preparations were made, storms struck the fleet. The gales kept up for two weeks. Men froze or numbly fell off their yards into the sea. Vessels were swept away from the fleet and onto the rocky coasts. There were more than three thousand sick men in the Armada by the time the *San Martín*'s journal recorded its last entry: "Having doubled the last islands of Scotland, to the north, we are steering for Spain with a west-north-west-wind."

Still they had to weather the Irish coast, where more dozens of vessels were driven aground and where castaways' skulls were beaten in by Irish soldiers. Aboard the *San Martín* the Duke of Medina-Sidonia collapsed at last. He had scarcely left his deck from the time he had first sighted the English off the Lizard. Now, in fever and delirium, he knew virtually nothing of the bitter, nineteen-day voyage back to Spain.

At daybreak on September 21, the lookout at the *San Martín*'s masthead cried out the landfall. But as the flagship neared the harbor of Santander, Spain, the wind died and surging waves slowly pushed her toward the rocks. A distress signal was fired and pilot boats came out to tow her into deeper water. When she finally dropped anchor that day, 180 of her crew were dead. All had been a fortnight without fresh water. The duke was so weak that he could not sit up in the boat to which he was lowered. So desolate was he that he later wrote Philip II, "I will not serve again though it cost me my head." But certainly that September day, as he was slowly rowed ashore, the defeated duke craned his neck for a last look at the battered *San Martín*, swinging at her anchor.

The confident girls of Spain, who four months earlier had expected the Armada's sailors to return home with Lutheran slaves, were now replaced by chorus girls in England singing:

> Here the Britons, honour prizing;
> Ev'ry thought of death despising;
>   Roll'd triumphant o'er the wave.
> There the Spaniards, vainly firing;
> By themselves, and foes expiring,
>   Fly, or find a wat'ry grave.

More than half of the Armada's men did indeed find a watery grave. And fewer than half of the "Invincible Armada's" ships ever returned home. But of those that did, only the name of the *San Martín* still stands out—the galleon that entire English lines of battle could not sink, the flagship and symbol of an unprecedented enterprise that failed but will always be remembered as the most daring of its time.

IV

Pirate Ship: The REVENGE

A ship built to order . . . A string of captures . . . History closes in . . . The oddest sea battle . . . "God be merciful . . ."

An air of mystery and suspicion hung over the sloop that was taking shape on the stocks in Bridgetown, Barbados, in 1717. On the surface there was little to make the vessel suspect. She was being built for Major Stede Bonnet, one of the island's well-known and prosperous planters. Whenever anyone asked the major, he said that he planned to take the sloop on trading voyages among the West Indies. This was a common occurrence; many planters also did some interisland trading. But why did this sloop need ten guns? And how did the major plan to occupy a crew of seventy men? Many Barbadians would have jumped to an obvious conclusion about the sloop, had it not been for the meekness, the foppish manners and the wealth of Major Bonnet. So everyone wondered about the sleek, heavily armed, shallow-draught little sloop, until her owner gave her a name. He christened her the *Revenge*—the favorite name for a pirate ship.

The *Revenge* had not had her name long before she went gliding out of Bridgetown's harbor in the dead of night. And right away she proved that she had been designed and built well for her job. She was fast, sturdy, capacious below, and yet she needed only a few feet of water. Thus the *Revenge*, this *Revenge*, was a unique vessel. She was a perfect example of the ideal pirate ship. But what was odd and quite untypical about her was that she was designed and built for the job.

Almost by definition, successful pirates were self-made men. Virtually every pirate became one through desperation or excessive greed. There was little incentive for anyone making a comfortable living to turn to piracy; it was the dirtiest and most dangerous business of the times. Accordingly a pirate ship, per se, was never commissioned for the purpose; a pirate ship was a captured ship. The vicissitudes of the profession dictated a preference for a certain kind of ship: a small, fast sloop with as shallow a draught and as broad a beam as feasible. But this was the type of vessel the pirates tried to capture and convert to their own purpose. It was never built to order, simply because no pirate was in a position to have one built to order.

In the early eighteenth century there were many such sloops built for trading voyages. They were not sloops in today's sense, of course; in the early eighteenth century a sloop could have two masts. And these West Indian traders were essentially not a great deal changed from galleons like the *San Martín*. The castles fore and aft were gone and the hull lay closer to the water. Generally the trading vessels were somewhat smaller than the galleon. They were faster in light airs, of shallower draught and manageable with a smaller crew—in short a slight modernization of the galleon, adapted to local conditions. These traders were what the pirates tried to seize for themselves. A few minor alterations were then made. The mast was shortened and the boom extended if possible, so as to "get over the horizon" more quickly. The deck was cleared of all housing, pens, boat racks and other obstructions. More space was cleared below for a much larger crew. Bulwarks were built up for protection during engagements. Armament was added, usually up to ten guns but rarely more. The pirate vessel's most effective weapon was speed. Her mission was not to slug it out with the enemy. When a man-o'-war came in view the pirate ship fled, if she could. She preyed only on less heavily armed merchantmen, running up to them, and running away if the victim showed too much fight. This was a particular type of sailing, for which a fast, sturdy vessel seemed best. But this vessel was never built to order—except for Major Stede Bonnet's *Revenge*.

She had not been at sea more than a week when the first prospective prize was spotted. All that is known about the *Revenge*'s first victim is that she was the *Anne*, Captain Montgomery, out of Glasgow— and that she was quickly overhauled. Though the precise details are lost, the capture undoubtedly went like all the rest—the little sloop racing down on the merchantman; the black flag rippling to the mast-head, the shot across the merchantman's bow; and the merchantman slowly swinging into the wind and losing way. Pirate Captain Bonnet sent his deputies across in a boat. They ransacked the ship and

searched the captain, crew and passengers. The valuables were ferried
across to the hold of the *Revenge*. Then Major Bonnet permitted the
Anne to proceed on her way, to the relief of the *Anne*'s captain, who
well knew that they were getting off easily.

Captain and crew of the next prize were not so fortunate. It was
only a day or two after their first capture that Bonnet and his pirates
sighted another merchantman. Again the trading vessel was no match
in a race with the *Revenge*. Again capitulation came quickly. But this
time Bonnet gave his victim sterner treatment.

She was the *Turbet*, and she was from Barbados. Evidently Bonnet
did not know the captain of this ship from his home island; the name
of the *Turbet*'s skipper has been lost. In any case, Bonnet did not
want this captain and crew proceeding on to Barbados and confirming
what so many suspected by now: that Major Stede Bonnet was on a
voyage not of trading but of piracy. So the captain and crew of the
Turbet were crowded aboard the *Revenge*, to be set ashore at the
next wood-and-water stop, and their vessel was burned.

The *Turbet* was followed by the *Endeavour*, the *Endeavour* by the
Young. And so they fell to Bonnet's *Revenge*. No merchantman was
swift enough to escape her, and no man-o'-war could catch her. For
more than a year Major Bonnet cruised the American coast, from the
West Indies all the way north to Long Island Sound, where he sold
his captured cargoes to New York merchants. For a few weeks Bonnet joined forces with a more famous pirate: Blackbeard. Bonnet soon
discovered, however, that joining forces with Blackbeard was a one-
sided affair, to put it mildly. He seized the first opportunity to continue cruising on his own.

His successes continued; no ship could match the little *Revenge*.
Bonnet had changed her name now, in hopes of confusing the dozens
of men-o'-war that were out searching for him; he had named the sloop
the *Royal James* and had even changed his own name to "Captain
Thomas." But it was still Major Stede Bonnet and the same unbeatable
Revenge.

Against all types of vessels she had proved her superior speed and
maneuverability. But now she was about to face another test: her
ability to slip in and out of the shallow coves, inlets and rivers of

the West Indies and the mainland. This was the final proof of a good
pirate ship.

In the full flush of all his victories, Stede Bonnet did not realize
that he was fast becoming an anachronism. While he went on captur-
ing ship after ship, a concerted campaign was being carried out to
drive the pirates from the seas. Boston had already been closed down;
few merchants any longer dared risk the heavy penalties for dealing
in stolen merchandise, and any pirates who tried to sneak into the
harbor found that Boston was a "hanging town." So was Philadelphia.
Some merchants willing to deal with pirates could be found in New
York, but they dealt at arm's length, sending their middlemen all the
way down the length of the sound to the end of Long Island; and
the prices they offered were a lot less than they once had been.
Meanwhile more naval vessels sailed along the coast looking for
pirates, and week by week the raiders were being swept from the
ocean. Although Stede Bonnet did not know it, the whole southern
coast was aroused and eager to put an end to piracy.

There was no doubt that Bonnet himself had become a menace.
Within a few weeks of cruising off the Carolina coast, he captured
a ship carrying rum, two more with cargoes of tobacco, another with
pork and bacon, a schooner loaded with leather, two vessels carrying
specie, another loaded with molasses, rum, cotton and cash. A dozen
vessels yielded their cargoes to Bonnet at gunpoint, before the
major decided that the time had come to go into hiding and refurbish
the *Revenge*.

In his wake followed two vessels which he had kept as prizes, to
carry some of the cargoes he had captured. Bonnet led them along the
coast to Cape Fear and slipped up the river with the tide until he
found an anchorage where his masts could not be spotted from the
sea. Everyone went to work quickly; the longer they stayed here,
the greater chance they took that a pursuer would find them. If one
did, they were trapped.

Quickly the *Revenge*'s spars were sent down. Most of her gear was
taken ashore. Long lines were strung from her masts to the trees
ashore. And as the men strained at the pulleys, the pirate ship was

hauled over on her side in the shallow water.

The men went to work hacking off the barnacles and digging out the wood-boring teredo worm. They found the sloop's bottom so fouled that many of her planks and even some of her timbers had to be replaced. Bonnet sent some of his men scouting downriver, where they discovered that a little shallop had come to anchor in the river mouth. In the dark of night the pirates slipped up to the shallop in a boat, swung aboard and overpowered the small crew before the victims knew what had happened. The crew was put ashore and the shallop was sailed upriver, to be cannibalized to repair the pirate ship.

Evidently the shallop's crew made good time overland to Charleston. There the news quickly spread: there was a pirate ship hiding in Cape Fear River.

Thereupon a Charlestonian presented himself to South Carolina's Governor Robert Johnson, and asked him permission to go after the pirate. The odd coincidence was that this volunteer pirate-chaser was, like his quarry, a retired officer of the British Army. His name was Colonel William Rhett, and he shortly assembled 2 sloops of war, 16 guns and 130 men to run down the pirate hiding in behind Cape Fear.

On the evening of September 26, 1718, Colonel Rhett's two sloops sailed around what are now known as Frying Pan Shoals and into the mouth of the river. Once in the river the pursuers could make out, in the dying light, the masts of the three pirate vessels behind the dunes. The *Revenge* (under her new name of the *Royal James*) was repaired, her bottom cleaned and her spars in place again. With her two prizes, she was ready to sail next morning downriver and out to the open sea.

Stede Bonnet watched the masts of the two sloops inching up the river, and quickly prepared to take two more prizes. Then, as he watched, the oncoming sloops came to a halt. Bonnet sent a boat down for a look. It was shortly back with the news: the two sloops were aground on a bar, blocking the exit to the sea. And they were heavily armed pirate-chasers. The *Revenge* was trapped.

Through the night Bonnet prepared for the morning's fighting. He was sure that his pursuer, having once gone aground, would not try to come any farther up the river in the dark when the tide rose again.

But the tide would be at flood once more at just about dawn, and that would be the time when Bonnet and his pirates would have to make their run for the open sea. If they did not, the armed sloops would come up after them.

Bonnet was faced with only a few alternatives. He could send one of his prizes downriver alone as a decoy; while his pursuers attacked it he could make his dash in the *Revenge*. But he knew that that would not work; the pirate-chasers would not be lured into full battle against one of the prizes, and Bonnet could be sure that they had done enough reconnaissance along the river bank to know which was the pirate ship and which were the prizes. He could send the *Revenge* herself down as a sacrifice. They could not take the chance of letting her past, and would have to attack her. But Bonnet evidently guessed that the pursuers would attack with only one sloop, holding the other in readiness to catch Bonnet if he tried to slip by in one of the prizes. If they did, he would be caught, because the armed sloop could make short work of either of the unarmed prizes. So, trying to think a step ahead of his pursuers, Bonnet decided to run the gantlet in the *Revenge*. If the pirate-chasers attacked him with only one sloop, holding the other in reserve, he could probably shoot his way out aboard the heavily armed *Revenge*. So everyone converged on the *Revenge*, preparing her for the morning, when she would fight for her life.

From the hold came the heavy cloth wrappings, which were draped and hung over bulwarks, fife rails, benches and all wooden sections that might suddenly be knocked into flying splinters. The light sails were sent down and stowed below; they were replaced by heavier canvas soaked in alum to retard fire. The important running rigging was doubled, and some of the standing rigging was replaced by chain to withstand flying shot. Extra tiller ropes of rawhide were placed near the helm. Oakum plugs were distributed along the rail, ready to fill the shot holes in the bulwarks. Blankets were piled around the water tubs, to be soaked and hung over the powder magazine; others would be thrown over any fires that sprang up. The sky was paling into dawn by the time Bonnet and his men reached the most important part of their preparations: the weapons.

The gun carriages were greased. The barrels were cleaned. Extra

guns, pistols, cutlasses and pikes were stacked near all the battle stations. The grenades were prepared—square bottles filled with powder
and pistol shot. So were the "stinkpots," the jars filled with sulphur
to be lit and tossed on the enemy's deck. Along the rail Bonnet super-
vised the placement of the culverins, the broad-muzzled blunderbusses
that were loaded with spikes, nails and jagged pieces of glass. And
then, as the sky began to redden in the east, the men strapped on their
personal weapons: cutlass at the hip and half a dozen pistols slung on
belts crisscrossed on the chest. At the *Revenge*'s guns it was time to wet
the sponges, light the slow matches and swing open the gun ports
along the ship's side.

Dawn brought a gentle breeze. Bonnet studied the tide, which had
already started running out. Better to go into battle before the sloops
came up after him. He gave the order: up anchor.

Slowly the *Revenge* gained way, her sails filling gently and the water
trickling past as the helmsman pointed her for the bend. As they neared
the point, everyone could see the masts of the two sloops of war. Their
sails were up and they were waiting around the bend.

Below, in the mouth of the river, Colonel Rhett watched the pirate
sloop come toward the bend. Upping anchor, he ordered both of his
vessels to tack back and forth until the quarry came in view. There
was no sign of the pirate's two prizes, so he decided to concentrate on
the one oncoming vessel. Whether he divined Bonnet's plan or
whether he did not consider the possibility of the prizes slipping by,
no one knows. In any case, both armed sloops—the *Henry*, with Rhett
aboard, and the *Sea Nymph*—were waiting for the one pirate sloop
when Bonnet's *Revenge* came racing into view.

This was the *Revenge*'s crucial test, the final trial of her design as
a pirate vessel. She had to be fast and maneuverable to run past the
armed sloops; she had to have shallow enough draft to slip over sand
bars too near the surface for her pursurers; and, if caught, she had to
have enough fire power to cripple them before they could surround
her or shoot her sails and rigging to bits.

She passed the first test going strong. Partly because of greater
momentum than the tacking sloops, but mostly because of her sleek
design, the *Revenge* shot past the *Sea Nymph* and bore down on the

Henry. Colonel Rhett was turning the *Henry* about and into the path of the *Revenge,* so Bonnet had to wear off.

Now came the second test. The *Revenge* was bottled up if she could not swing out of the channel and around the *Henry.* And if Bonnet tacked to slip under the *Henry*'s stern, the *Revenge* would lose her advantage of speed. So Bonnet took a chance.

Edging gingerly nearer and nearer the river bank, he kept the sloop running downriver. While the *Henry* was still gaining speed, the *Revenge* crept up on her, went abreast of her, passed her and left her a hundred yards astern. In a moment Bonnet could swing back into the channel. Ahead lay the entrance to the river, and beyond that the open Atlantic.

Then came a crunching, shuddering lurch. The *Revenge* had struck. The spars swung wildly, the masts creaked and the sails flapped. The helmsman swung the wheel with no result. The *Revenge* was hard aground. Astern, still gaining speed and coming down on her fast, was the *Henry.*

But the *Revenge*'s luck had not deserted her yet. The *Henry* had just come within range when there was the same thumping and slatting of sails, as she too ran aground. Farther astern, out of range but following the *Henry,* the *Sea Nymph* too slid onto a bar.

It was no consolation to realize that the two pursuing sloops had grounded in water the *Revenge* had just sailed through. She was now caught fast, and she was within range of the *Henry*'s guns.

Now came one of the oddest sea battles in history. Pirate vessels and their pursuers had shot it out before when both were stuck on sand bars. One of the best methods for catching a fleet pirate vessel was to run her to ground in a tidal river, where she could not speed away from her pursuer. In fact, two months after this battle, the great Blackbeard would finally be caught when his ship went aground in Ocracoke Inlet. But never before had two British Army officers, one turned pirate and one turned pirate-hunter, fought it out from ships that heeled over onto their sides as the ebbing tide left them high and dry. Even the vessels' guns exchanged only a brief fire, so fast did the tide run out. And with the tide went the luck of the *Revenge.* As she heeled over, her guns could not be brought to bear.

Bonnet's men heaved at the heavy tackle, pushed at the hand spikes and pounded wedges under the guns. But the *Revenge* was too far over on her side.

So was the *Henry*, and in a more vulnerable position. While the *Revenge* had rolled her deck away from the *Henry*, the pirate-chaser had rolled so that her deck was exposed to the pirates. Peering over the bulwarks and through the gun ports, they could cover the *Henry*'s deck with a withering volley of small-arms fire. This they promptly did. While the tide receded, turned and started back in, Bonnet and his men sprayed the *Henry*'s deck from bow to stern. The return fire ricocheted off the *Revenge*'s broad side. But the pirates' fusillades chewed up the *Henry*'s deck, riddled the sails and cut some of the rigging. Rhett and his men kept under cover, rarely creeping out to exchange fire. Still, ten men were killed and fourteen wounded, so effective was the marksmanship from the *Revenge*.

But it was not enough. Without his heavy guns Bonnet could not cripple the *Henry*. And the *Sea Nymph* lay out of range. The pirates' only hope was that the incoming tide would float the *Revenge* first.

It did not. While the *Revenge* was still regaining an even keel, there were cheers from the *Henry* as she slowly moved away. Rhett took her out into the channel to make a few quick repairs and to prime and load his guns. The *Sea Nymph* floated free and joined the *Henry*. Still the *Revenge* stuck fast. Evidently her speed had driven her into the sand with such force that she might not float even at high tide.

Shortly she did float, but by then it was too late. With all guns out and the smoke from their slow matches curling into the dying breeze, the *Henry* and the *Sea Nymph* swung into position between the *Revenge* and the river mouth, and waited for her to open fire.

Instead a white flag fluttered to the masthead of the *Revenge*. Major Stede Bonnet knew when his—and his ship's—luck had run out.

With much pomp and correctness the major surrendered to the colonel. Captor and captured sailed into Charleston Harbor, where the pirates were sent ashore to await trial in prison. What happened to the *Revenge* after her odd battle is not known. No doubt the vessel designed as a pirate ship was set to catching pirate ships. But we do know what happened to the man who designed her and commanded her.

All of Bonnet's men, except four who proved that they had been forced to turn pirate, were found guilty. On November 8, 1711, at White Point, Charleston, they were publicly hanged. Bonnet himself escaped from his prison. But his luck was indeed finished. He was recaptured, tried and found guilty.

Judge Nicholas Trott, studying the still dandyish figure before him, decided to give the man a long, belated lecture on the error of his ways. "You being a gentleman that have had the advantage of a liberal education, and being generally esteemed a man of letters, I believe it will be needless for me to explain to you the nature of repentance and faith in Christ," the judge said, "they being so fully and so often mentioned in the Scriptures that you cannot but know them." Nevertheless, the judge held forth on the subject of Bonnet's sins, his need for "true penintence" and the little time left for seeking salvation. The speech lasted for nearly half an hour, and worthy though it was, complete with a sprinkling of quotations from the Scriptures, Major Stede Bonnet must have been considerably annoyed. The fact was that he had fled his home in the first place to escape the nagging tongue of his wife. And here he stood, in the final moments of his life, being nagged by a judge. Perhaps he was even a bit relieved when the peroration was at length reached, and the "gentleman pirate" heard the words:

"The sentence that the law hath appointed to pass upon you for your offenses, and which this court doth award, is that you, the said Stede Bonnet, shall go from hence to the place from whence you came, and from thence to the place of execution, where you shall be hanged by the neck till you are dead. And the God of infinite mercy be merciful to your soul."

V

Ship-of-the-Line: The VICTORY

*Proud ship and prouder man . . . The invasion mounts
"I am ready" . . . A ragged crescent . . . The "Nelson
touch" . . . "Victory! How you distract my poor brain!"*

The story of the ship is inseparable from the story of the man. Their histories started together: when the keel of the British warship *Victory* was laid down, on the twenty-third of July in 1759, Horatio Nelson was ten months old, the son of a little-known Episcopal rector. His family's only claim to even local fame was the fact that Horatio's great-great-grandmother had been sister to Sir Robert Walpole, Earl of Oxford. In fact, at the outset of the two careers, the prospect for the ship looked brighter than the prospect for the young man. She was officially a first-rate ship-of-the-line. She stood at the head of a list of twelve ships commissioned by the ministers of George II, in the "Year of Victories"—the year which provided the climax of the Seven Years' War, the year of Surat and Quebec, of Lagos and Quiberon Bay. And because she stood at the head of the list, she received the name of *Victory*.

It was already a proud name, dating back almost two centuries. The first *Victory*, purchased by the Royal Navy in 1561, had helped smash the Armada (Chapter III). *Victory* II had won battle honors at Dover and the Texel, Scheveningen and Solebay. The third had shone at Barfleur. The fourth had set a precedent of tragedy as well as honor: she had been lost in the Channel with all hands in 1744. The fifth, Nelson's *Victory*, would carry on the tradition, of honor and tragedy.

She was the largest of all the *Victories*. She mounted one hundred guns, bristling from three decks that rose, deck on deck, from her water line. The range of her guns was up to one and a half miles, and at five hundred yards her cannon balls could pierce three feet of timber. She was registered at 2,163 tons, and 125 fathoms of hempen cable 9 inches in diameter were required just to hold her at anchor. She was 226 feet long, 52 feet across, with a 150-foot-long keel made of teak. In fact, she was one of the largest ships ever built up to that time.

The British Navy depended for its life on ships like the *Victory*. Such vessels as frigates, corvettes and other smaller ships had their specialized duties, and nearly all of them fought at one time or another. But the first line of battle was taken by the ships-of-the-line, the mastodonic, powerfully armed vessels like the *Victory*. Her design was little changed from that of a century earlier; the line of her bulwarks from bow to stern was straighter, but the hull, the rigging and even the elaborate carved work projecting from her bow resembled that of the ships in the navy of Charles II. Yet the ship-of-the-line would remain the same for at least another century—in fact, until steam replaced sail in the navies of the world.

The *Victory* herself was built to last, with a heavy double-layered hull two feet thick, made of stout English oak. (Just in the past few years the Royal Navy has been carving out sections of her innards in a battle against the deathwatch beetle; in the *Victory*'s deepest recesses, up against the keel itself, they have found timbers that were hand-carved, with ornate and meticulous care, two centuries ago.) It is no wonder that it took six years to build her. By the time she was launched, the war for which she had been commissioned was over. So she sat at anchor, went on occasional duty cruises and waited for the action that in those days was sure to come. And it was while she waited, at anchor in the Medway, on January of 1771, that she was first seen by young Horatio Nelson, a twelve-year-old boy joining his first ship as a midshipman.

There still was no sign of the Nelson to come. His ship was H.M.S. *Raissonable*, and her captain was young Nelson's uncle, Maurice Suckling. Horatio was one of eight children, barely supported by a widowed father; the boy's mother had died when he was nine. He was frail and weakened by the ague always prevalent at the time, but he asked for service at sea when he noticed that his uncle was to command the *Raissonable*. His uncle's reaction had been: "What has poor Horatio done, who is so weak, that he above all the rest should be sent to rough it out at sea? But let him come; and the first time we go into action a cannon ball may knock off his head and provide for him at once."

Horatio served aboard the *Raissonable*, transferred to the *Dreadnought* for a cruise to the West Indies, and returned "a practical seaman," as he wrote later, "with a horror of the Royal Navy." For a while he served as a pilot, learning every shoal and rock of the way from Chatham to the Tower of London and down the Swin Channel to the North Foreland. This was too dull. He enlisted aboard a ship sailing to the Arctic. Then he sailed to the East Indies, from Bengal to Bussorah. He sailed the wintry North Atlantic on convoy duty. He returned to the West Indies, chasing privateers in the American Revolution. He cruised the North Sea and the Mediterranean. He rose rapidly through the ranks, partly because his uncle achieved prominence in the Royal Navy and kept a watchful eye on him, but mostly because Nelson drove himself on toward fame, spurred by an overpowering ambition. By 1794 he had risen through lieutenant to captain and was in command of the *Agamemnon*, heading for duty off Corsica. Here he and the *Victory* crossed paths again.

Nelson led a marine attack on the French positions at Calvi, on Corsica. The marines, many of them from the *Victory*, took the town after a bitter battle in which a shot struck the ground near the young captain and drove a shower of sand into his right eye. He could never see out of it again. Calvi was taken and Nelson was chiefly responsible for the success of the mission. For the first time, but not the last, Nelson and the men of the *Victory* won an engagement at high cost.

The paths of man and ship parted again. The *Victory* went to Portsmouth for refit, and then back to the Mediterranean. Largely as a result of a battle off Cape Hyères, with the *Victory* present but Nelson absent, British control of the Mediterranean was lost. It was not regained until three years later, by Nelson at the Battle of the Nile.

The long intermittent war against the French went on. The *Victory* served as a hospital ship. She saw action off Cape Saint Vincent, in a battle that was won mainly because of the actions by Nelson aboard his ship, the *Captain*. But not until 1803 did the *Victory's* great era dawn. She was placed under the command of Nelson.

The young midshipman who had first seen the *Victory* at age twelve was now forty-five years old. In three decades he had undergone a considerable sea change. He was now a heroic figure of a man. Physically he was still far from robust. He stood only five feet six inches tall. His frail figure had been so weakened by long cruises in the American Revolution that he had been taken home to Bath unable to walk; it had taken three months for him to recover. He had lost not only his right eye but his right arm as well—in an incident that revealed much of the manner of the man.

It happened during a landing action against the town of Santa Cruz. The town was too well prepared for the assault. To the eerie accompaniment of church bells ringing the warning and shore batteries thundering the defense, Nelson was shot through the right elbow just as he stepped ashore to lead the assault. He bound up the spurting arteries himself and tried to continue the attack, and when he was finally forced aboard a boat and rowed out to his ship he pulled himself aboard with his good arm, saying, "Tell the surgeon to make haste and get his instruments. I know I must lose my right arm, so the sooner it is off the better." He was that kind of fighter. (Many years later, while Nelson was being acclaimed by crowds of Englishmen after the Peace of Amiens, he recognized a man who had attended him after the amputation. He beckoned the man forward, shook his hand and gave him a remembrance. The man took from his shirt a piece of lace which he had torn from Nelson's arm at the time, explaining that he had preserved it ever since. It was that kind of navy.)

The Nelson who now took command of the *Victory* was a paradox of a man. He could say to his men: ". . . you must always implicitly obey orders, without attempting to form any opinion of your own respecting their propriety." And he could say to his fellow officers: "I am acting not only without the orders of my commander in chief, but in some measure contrary to him. However, I have not only the support of His Majesty's ministers . . . but a consciousness that I am doing what is right and proper for the service of our king and country." Always he expected his superiors to tolerate in him what he would never countenance in his own men.

His vanity even took the form of appearing "weighed down," as his

contemporaries put it, with his medals at every public function. Yet
he could show humility. Once after nearly being shipwrecked he
wrote home:

I believe firmly it was the Almighty's goodness, to check my consum-
mate vanity. I hope it has made be a better officer, as I feel confident it has
made me a better man. Figure to yourself, on Sunday evening at sunset, a
vain man walking in his cabin, with a squadron around him who looked
up to their chief to lead him to glory. . . . Figure to yourself, on Monday
morning when the sun rose, this proud man, his ship dismasted, his fleet
dispersed and himself in such distress. . . .

But Nelson was constantly surrounded by the stuff on which over-
weening pride is fed. An example is that of the man who was asked
why he addressed a letter simply, "Horatio Nelson, Genoa," and replied, "Sir, there is but one Horatio Nelson in the world." Public
recognition was even more adulatory. England made him Baron Nelson
of the Nile and of Burnham-Thorpe in 1798, then a viscount after the
Battle of Copenhagen in 1801. Even Naples, that place he called "a
country of fiddlers and poets, whores and scoundrels," made him
Duke of Bronte, a title he was proud always to assert. But he earned
his fame. He had no conception of fear. After one series of battles
he took the *Agamemnon* into port in such shape that she carried not a
spar or sail that did not need mending, and her hull had to be wrapped
with cables to keep it from breaking apart. When Nelson went into
battle he flew England's colors in half a dozen places, so that even
if the masts were knocked down the colors would still fly. Nelson
was himself a poor shot. When he went hunting, his companions
feared for their lives because of his habit of shooting without even
lifting the shotgun to his shoulder; and he rarely hit his target. But
he was one of the great tacticians of history, as he was about to demonstrate aboard the *Victory*.

Above all, Lord Nelson lived with a sense of destiny. To him life
was meant to be devoted to the service of his country above—and to
the exclusion of—all else. And life to Nelson, in this year of 1803,
meant the destruction of the massive fleet of French and Spanish
ships which threatened the Channel, the control of Europe, and Eng-

land itself. This was the hard duty which Nelson welcomed. Both his weapon and his home was the *Victory*.

She too was changed from the ship the young midshipman had seen thirty-three years earlier, even from the ship which had seen action alongside him in the Mediterranean. At Chatham she had undergone her most extensive refit. She had been practically rebuilt, over a period that had taken nearly two years. From her bow, where she was given a new figurehead, to her stern, which was enclosed and surmounted with the three lanterns of an admiral, she was completely refurbished. And she was surprisingly fast for a stately ship-of-the-line. Like Nelson, the *Victory* was ready for her time of destiny.

Destiny took a strange turn at first. Aboard the *Victory* Nelson found the Combined French-Spanish Fleet that he had been seeking. He moved swiftly to trap the fleet in Toulon, where it had fled. But the wind turned against him, and while he tacked back and forth against it, complaining, "Dead foul! Dead foul!" the enemy fleet, under the French Admiral Villeneuve, got out and away across the Atlantic. This was a second time for Villeneuve; he had been the only French admiral to escape from Nelson after the Battle of the Nile. Now Nelson followed him, in an odd and frustrating chase that went all the way across the Atlantic, in among the West Indies and back to Europe again. When Nelson went ashore at Gibraltar, it was the first time he had set foot on land in two years. And it was a month later before the *Victory* came gliding into England's Portsmouth Harbor and Nelson debarked for a leave.

He knew it would be short, because he knew that Villeneuve's refuge in Ferrol would be short also. Sooner or later the great enemy fleet would be ready to move out again. That would mean that Napoleon was ready to launch his long-expected, all-out assault on England itself, in a final bid for the control of all Europe. It would be only a matter of time, but Nelson little realized how short that time would be.

While Admiral Cuthbert Collingwood kept watch on Villeneuve and his fleet in Ferrol, Nelson retired to his estate at Merton, in Surrey. Here he settled down to enjoy his brief respite, in a curious menage.

Nelson's estate at Merton was managed not by his wife but by his notorious mistress. A younger Horatio had, in the West Indies eighteen years earlier, married one Fanny Nisbet, the young widow of a Dr. Nisbet of the island of Nevis. That was in March of 1787. But this was August of 1805, and much had happened in nearly two decades. The most important thing that had happened was the meeting of Nelson and Emma Hamilton.

She had been born Emma Hart, the daughter of a smith of Neston, Cheshire. She had had her first experience in love with a naval officer. Others followed, including Sir Harry Fetherstonehaugh, who fathered her first child. Her next provider was Charles Greville, who set her up in a London flat and who also happened to be nephew to Sir William Hamilton. Sir William was a dilettante widower whose wife had left him with a comfortable fortune, freeing him to indulge his hobbies: classical archaeology and the study of earthquakes. For thirty-four years he was Britain's plenipotentiary to the Bourbon Court, and it was on a trip home to England that he first spied his nephew's comely mistress. In the manner of the times Greville sold Emma to his uncle, who became so infatuated with her that he shortly married her. Thus Emma Hart, former trollop, became Lady Hamilton. And thus Emma was in Naples with her ambassador husband when Horatio Nelson arrived after his victory at the Nile.

He was forty, with a black patch where his right eye had been and an empty sleeve in place of his right arm. But he was the romantic hero of all Europe, and on Emma Hamilton's curving balcony, with a view of Vesuvius to the south and Capri across the bay, the mutual seduction took place. Sir William was still hale and hearty in his late sixties (he had recently climbed Vesuvius for the twenty-second time), but he consented to the liaison. Later, on April 6, 1803, in England, he died in Emma's arms, his hand held fast in the hand of Nelson.

And now Emma, Lady Hamilton, usurped the place sadly resigned by Fanny, Lady Nelson. There was no divorce, simply an arrangement understood and accepted by all concerned. To Merton, presided over by Emma Hamilton and swarming with friends and relatives, Nelson retired, to rest for the great battle he knew was to come.

It was the first time Nelson had been home in two years and three

months. He walked through Merton's green gardens, listened to the
call of the birds and watched the flow of the River Wandle, which he
had nicknamed "The Nile." He visited with an uncle, fresh back from
far-off Africa with a crown bird and a civet cat. Nelson seemed to
enjoy playing the host. He was genial, if quiet, at table with the dozen
or more guests who were usually staying at Merton. After dinner he
generally cut short the talk over the cigars in the library and led the
men to join the ladies in the drawing room. Despite the many house
guests he seemed to find time alone with Emma, as well as with Emma's
daughter Horatia, who was four and a half and "uncommonly quick";
she could write a letter, was learning French and Italian and could
play the piano. But often Nelson could not be found in the big house;
he would be out in the summerhouse (which he called "the quarterdeck"), with his old friend Captain Keats, planning the strategy he intended to use against Villeneuve.

But where was Villeneuve? Nelson had been at Merton only a week
when the word came: Villeneuve and his fleet had slipped out of
Ferrol. Where had they gone? Nelson pondered the question and left
for London. If Villeneuve had gone off again to the West Indies, there
was not much to worry about. But Nelson did not think so. He felt
that Villeneuve would not take so big a fleet across the Atlantic so
soon again; he had probably gone to Toulon or Cádiz. That they
should worry about. It presaged the worst news of all: invasion.

There was a pause in the conversation before Prime Minister Pitt
asked: "Now, who is to take command?"

Nelson replied, "You cannot have a better man than the present one
—Collingwood."

"No, that won't do. You must take the command."

Nelson tried to argue, but his heart was not in it. He was quickly
overruled. Pitt explained that there was no time to lose, and asked:
Could Nelson be ready in three days?

"I am ready now."

Next day the report came in: Villeneuve was in Cádiz.

But preparations moved slowly and, while Collingwood kept watch
on Villeneuve and his ships, the *Victory* was readied for battle. On
September 13, Nelson made his last tour of Merton, with Emma on

his arm. They dined alone. And late that night Nelson walked softly into Horatia's room.

The slight form on the little bed slept soundly, the blanket rising and falling evenly. There was no sound save the rustle of curtains at the open window. For a long time Nelson looked down at the sleeping figure. Then he knelt at the side of the bed and prayed. He rose, looked at her once more and tiptoed from the room.

Minutes later he was bidding Emma good-by and the chaise was clattering off toward Portsmouth. A few hours before dawn he sat in a tavern while his horses were being changed and wrote in his diary: "Friday night at half-past ten, drove from dear, dear Merton, where I left all which I hold dear in this world, to go to serve my king and country. . . ."

Waiting for him at Portsmouth was the *Victory*. During Nelson's respite at Merton the big ship had swung to her anchor in Portsmouth harbor. She should have gone into dry dock, but the uncertainty of Villeneuve's movements had meant that she had to be kept on the alert. Her armament was increased to 104 guns. Wide bands of black and yellow were painted along her sides. Hammocks were slung on the lower gun deck, and mess tables were suspended between the guns; living space had somehow to be provided for 850 men. Everywhere there was bustle as the big ship was repaired, inspected and provisioned. Her capstans groaned as the men walked in circles hoisting the stores aboard: 35 tons of powder, 120 tons of shot, 45 tons of biscuits, 25 tons of pork, 10 tons of flour, 2 tons of butter, uncounted gallons of rum. Across the whole width of the ship, in the stern section of the upper gun deck, the spacious day cabin and dining cabin and the cramped sleeping quarters were prepared for the man who had sent his luggage on ahead and was now racing through the night to Portsmouth and the *Victory*.

Nelson reached the George Inn in Portsmouth in time for a 6 A.M. breakfast on the morning of September 15. There followed a hurried, secret conference with the captains of the *Royal Sovereign*, the *Defiance* and the *Agamemnon*, which were at Spithead and not yet ready to put to sea with the *Victory*. A short rest to recover from the all-night journey, a letter to "My dearest" Emma—and Nelson was ready to go aboard.

It was noon. Saturday crowds filled High Street outside the inn's entrance. To avoid them Nelson slipped out the back way and down the flagstoned alleyway. But at the corner he was discovered and the crowds swirled around him. Slowly working his way through the throng, Nelson greeted them. He was sorry, he said, as they reached out to him, that he did not have two arms so he could shake hands with them all. Some wished him good luck. Some called out blessings. Some dropped to their knees, took off their caps and prayed for him. A few cried.

On the Southsea beach, where the bathing machines were drawn up in lines like sentry boxes on the sand, the crowd followed him to the water's edge. The admiral's barge waited for him, the sailors' oars held aloft as he stepped aboard. In the flat calm the barge slid swiftly away from the shore. Nelson stood up and waved. Some of the people waded out into the water, still calling after him. He turned to Captain Hardy, the *Victory*'s master. "I had their huzzas before," he said. "I have their hearts now."

The *Victory* waited, swinging on one anchor at Saint Helens. As Nelson was piped aboard, sailors cheered and Portsmouth officials gathered around him; they had come out to the *Victory* to wish him luck. Nelson invited them to stay for a ceremonial dinner.

It was a pleasant affair, with many toasts to victory and the *Victory*. But an air of tension hung over the festivities. Like the plain people on the shore, the politicians of Portsmouth were keenly aware that England's future depended upon the coming battle. Everyone had heard of the huge invasion camp at Boulogne, with as many as 150,000 men and 400 cannon concentrated for the cross-Channel attack. Elements of Villeneuve's fleet were said to be scouting the Channel, and some two thousand small boats were supposedly ready to follow in the wake of the Combined Fleet and make the landing on the English coast. Despite these reasons for anxiety, Nelson appeared to be relaxed and confident throughout the dinner. But later that evening he motioned to one of the town officials and drew him aside to ask him if he could look into the possibility of some kind of pension for Lady

Hamilton. He had a presentiment, he explained, that he might not return from this engagement alive.

Next morning at eight the *Victory* weighed anchor. With the frigate *Euryalus* accompanying her, she started down the harbor. A boat came out, bearing a letter that had been rushed down from Merton. At the big round table in his cabin Nelson left-handedly scrawled a note.

MY BELOVED EMMA,

I cannot even read your letter. . . . The wind is quite fair and fresh. We go too swift for the boat. May Heaven bless you and Horatia. . . . Farewell.

The fair wind now turned against the *Victory* and her crew, blowing hard and into their teeth during that day and night. Slowly the flagship and her escorting frigate worked their way down the coast. Off Plymouth next morning the weather was still nasty. Two seventy-four-gunners were waiting there to rendezvous with the *Victory*. Nelson signaled them to join him, doubting that they could. But they made it, coming up with him off the Lizard. By that time the wind had died to a near-calm.

Two days later the *Victory* and her escorts were thirty leagues southwest of the Scillies. Coming down on them was the frigate *Decade* bringing news from the fleet waiting off Cádiz: Villeneuve was still in harbor. The *Decade* went on her way to England, while Nelson sent the *Victory*'s companion, the *Euryalus*, ahead to Lisbon with messages for the British consul and Collingwood. Every man possible should be secured for action, but no mention should be made that Nelson was arriving. The enemy should not be warned that the British fleet was assembling.

By dawn of the twenty-eighth a British bomb ketch appeared on the horizon. A little later Nelson could make out the white topsails of the waiting fleet. There were now eighteen British ships-of-the-line off Cádiz, with more support on the way. The fleet was gathering for the kill.

September 29 was Nelson's forty-seventh birthday. From the

British fleet's position off Cádiz he could detect the scent of orange groves, carried to the *Victory* by a warm breeze from the mainland a few miles away. With his glass Nelson could see thirty-six enemy men-of-war in Cádiz harbor "looking me in the face." There were no signals from the *Victory* to the other ships, but invitations went out by boat for a birthday party to be held aboard the big flagship that evening. Fifteen officers dined and watched a theatrical production put on by some of the sailors. All went to their bunks early. It was a hot, still night, heavy with the expectancy that Villeneuve might try to slip out any time now. Aboard the *Victory*, as she rolled and creaked with the swell, Nelson slept soundly. But, inexplicably, he woke at 4 A.M. and could not get to sleep again.

That day he presented his battle plan.

The captains who gathered around the big table in the *Victory's* day cabin well knew the problems they faced. Inside Cádiz Harbor Villeneuve had nearly forty ships, one of the biggest naval forces ever assembled. The British fleet had swelled to nearly thirty, and new ships came racing to the rendezvous every day. Thus the central problem: how to engage two such enormous and unmanageable fleets? As naval battles like this had grown in scope through the years, the British had developed a classic battle plan: the ships were ranged in one long line and sent plowing alongside the enemy's formation to blast away, broadside for broadside, until the stouter-timbered and the better-armed reduced the others to shattered hulks. But with thirty or more ships on each side, this kind of maneuver seemed extremely difficult if not impossible.

Consider the difficulties. How could all these big ships be kept from running afoul on each other? Which ships would attack which ships of the enemy? How could Nelson plan the pattern of his attack when he had no way of knowing what the speed of his ships would be? It might be nearly zero, in a calm, with rolling swells sweeping his ships in the wrong direction. The only communication was by signal flags flown aboard the *Victory*. Nelson could not be sure that they would be seen in the smoke of battle, or that they could be obeyed if they were seen.

That is why traditional British naval strategy of the time generally consisted of sending one long line of ships into action. But could this be done successfully with so many ships?

These were the questions in the minds of the captains as they studied the spare figure seated at the head of the table, his dead eye unseeing, his empty sleeve pinned to his coat, his chest encrusted with the embroidered rosettes of his decorations. And as they listened to him, he answered their unspoken questions.

First, he planned to solve the problem of the long battle line by abandoning it. He would divide his fleet into three divisions; the fleet would go into battle in three lines. Not only that, the fleet would henceforth sail in these three divisions, so that the sailing formation would be the battle formation. No minutes would be wasted maneuvering into battle formation when the enemy was sighted. The fleet would be ready at any hour, day or night.

Once the battle was joined, each division would have a separate assignment. One would consist of fifteen ships; these fifteen would go after twelve ships in the rear of the enemy's line. The second division would fight off whatever enemy ships managed to swing around and come to the aid of the embattled rear. The third division, composed mainly of fast seventy-fours, would support whichever of the first two divisions needed help; if none was required, this third division would make for the center of the enemy line and try to capture the enemy's commander in chief.

Thus Nelson planned for a complete turnabout of the traditional single-line, ship-to-ship tactics. He would concentrate most of his attack on one part of the enemy fleet, endeavoring to put most of it out of action while the cumbersome ships forward were working their way about and back to the rear. He realized that the battle itself might not work out that way. But he added that "no captain can do very wrong if he places his ship alongside that of an enemy."

This decentralization of attack was novel but not unheard of. In earlier battles sections of a fleet had been given separate duties and missions. What was revolutionary was Nelson's addition: once he gave the signal for the general method and direction of attack, each commander of each squadron would be on his own, to direct his squadron's actions as he saw fit. This was a complete break with accepted naval strategy; always the single commander in chief directed the entire battle by signals from the flagship. Not Nelson at Trafalgar. By his plan, the plan he had worked out in the summerhouse at Merton, the enemy would be attacked not by one lumbering line of battle but by three separate, highly maneuverable, totally unpredictable fleets. That was the plan. As Nelson wrote Emma, "it was new—it was singular—it was simple." And it went through his captains "like an electric shock." The meeting broke up with the captains muttering, "It must succeed, if only they will allow us to get at them." This was, as Nelson himself called it with pardonable pride, "the Nelson touch."

How, then, would Nelson's captains "get at them"? When would Villeneuve and his Combined French and Spanish Fleet come out? Nelson conjectured that perhaps his ships were too close to Cádiz; they were only fifteen to twenty miles outside the harbor. So he moved the main body of his fleet fifty miles to westward. But now he courted the greater danger that Villeneuve might slip out of the trap. Nelson ordered a squadron of seventy-fours to cruise near the harbor. "Let me know every movement," he told the squadron's commander. "Watch all points, and all winds and weather. . . . I shall depend on you." And to London he sent an urgent appeal for more fast frigates: "Send me more *eyes!*"

He had guessed correctly that Villeneuve was afraid to come out. In fact, Napoleon had had to threaten to replace Villeneuve if he did not put to sea. Now Villeneuve met with his captains. All agreed to set sail. But all agreed also to avoid battle if they could.

Aboard the *Victory* Nelson received an intelligence report: the enemy was getting troops on board. Some ships were already bending on their topsails. That was October 5. Four days later came the news that all but one of the Combined Fleet were loading stores, canceling leaves and testing topgallant sails in the breeze. There were more than thirty in the enemy fleet, including fifteen Spanish ships-of-the-line, four of them mounting 100-130 guns each; four French eighty-gun ships; fourteen seventy-fours; five frigates; two gun brigs. Nelson had twenty-seven ships, none of them more heavily armed than his 104-gun *Victory*.

Still Villeneuve delayed, and still Nelson waited. On the night of the tenth it rained, to the vexation of some of the captains who were having their ships painted black and yellow like the *Victory*. By the thirteenth the *Agamemnon* and the frigate *Amiable* joined the waiting fleet. On the night of the eighteenth Nelson wrote in his journal: "Wind easterly. The Combined Fleets cannot have finer weather to put to sea." In the morning a boat went from the *Victory* to the *Royal Sovereign* with a message to Collingwood. "What a beautiful day! Will you be tempted out of your ship?" But before Collingwood could reply, the warning signal went up. The Combined Fleet was moving out of Cádiz.

Villeneuve had started out at 7 A.M. At first he had been delayed by calms. But in the afternoon a freshening breeze came up. Slowly gathering speed, the gigantic formation moved ponderously out to sea.

And on the horizon two British frigates watched. The fleet set off on a northward course. Word flashed to the *Victory*. From ship to ship in the British fleet the signal rippled to the masthead. And below, in his cabin in the *Victory*, Nelson wrote two letters.

My dearest, beloved Emma . . . The signal has been made. . . . May the God of Battles crown my endeavours with success. . . . May Heaven bless you. . . .

The second letter was significant because it was addressed to the young girl whom Nelson had always called his "foster daughter." This one started: "My dearest angel . . ." and it was signed: "Your father."

By nightfall the enemy was reported still on a northward course. And at dinner Nelson said to one of his officers that if he was killed he wanted to be buried in St. Paul's, not Westminster Abbey. He had heard that the Abbey was built on marshy ground and might someday sink. St. Paul's, he said, was on a rise and would stand forever.

As dawn came on the twentieth, Nelson's fleet was nearing the land. It was raining. There was no sign of the enemy. Nelson headed northwest. Where was the Combined Fleet?

It was just out of sight to the north, lying to while Villeneuve and his captains held another conference. They decided to head northwest.

The captains returned to their ships, and all sails filled again as the big fleet fell off on the new tack. And aboard one of the Spanish ships a commodore muttered to a subordinate: "This fleet is doomed. The French admiral does not know his business." Then he ordered his crew to assemble on deck for prayers.

Slowly during the morning of the twentieth the sky cleared and the wind shifted. Aboard the *Victory* Nelson added a postscript to his letter to Emma: he was afraid there might not be enough wind for the French and Spanish to clear the shoals of Cape Trafalgar. Out of his sight, the Combined Fleet might slip back into Cádiz Harbor. Where *was* Villeneuve?

Then came the signal, telegraphed from Blackwood aboard the frigate *Euryalus*. He could count nineteen . . . twenty-five . . . thirty-four enemy sail, all at sea. Nelson replied: keep track of them. To one of his officers he said, "The twenty-first will be the day."

Through the night of the twentieth the breeze dropped off. A heavy swell started to roll in from the west. Nelson slept for a few hours, and rose before dawn to order the shift of course. He estimated that for part of the previous day and night they had been sailing parallel to the course of the enemy. Villeneuve had now been drawn far enough away from Cádiz. He was beyond the point of no return.

The night sky above the *Victory* lit up with Bengal fires as the signal was given. Slowly the *Victory* led the fleet around to the north-east, as the British moved in to attack.

Nelson was on the *Victory*'s quarterdeck waiting for daylight. When it came, he saw the enemy—a long double row of ships hazily outlined against the cliffs of Trafalgar far in the background. They seemed to stretch from horizon to horizon, and already Nelson could see that Villeneuve had more big ships-of-the-line than he had.

Villeneuve could see the British fleet too. Earlier, in the darkness, he had watched the faraway signal fires light the sky. Now he studied the British fleet and made his decision: to run for it, back into Cádiz if he could make it.

But he quickly learned what Nelson had already guessed. He was too late. The distance was too great. The British were too close. The wind had virtually disappeared and the heavy swells from the west made maneuvering difficult as the ships of the Combined Fleet tried to come about.

Nelson watched the French and Spanish ships swinging in apparently aimless circles, and gave the command "Bear up and steer east" to intercept Villeneuve's course.

Gradually, rolling to the same swells, the *Victory* and the rest of the British fleet headed into action. The *Victory* led twelve ships in the northern column. Off to leeward, aboard the *Royal Sovereign*, Collingwood led fourteen ships straight for the center of the enemy formation. And as Collingwood dressed for action, he suggested to one of his lieutenants that he replace his boots with shoes and silk stockings; they would be "so much more manageable for the surgeon."

As the French and Spanish ships tried to make up a line of battle, Nelson watched from the *Victory*'s quarterdeck. Although even her studding sails were set, the *Victory* barely moved eastward, frequently losing her wind as she rolled to the swells. At this pace it would be two to three hours before the battle was joined. But already Nelson's fleet was in formation, while the enemy was drifting into a wide, ragged crescent, curving toward the incoming British. Nelson studied his fleet with satisfaction, striding from side to side on the *Victory*'s quarterdeck.

Watching him, Dr. William Beatty, the *Victory*'s surgeon, worried about the admiral's safety. Nelson was wearing the undress uniform coat he had worn since leaving Portsmouth. His sword was not at his side, and the coat had no medals pinned to it. But on its left breast were the embroidered rosettes of his orders of knighthood. Dr. Beatty turned to one of Nelson's secretaries and suggested that someone warn the admiral about those embroidered decorations. The enemy was likely to have Tyrolese sharpshooters in the tops, and the decorations would make a perfect target. It would be a good idea to cover them or change coats. The secretary replied that he did not think the admiral would take kindly to such a suggestion.

It was time, Nelson announced, to make a final tour of the ship. With Captain Hardy and a knot of aides following him, he looked into nearly every corner of the *Victory*. At the forecastle he checked the carronades, the short guns that fired huge amounts of shot at close range with such effectiveness that they were nicknamed "smashers." They were now being loaded with round shot and musket balls. One of these carronades, packed with three hundred balls, would be first to fire on the enemy. On the middle gun deck, behind the stove, sea water was being distilled; the fresh water would be needed by the *Victory*'s surgeon when his grisly work commenced. In the center of the orlop deck, so-called because it "o'erlaps" the ship's hold, the powder magazine bustled with activity. On felt soles the gunner and his mates shuffled about filling their charges. Soon, before going into action, the grand magazine would be locked, so it could be flooded if fire came too near the thirty-five tons of power—enough to blow the *Victory* out of the water. But it was the lower gun deck that Nelson inspected longest.

Here were the *Victory*'s vitals. Here were the work area and the eating and sleeping quarters of 225 of the ship's 850 men—Englishmen and Germans, Dutch and Swiss and Americans, even a few Frenchmen and Spaniards. Here were the hammocks, now folded up along the bulwarks to guard against flying splinters, and the mess tables, now being taken down to be towed astern until the battle was over. Here, at the bow, were the anchor hawseholes, which Nelson inspected; he complimented the men on how well the holes were barricaded against enemy fire and the sea. He also gave the gunners a pep talk, enjoining them not to waste a shot. The gun crews, fifteen men to a gun, stripped to the waist and wearing handkerchiefs around their heads to deaden the noise, gave the admiral a short cheer.

These men were the architects of victory or defeat. Whatever her speed, which was impressive with any wind; whatever her ability to withstand the pounding of the enemy, and this too was impressive —the *Victory*'s main purpose was to inflict damage on the enemy. This depended upon her guns, 104 of them mounted in three tiers. She carried virtually every kind known to marine warfare. There was grapeshot, three tiers of iron balls, all connected by an iron pin and packed in a canvas bag; when fired, they spread out like gigantic shotgun pellets. There was fagot shot, an iron cylinder sliced into pieces and held together by string until fired; when the pieces sprayed into the enemy, they sliced his rigging and shredded his sails. There was bar shot; shaped like a dumbbell or iron spades slung on a ring, it whirred through halyards and standard rigging like flying knives. There was chain shot, which wrapped around anything it struck. There was elongating shot, which spread out even longer than chain shot, and cut down shrouds and stays, sending the enemy's masts crashing over the side. There was even hot shot, ordinary cannon balls heated white-hot before being shot at the enemy to set him afire. But the most important weapons were the big thirty-two-pound guns. Weighing almost three tons each, measuring nine feet long, these "long nines" could loft their thirty-two-pound shot one and a half miles. At close quarters they could fire a double shot, without great accuracy but with tremendous impact.

All these guns, all this variety of shot, all the hundreds of gunners were ready and alert. Even the slow matches, to touch off the powder in the guns, were lit and smoking. Nelson inspected this efficient workshop of the *Victory* and climbed back the steep steps to the quarterdeck.

It was nearly 10 A.M. The Combined Fleet lay off near the horizon, almost as much out of reach as it had been an hour earlier. The nearcalm showed no signs of turning to breeze. The only sounds were the creak of the *Victory*'s spars, the slat of her sails and the rasping of cutlasses being sharpened by the marines. Nelson paced the deck with more anxiety. If only a slight wind would come up, he would be less at the mercy of the rolling sea. He studied the Combined Fleet once more and then went below.

Throughout the ship were hinged bulkheads. Now they were swung up or down, out of the way so as to provide easy access the length of each deck. Nelson's quarters were virtually empty. The hinged bulkheads were drawn up and what had been day cabin and dining cabin were now a cavernous part of the ship. All that remained was his desk; on it were his sword and personal notebook. Everything else, from his large round dining table to his Wedgwood spittoon, was either stowed away in the hold or towed in boats astern, to be brought back aboard after the battle. Even the rug had been rolled up, leaving bare the checkerboard sailcloth covering on the cabin deck. Nothing was left to litter, shatter or splinter. The *Victory* was stripped for action. In the empty cabin Nelson sat at his desk and opened his note-book. In it he wrote a prayer for "a great and glorious victory."

Lieutenant John Pasco was acting signal officer of the *Victory*. His rank entitled him to be executive officer, but somehow this had been overlooked. Pasco decided to ask the admiral to assign him to his proper duties. He walked under the upswung bulkheads into the cabin, and found Lord Nelson on his knees.

Nelson's back was turned to him. Pasco waited until the admiral finished his prayer and rose, then accompanied him onto deck. He forgot all about his request.

The enemy was nearer. But the *Victory*'s speed, which had been almost three knots, was down to one and a half. It would take longer to close, and maneuvering for advantage would be slow-motion, if possible. Scarcely a ripple marked the sea, but still the swell rolled in from the west. There was not a cloud in the sky, and the water was a rich blue. It was a little after eleven, and Nelson estimated that it would be about an hour before he could engage Villeneuve. But this time he had him. The Frenchman has escaped all the way across the Atlantic before, and into Cádiz Harbor later. He would not escape now.

They were close enough to study the Combined Fleet's formation, which was still a haphazard crescent instead of a straight, tight line. The calm was working against the enemy too. But his force looked larger. Nelson counted more big three-deckers than he had expected. He studied them through his glass—the huge *Santissima Trinidad*, sparkling with a fresh coat of vermilion and white; the lumbering *Bucentaire*, flying the flag of the commander in chief. Only barely making headway, they seemed to lie there, guns bristling through open ports, waiting.

On the *Victory*'s deck the band struck up: "Rule Britannia" and then "Britons Strike Home." Nelson turned to an aide and ordered everyone to his station. Dr. Beatty asked Captain Hardy if he wouldn't warn Nelson about those rosettes embroidered on his coat. Hardy said he would. Beatty went below to await the wounded.

Lieutenant Pasco, the signal officer, was still at Nelson's side. "Mr. Pasco," Nelson said, "I'll now amuse the fleet. I wish to say to the fleet, 'England confides that every man will do his duty.' You must be quick, for I have one more signal to make, which is for close action."

Pasco suggested that he could be quicker if he used the word "expects" instead of "confides." In the signal code they were using, "expects" would save seven hoists. Nelson agreed: "Make it directly."

Off to the south of the *Victory* Collingwood, urging the *Royal Sovereign* nearer to the enemy line, watched the flags flutter up the masts of the *Victory*. "I wish Nelson would leave off making signals," he muttered. "We all know what we are about." But as word after word of the message was repeated through the fleet, there was a chorus of cheers.

The cheers could be heard dimly aboard the *Victory* as Nelson said, "Now: number 16." The signal for close action went up. It was to remain at the *Victory*'s masthead until it was shot away.

Nelson turned to watch the *Royal Sovereign*, which was closing nearer and nearer to the enemy line. Hardy took the opportunity of a moment of silence and gingerly mentioned the decorations on Nelson's uniform, reminding him that they made him an awfully good target for sharpshooters in the enemy tops. Nelson agreed. But, he added after a moment, it was too late now "to be shifting a coat." He strode to the starboard rail to watch the *Royal Sovereign* go into action.

The *Royal Sovereign* had a new copper bottom, one which the *Victory* badly needed but had been deprived of because she had stayed on alert all the time Nelson had been at Merton. With her clean hull, the *Royal Sovereign* forged ahead and, at exactly 11:40 A.M., launched the Battle of Trafalgar.

She hit the enemy line at about its mid-point, simultaneously exchanging fire with half a dozen French and Spanish ships. Despite their broadsides she broke the line, passing close under the stern of the big *Santa Anna*, which flew the flag of the fleet's vice commander. Minutes later the British ship *Revenge* came into action, taking some of the pressure off the *Royal Sovereign*. Nelson watched with satisfaction as the enemy line broke—and then a splash off the *Victory*'s bow told him that the flagship was in action too.

The next enemy cannon ball fell alongside. The next one went over the *Victory*. Two more splashed around her, and the sixth found the range, tearing through the main topgallant sail. There was a brief, ominous silence, and then seven or eight broadsides thundered at the *Victory* all at once.

Round shot whirred across the deck like gigantic hail. An aide standing beside Captain Hardy was torn nearly in two. Marines tossed the body over the side before the blood could make the deck too slippery. Whipple, the captain's clerk, was called to take his place; a few minutes later another broadside killed him.

The *Victory* was now suffering the unequal punishment that is inevitable in the first stage of a head-on attack against a naval line of battle. During the approach, until the *Victory* could break the line, she was virtually at the mercy of the enemy gunners. Her guns could not be trained forward but, while she came down on them, most of the port guns of the Combined Fleet could be trained on her. During this stage the enemy was in effect performing the classic maneuver of crossing the *Victory*'s "T." Nelson had allowed for this; it was the price the British fleet had to pay in order to break the enemy's formation into separate groups to be attacked piecemeal. Nelson was gambling that this disruption of the normal line of battle would overcome the enemy with a smaller British loss than the accepted broadside-to-broadside line of battle engagement. This strategy accepted the fact that the attacker would have to take brutal punishment at first in order to achieve surprise and victory at the end.

Normally this punishing first stage would not last more than a few minutes, while the attacker flew downwind into the enemy line. But now the breeze died completely. Becalmed, rolling helplessly in the swells, the *Victory* could only lie there and take it.

For nearly half an hour she took it, while shot ripped through her sails, splintered her spars and pounded at her thick sides. This was the sort of work the *Victory* was built for, with her double-thick walls of prime oak. But not even a floating fortress like the *Victory* could last forever in such a hail of iron. Her sails and rigging took the worst beating; the French and Spanish gunners obviously had orders to "go for the tops" and were concentrating on masts and spars. The *Victory*'s sails were soon riddled. Within minutes her mizzen topmast cracked and split away, falling overside in a tangle of shrouds and torn sail. A lower shot killed eight marines on the poop deck. Another smashed the wheel. The *Victory* would now have to be steered by rawhide ropes and tackle attached to the tiller on the lower gun deck, to commands shouted from the quarterdeck above. Another shot slammed through four thicknesses of hammocks stuffed in the nettings along the rail, and struck the fore brace bitts on the quarter-deck, where Nelson and Hardy were pacing up and down. They paused. A flying splinter had ripped a buckle from Hardy's shoe. Nelson said, "This is too warm work to last long." They resumed their pacing, from the shattered wheel to the cabin hatch.

By now the whole ship was enveloped in a cloud of acrid smoke. More and more men were falling. The dead were heaved overboard, and the wounded were carried below to the surgical quarters of Dr. Beatty. Still the gunners had to sit out the barrage until the *Victory* could swing around and bring her guns to bear.

But then the smoke clouds began to move. A faint breeze was rising. What was left of the *Victory*'s sails started to swell with it. And Nelson gave the order: to starboard.

Slowly the *Victory* turned. Riding the light breeze, she moved diagonally up to the enemy line. Into view of the port gunners came the stern of the huge French ship-of-the-line *Bucentaire*. For another minute or two Nelson waited, while the *Bucentaire* came so close that her tricolor almost brushed the *Victory*'s yardarm. The stern windows of the *Bucentaire* were alongside when Nelson gave the next order: fire.

The *Victory* rocked with the force of the broadside. In one thundering barrage she let go with every gun that could be brought to bear. The carronade in the bow, packed with three hundred musket balls and round shot, sent the entire charge through the *Bucentaire*'s stern windows. All fifty guns along the *Victory*'s port side, double- and triple-shotted, struck the Frenchman in the single blast. In that one broadside three hundred men aboard the *Bucentaire* were killed or wounded and twenty guns were smashed. As the *Victory* moved slowly past while her gunners reloaded, a shower of black dust and splinters fell on her deck.

The intended tactic for the *Victory* was to move on through the line, cutting out half a dozen ships to finish off with the help of the other British ships following on her heel. They were now in the heart of the enemy's double line, and Hardy, going forward to look through the blinding clouds of smoke, returned to report that they could not sail through. The rest of the line was, he said, "closed like a forest." They would have to crash into one of the enemy ships. Nelson replied: "Take your choice."

Ranging up across the *Victory*'s bow was the French seventy-four-gun *Redoubtable*, with grappling hooks lashed to her yardarms. The two ships struck, rebounded and struck again. The *Redoubtable*'s grapnels caught the *Victory*'s rigging and immediately the Frenchmen lowered the *Redoubtable*'s main yard to provide a boarding bridge to the *Victory*'s deck. While the enemy sprayed the *Victory* with small-arms fire, langrage and grenades, a boarding party formed up near the lowered main yard.

At that point there was another violent thump as the British ninety-eight-gun *Temeraire* crashed into the melee, her rigging catching foul of the *Redoubtable*'s bowsprit. But the *Victory*'s gunners kept up their fire. From their port side they had a clear shot at the Spanish ship *Santissima Trinidad*, not far ahead of the *Bucentaire*, and they slammed her with broadside after broadside. The *Redoubtable*, however, was locked so close that some of the *Victory*'s gunners were firing right in her gunports, and receiving fire the same way. So close were the two hulls that the gun crews had to use jointed sponges and rammers; there was not enough space for the ordinary long handles.

The carnage below was increased by the accuracy of the French small-arms fire. But on deck it was worse. The *Redoubtable*'s tops were packed with sharpshooters, shielded by breastworks built on the platforms of the main and mizzen masts, and these riflemen and grenade throwers were deluging the *Victory*'s deck in an attempt to clear the way for the boarding party. From the *Redoubtable*'s mizzen-top there was a clear view of the *Victory*'s quarterdeck forty-five yards below, and of the two figures still pacing back and forth between the helm and the cabin hatch.

The two officers said nothing as they continued their pacing. The

Victory could not maneuver so long as she was locked to the *Redoubtable* and *Temeraire*. It was a test of the gun crews and of the stoutness of the *Victory*. Nelson's strategy was now in effect. The enemy line was broken into a number of groups, each battling against groups of British attackers. With the long line broken, it was no longer a simple test of combined broadside against broadside, in which the larger force of the enemy could have been expected to win. Now the smaller British force had the initiative, as each British captain picked out his target. And from all he could see Nelson could conclude that nearly all his captains were using the initiative well. They had certainly mixed it up. The advantage of the Combined Fleet was lost and it was an even battle. The "Nelson touch" was working, so far.

There was no further order for Nelson to give at the moment, and any conversation could probably not have been heard by Hardy over the pounding of the guns, the crashing of spars and the cracking of rifles. So the two men paced the quarterdeck from helm to cabin hatch—an oddly mismatched pair with Hardy's six feet four and one-half inches alongside Nelson's five feet six inches.

It was 1:35, and they had just turned from the hatchway when Hardy realized that Nelson was not beside him. He turned. Nelson was on his knees, supporting himself on the deck with his left hand. Then his arm gave way and Nelson fell.

The sergeant major of the marines and two seamen were already over him, raising him on his left side as Hardy kneeled beside him.

"Hardy," Nelson said, "I believe they have done it at last."

The stumbling trip from the open quarterdeck down the steep blood-slicked steps to the cockpit, headquarters of Dr. Beatty, was a descent into the inferno. This section of the orlop deck where the doctor was performing his surgical operations was lit by lanterns which feebly illuminated the big room. The low ceiling magnified the cries of the wounded, for whom there was no anesthetic but rum during the amputations. The deck was painted red, to camouflage the slime of blood that washed into the scuppers. Dr. Beatty did not at first recognize his newest patient. Nelson had draped a handkerchief over his face and the decorations which had attracted the French sharpshooters; the admiral did not want his men to see, at this psychological moment in the battle, that he had been hit. Beatty went on with his work—until one of the seamen told him the news: the slight figure sprawled on a cot against the knee of the ship was Nelson.

Beatty went over to him. The handkerchief had been removed, but Nelson did not recognize the doctor in the dim light. Beatty undressed him and examined him. The wound was in the chest, and the musket ball had apparently lodged in the spine. Beatty covered him with a sheet and asked him how he felt. Nelson finally realized who Beatty was, and answered his questions quietly. He had no sensation in the lower part of his body. He had felt no pain at all in the first few minutes, but it was getting to him now. He could feel "a gush of blood every minute" in his chest. Beatty felt the admiral's pulse; it was above normal. He noted that Nelson's breath was short and difficult. Where, he asked, was the pain centered? Nelson said it was in his spine, where the musket ball had lodged. "I felt it break my back," he said.

Realizing there was nothing he could do, Beatty rushed off to answer a cry of emergency. His assistants, their blood-reddened arms glinting in the light of the swaying lanterns, massaged Nelson's arms and legs to keep up the circulation. Walter Burke, a surgeon's attendant, tried to cheer the Admiral. Nelson would live to take home the news of the *Victory*'s success, he said. Nelson replied: "Nonsense, Mr. Burke . . . My sufferings are great, but they will soon be over." Then he asked for Hardy. Someone dashed up the companionway to fetch him.

Nelson closed his eyes and for a while was silent, listening to the noises around him—the shrieks of the butchery nearby, the stampings and poundings on the gun deck above his head, and the echoing thunder of the *Victory*'s guns. When he opened his eyes he looked about, unseeing, and asked where Hardy was. "Will no one bring Hardy to me?" he asked. "He must be killed."

A young seaman with a bandage covering his flesh wound stepped up and replied with perfect naval formality: "Circumstances reflecting the fleet require Captain Hardy's presence on deck, but he will avail himself of the first favorable moment to visit his lordship." Nelson, unable to see the young man, smiled and asked who brought this message. The young sailor replied, "It is Mr. Buckeley, my Lord." Nelson recognized the name of the son of an old shipmate. "It is his voice," he said. "Remember me to your father."

Beatty returned, but he could do nothing, not even to relieve Nelson's suffering, which by now was obviously severe. Nelson lay on the cot, his eyes closed, his mouth clenched firmly as each spasm shot through him. As if from far away, the booming of the *Victory*'s guns and intermittent choruses of cheers reminded them that the battle still went on. Oblivious of its outcome, Burke propped the pillow under the admiral's head while Reverend Scott, the *Victory*'s chaplain, ceaselessly massaged Nelson's chest.

Each time the *Victory* fired a concentrated broadside the ship rocked heavily. Then there came a violent lurch. The *Victory* had broken free from entanglement with the *Temeraire* and the *Redoubtable*. Nelson stirred, opened his eyes, but closed them without comment.

It was half an hour before Hardy came down the companionway and stooped over the body on the cot. Nelson opened his eyes again but could not see him. Hardy had to identify himself. Nelson asked in a half-whisper, "Well, Hardy, how goes the battle? How goes the day with us?"

"Very well, my Lord," Hardy replied. "We have got twelve or fourteen of the enemy's ships in our possession. But five of their van have attacked and show an intention of bearing down on the *Victory*." Hastily and reassuringly he added, "I have therefore called two or three of our fresh ships round us and have no doubt of giving them a drubbing."

Nelson seemed not to be listening. But he asked, "I hope none of *our* ships have struck, Hardy?"

"No, my Lord. There is no fear of that."

Dr. Beatty joined the little group around Nelson's cot. Hardy asked him, in a low whisper, if there was any hope. Nelson replied before Beatty could.

"No. It is impossible. My back is shot through. Beatty will tell you."

Beatty could only nod silently. Hardy reached down and took Nelson's hand for a moment. Then he turned and climbed back up the companionway.

Nelson turned his head, trying to see Dr. Beatty as he ordered him to go and tend to the others; he could do nothing more here; he was only wasting his time. But a few minutes later Nelson sent for the doctor again, and as Beatty rushed up, the admiral said, "I sent for you to say what I forgot to tell you before—that all power of motion and feeling below my heart are gone."

Beatty replied: "My Lord, unhappily for our country, nothing further can be done for you." The doctor walked a few steps away and put his hand over his eyes, as Nelson replied, almost too softly to be heard, "I know." He paused and whispered, "God be praised, I have done my duty."

There followed a tremendous roar, rocking the ship on her side. The *Victory* was loosing a powerful, co-ordinated broadside at the now fleeing enemy. Nelson moaned.

"Oh, *Victory! Victory!* How you distract my poor brain!"

And then came silence. The *Victory* had fired her last broadside of the battle. The enemy ships had been captured or had fled. The echoing din of the orlop deck subsided into heavy silence broken only by the bump of a broken spar above, the ripple of the water along the sides, the muted groan of a wounded seaman. Then there was the sound of feet clumping down the companionway and Hardy was leaning over the still figure again. Nelson did not open his eyes.

Hardy reached down and took Nelson's hand. He had come, he announced, to congratulate his lordship "on a brilliant victory which is complete." The enemy had been put to rout and at least fourteen ships had been captured.

Nelson did not answer at first. Then he whispered, "That is well. But I bargained for twenty."

Still holding Hardy's hand, Nelson said, "Don't throw me overboard, Hardy."

Hardy was startled. "Oh, no. Certainly not."

"You know what to do," Nelson whispered. "And take care of

my dear Lady Hamilton, Hardy. Take care of poor Lady Hamilton."

His labored breathing could now be heard clearly through the room. He whispered, "Kiss me, Hardy."

Hardy knelt and touched Nelson's forehead with his lips. Nelson said, "God bless you, Hardy."

The captain rose, stood looking down on the frail figure for the last time, and then tiptoed to the companionway. His duty now was to report to the rest of the fleet.

Chaplain Scott continued to massage Nelson's chest. Nelson whispered to him, "I have not been a great sinner, Doctor. Remember that I leave Lady Hamilton and my daughter as a legacy to my country. . . . Never forget Horatia. . . ." And then: "Thank God, I have done my duty. . . ."

Dr. Beatty, returning and kneeling over the admiral, could find no pulse. He had to tap the chaplain on the shoulder and tell him, with a silent shake of the head, that he need no longer chafe Nelson's lifeless chest.

The Battle of Trafalgar was one of history's turning points. Of the Combined Fleet's thirty-three ships, only eleven made it back to Cádiz, and none of them ever fought again. The annihilation of the French and Spanish Fleets shattered forever Napoleon's dream of invading England. Just as the Battle of Britain, fought mostly in the air over the Channel in World War II, drove Hitler back across Europe, so the sea battle off Trafalgar's cape sent Napoleon off overland— to Leipzig, Moscow and Waterloo. But the price was high: more than 1,500 British casualties, of whom more than 450 died, including Lord Nelson.

His cabin was converted into a mortuary chapel. The furniture which had been removed and towed astern during the battle was stowed elsewhere, and the bare cabin housed only the large cask of brandy in which Nelson's body was preserved through the voyage home. And aboard one of the ships of the British fleet, as the word spread, a sailor wrote home: "God bless you! Chaps that fight like the Devil sit down and cry like a wench."

A few days later Samuel Taylor Coleridge noted that when the news reached him in Naples, "Numbers stopped and shook hands with me, because they had seen the tears on my cheek and conjectured that I was an Englishman; and some, as they held my hand, burst themselves into tears."

But the *Victory* survived. Battered by the battle, smashed by a tempest that swept down on the fleet next day, she reached port in Gibraltar, making a foot of water every hour and keeping her men at the pumps. At Gibraltar she underwent emergency repairs, and on November 4 she set sail for home. The voyage, through more autumn storms and under jury rig, took a month. It was not until early on the morning of December 5 that the *Victory* made her entrance into Portsmouth Harbor. A larger crowd than the one that had cheered Nelson and the *Victory* into battle now watched as the big ship came home, with her admiral's flag at half-mast.

The reports and messages were written. Dr. Beatty examined Nelson's body and inscribed his official report: the bullet "entered the left side of the spine . . . fractured the left transverse process of the sixth dorsal vertebra, wounded the medulla spinalis and, fracturing the right transverse process of the seventh vertebra, made its way from the right side of the spine . . . through the muscles of the back and lodged therein. . . . On removing the ball, a portion of the gold lace and pad of the epaulette, together with a small piece of His Lordship's coat, was found firmly attached to it." Meanwhile a less official message sped from Chaplain Scott to the Surrey home of Mrs. Cadogan, Emma Hamilton's mother: "Hasten the very moment you receive this, to dear Lady Hamilton, and prepare her for the very greatest of misfortunes."

Emma Hamilton took the news with fortitude at first. But, as Nelson's wife and blood relatives received pensions and honors and everyone conveniently forgot his wishes for her and Horatia, Emma sank into despair. She was arrested for debt. When released, she sailed for France. There she devoted her dwindling energies and finances to Horatia. She died, in near-poverty, in 1815 and was buried in Richmond, France. Horatia married a minister and lived to be eighty-one, never knowing for certain what was established only after her death—that Nelson was indeed her father.

One wish of Nelson's was observed. He was buried at St. Paul's, after a day-long funeral on January 9. And on that day Nelson's flag was lowered, from its midway point on the *Victory*'s mast, for the last time.

For the *Victory* the war against Napoleon went on. It took nearly two months to repair her scarred sides, her shattered interiors and her broken masts. In January of 1809 she was one of the ships bringing home Sir John Moore's army from Coruña. Then she sailed to the Baltic, under the flag of Admiral Saumarez. But she never distinguished herself again as she had at Trafalgar under Nelson. By 1812, despite British reverses at sea in the war against the Americans, the *Victory* was sent into dry dock for another refit. She never sailed into battle again.

She went into reserve, then became the flagship of the Portsmouth Command. For a full century she performed ceremonial duties, until in 1922 her timbers finally began to rot. But England had not forgotten her. A public appeal brought more than £100,000—enough to restore her to "Trafalgar condition."

That is her condition today. She sits in Portsmouth Navy Yard, on her steel cradles in the oldest graving dock in the world. More than a quarter-million visitors from all over the world come to see her every year. Her minor vicissitudes go on: in a World War II air raid a German bomb blew a hole in her port bow; it was repaired. Today workmen are continually kept busy replacing parts of her hull in a long battle against the deathwatch beetle. But the *Victory*, once only a typical eighteenth-century ship-of-the-line, has long since become far more than that. Like the soaring pillar that memorializes Lord Nelson in London's Trafalgar Square, the shining yellow and black hull and the towering masts of the *Victory* remain a symbol of a proud nation's never-to-be-forgotten naval glory.

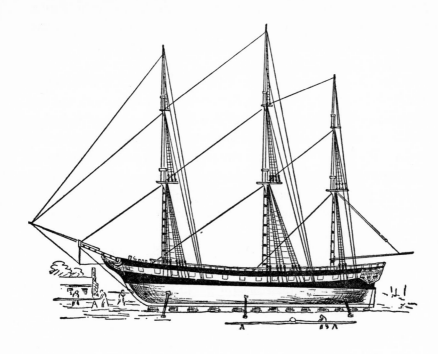

VI

Frigate: The CONSTELLATION

A weapon against the Dey . . . Pyrrhic victory off Saint Kitts . . . "War" against the Barbary pirates . . . Frustration in 1812 . . . A scandalized name

She was conceived with the United States Navy. But she took a long time aborning. And it is fortunate that her career did not epitomize that of the Navy, for rarely in history has one ship had so much plain hard luck. Not only was the frigate *Constellation* embarrassed in battle, repeatedly deprived of rightful glory and cheated out of an entire war, but whatever fate deals with ships has even gone so far as to scandalize her name.

Fate started early. The *Constellation* was authorized in the Naval Act of 1794, which laid the plans for the first real U.S. Navy. Of the thirty-five warships of the Continental Navy, exactly one remained in American hands when the Revolution ended. Only the privateers were still in action. And what little was left of an official Navy disappeared altogether when its entire personnel was disbanded for economy reasons.

So the new nation was in no position to remonstrate with the Dey of Algiers when in 1793 his warships started to plunder American merchantmen in and around the Mediterranean. During October and November of that year alone, eleven ships were taken and 113 Americans were imprisoned and held for ransom. Consuls general represented the U.S. at the Barbary States in those days, and it was humbling to hear that some of them were forced to enter the Dey's presence by creeping under wooden bars and kissing his hand.

Such reports—and the continually rising ransom prices—finally stirred the U.S. government to call the Dey's bluff. The Naval Act of 1794 called for six frigates, three of forty-four guns each, of which the *Constitution* was one, and three of thirty-six guns, one of them the *Constellation*. Congress let the bill squeak through, by a margin of two votes, but only after attaching a rider stipulating that all work on the frigates would be halted if a treaty were reached.

The *Constellation*'s troubles started at once. Three designers fought over the plans. Finally construction started in Baltimore, but the work went slowly and amidst considerable confusion. A year after the passage of the Naval Act, only the bare ribs of the *Constellation* were finished. Supplies of cordage and live oak were fouled up somewhere. Then, to cap everything off, a peace treaty was negotiated with Algiers. All work on the frigates stopped immediately. There followed more arguments in Congress, at the end of which a supplementary act was passed authorizing the completion of three of the frigates. One was the *Constellation*.

On September 7, 1797, three years after the original go-ahead signal, the frigate *Constellation* was finally launched. She was large for a frigate of her time. The term frigate, in fact, had at one time or another designated everything from an oared galley in the sixteenth century to one of Britain's medium-sized naval vessels in the mid-seventeenth century. By the time of the *Constellation*, however, a frigate was generally a flush-decked vessel carrying thirty to forty guns. The *Constellation* was similar to foreign thirty-six-gunners, but she was larger and she was rated for thirty-eight guns by the time she was completed. Her flush deck was 163 feet long, and her over-all length of 164 feet was greater than that of many British and French frigates. Her size represented an American decision not to compete with the British in the construction of great floating fortresses like the *Victory*. America chose instead to concentrate on the frigate, but to make it a powerful naval weapon. The *Constellation* was sixty-two feet shorter than the *Victory* and carried sixty-two fewer guns, and thus was no match for such a huge ship-of-the-line. But she and the other new American frigates were designed to overpower any foreign vessel of their class. Some of the American frigates would indeed demonstrate their superiority over their British counterparts in the War of 1812; the *Constellation* would not, alas, be one of these.

By the time she was launched, the government had forgotten all about the Barbary pirates. American merchant ships were now having too much trouble with the French. As part of their war effort against the British the French were seizing and sometimes sinking or burning neutral American ships suspected of carrying goods to and from

England. An estimated 316 American vessels were captured between July, 1796, and July, 1797. Finally, so that no mistake would be made about its intentions, the French government recalled its minister and refused to accept one from the United States. The naval war that followed was undeclared, but it was war nevertheless.

The first captain of the *Constellation* was Thomas Truxton, a red-faced, bewigged, gouty martinet who schooled his junior officers so well that he is frequently called "The Father of the Navy." Truxton had been a sailor at twelve and had been impressed into the British Navy in his teens. He had been released, then captured again by the British during the Revolution. He had escaped from a British prison camp in the West Indies and had won his first American command at twenty. Truxton ran a taut ship, as evidenced by what happened when the *Constellation* got to sea.

With as large a force as could be scraped up, the *Constellation* sailed for the West Indies, to search out and attack elements of the French Navy at one of their main bases. And for once the *Constellation* had a stroke of good luck. She was the first to sight a French warship.

It was the *Insurgente*, new and fast. But the *Constellation* was faster, and fifteen miles off the west coast of the island of Nevis, on February 9, 1799, the battle started.

Using a squally wind with all the skill gained in his privateering days, Truxton swept down on the *Insurgente*, managed to maneuver across her bow and sent a broadside of cannon balls, spikes and twisted metal screaming the length of her deck. But a lucky shot from the *Insurgente* neatly hit the *Constellation*'s foremast, splitting it so badly that the topmast would undoubtedly go over in a few minutes. In charge of the foretop was a midshipman named David Porter. He bawled below for orders to lower the yard and ease the strain, but at that point he could not make himself heard above the battle. Scrambling up to cut the slings himself, he lowered the yard and saved the mast only a few minutes before it would have crashed over and left the ship at the *Insurgente*'s mercy.

Despite freakish squalls and a crippled foretop, Captain Truxton somehow managed to work his way around the enemy, pouring more broadsides across her deck and up and down her length. Truxton's gun crews were well disciplined, and with reason. When one of the *Constellation*'s gunners, after watching the man next to him be decapitated by British shot, panicked and broke from his post, his gunnery officer pulled a pistol and shot him dead. The others stayed at their guns. Outgunned and outmaneuvered, the *Insurgente*'s Captain Barreaut struck his colors. Then, with the prize within Truxton's grasp, it was swept away.

The first lieutenant of the *Constellation* was John Rodgers; Truxton selected him and Midshipman Porter to secure the French ship and send the prisoners across to the *Constellation*'s brig. But as night fell, the wind increased to a gale. There were 173 Frenchmen still aboard the *Insurgente*, and they had taken advantage of the break; they had thrown all the irons overboard and had even jettisoned the hatch gratings, so there was no way to lock the prisoners below deck. Rodgers and Porter had eleven seamen with whom to control this rebellious crew. Stationing one man at each hatch with a loaded blunderbuss and a pile of muskets—and orders to shoot the first head that popped up—Rodgers directed the clearing of the bodies and wreckage from the decks. All night the storm increased, and by morning the plunging *Insurgente*, with jury rig and spliced bolt ropes, had been driven out of sight of the *Constellation*.

For three days, while the storm raged on, Rodgers, Porter and their little band of seamen fought to keep the 173 mutinous prisoners below and sail a ship that normally required a crew of three hundred even in good weather. Finally, bone-weary and sleeping on their feet, they managed to raise Saint Kitts. There Truxton paced the deck of the anchored *Constellation*, anxiously awaiting news of the *Insurgente* and his best young officers. For saving the prize despite all these fearsome difficulties, Rodgers was promoted to captain and Porter was raised on the spot from midshipman to lieutenant at nineteen.

But credit for overcoming so many mishaps must go to Truxton, and even more credit was to go to him later. Within a year of his battle with the *Insurgente*, he had sighted the French warship *Vengeance*, to southward of Saint Kitts. This time he surmounted even worse handicaps.

The *Vengeance* was bigger than the *Constellation*, but her decks were piled high with an overflow of her cargo, hogsheads of sugar bound for Martinique. Her skipper was not anxious to get into a fight under those circumstances. He ran for it, and for twelve hours Truxton tried to close with him, only to have the light wisps of wind die out at the last minute. Finally the wind picked up, just as darkness fell. Truxton would not wait; lighting battle lanterns, he beat to general quarters and sent the *Constellation* plunging alongside the heavier-gunned *Vengeance*.

Yardarm to yardarm they fought for five hours. By withholding fire until it could be delivered in concentrated broadsides, Truxton made his fewer guns more effective than those of the enemy, and the *Vengeance* struck her colors. But the French gunners had concentrated on the *Constellation*'s rigging and had managed to shoot away most of the shrouds supporting the mainmast. The maintop crew was under the command of Midshipman James Jarvis, age thirteen. Jarvis refused to leave his post, or let any of his men leave their posts, without orders. Just as the *Constellation* came up to accept the *Vengeance*'s surrender, the mainmast crashed. Thirteen-year-old Midshipman Jarvis and all but one of his crew were killed. And Truxton, his ship a cripple, had to stand helplessly watching his prize limp away.

It was not until later that he learned how bad his luck really had been. Twice during the battle the *Vengeance*'s captain had tried to surrender; but his signals had gone unnoticed in the din and cannon smoke. If Truxton had got alongside the *Vengeance* only a few minutes earlier, he would have made her a prize. As it was, she got away, and the *Constellation* crept into Port Royal, Jamaica, a week later without a spar or a fathom of rigging on main or mizzen.

Once again Captain Truxton had overcome what seemed like a jinx on his ship and had won. For accomplishing the seemingly impossible, he was voted a medal by Congress and received ceremonial swords, prize money and a six-hundred-guinea silver plate from Lloyd's of London.

But the jinx finally got Truxton. An officious and overbearing disciplinarian, he was also the best all-around captain in the young Navy. His successes against the French, however, made him even more conceited than before. Assigned to a new command in the Mediterranean, he got into a petty fight with the Navy Department over rank and seniority. Finally, discredited and maligned, he took off his blue coat and epaulets (but not his white naval wig, which he wore until the day he died). Not many Americans today know Thomas Truxton as well as they do John Paul Jones or Isaac Hull or David Farragut. They should.

The difference between the hard-luck *Constellation* under Truxton and under her other skippers was almost immediately apparent. On a particularly hapless cruise, running from the West Indies to New York, she sighted another warship, came up on her in the dark and exchanged shots before the skipper discovered that she was a British ship. This was embarrassing, and did little to improve the *Constellation*'s low morale. Her captain now was Alexander Murray—old, crotchety, deaf, with an unhappy habit of picking fights with his junior officers and disciplining them severely for minor infractions. (He returned from one cruise with two of his officers in irons, and so harsh had been his treatment of them that the Navy Department removed him from command.) On this cruise of the *Constellation* Murray had hardly recovered his temper when he sighted, chased and captured a three-masted French lugger—only to be informed by her disgusted captain that he had acted illegally because the war had ended. The *Constellation* was destined for more such comic-opera cruises now that Truxton was gone.

Meanwhile the Bashaw of Tripoli had captured some American prisoners and was holding them for ransom. But this time the Bashaw was bluntly notified that no ransom would be forthcoming. He "declared war." Off to the Mediterranean went a fleet including the *Constellation*.

During this war the frigate *Philadelphia* distinguished herself in a reverse way by running aground in the harbor of Tripoli while chasing a blockade runner. Stephen Decatur and a brave little band slipped into the harbor in a captured Tripolitan ketch and burned her. But there was not even the excitement of being captured for the *Constellation*. Presently a violent storm damaged her so much that she had to return to the States.

For nearly seven years she lay rotting in New York. Her spars and topmast were sent down. Her paint peeled. Barnacles encrusted her hull. Dry rot ate at her planks and even some of her main beams. That was what she was like at the outbreak of the War of 1812.

The War of 1812 was the time of glory for many of the new Navy's frigates. While the *United States* was beating the British *Macedonian*, the *Constitution* was winning her undying fame by defeating the *Java* and destroying the famous *Guerriére*. Meanwhile what of the *Constellation?* Enroute south for repairs, she had gone aground on a sand bar, turned over at low tide and sunk. She was raised and towed to Norfolk for refitting. It was January of 1813 before she was ready for sea again. Dropping down to Hampton Roads, she ran into a British blockade and turned back. During the rest of the War of 1812, while other frigates made America a world maritime power, the refitted but unfortunate *Constellation* lay in the James River, engaging in desultory target practice. Once she saw some "action" when a little band of British boats tried to land some troops near Norfolk. *Constellation* sailors and marines, almost delirious over the prospect of something to do, fired on the boats from the frigate, manned artillery on the shore and repulsed the landing. It was the *Constellation*'s only engagement in the entire war.

The Barbary pirates took advantage of the War of 1812 and again went on the rampage. Again they "declared war" on the United States. Again a Barbary "navy" captured the crews of two American ships and held them for ransom. Again a fleet that included the *Constellation* took off for the Mediterranean. With rare good luck the *Constellation* was in the lead when the fleet came upon the big Algerian flagship *Meshouda*. With her usual luck, the *Constellation* succeeded only in driving the *Meshouda* under the guns of two other American ships. They promptly made and got credit for the kill, an unusually important one that included the Algerian admiral Rais Hamida. The Dey shortly capitulated and most of the fleet sailed home, leaving the *Constellation* to the dreary job of enforcing the new treaty.

For the next forty-five years she had one uneventful cruise after another, in the West Indies, along the coasts of South America and across the Atlantic. In 1842 she went to the Far East but arrived too late to take part in the Opium War. In 1853-54 she spent a year in the repair yard again. By 1861 she had the unenviable task of patrolling the coast of Africa, chasing slavers.

It is another irony among the many of her life that the *Constellation*'s job in the Civil War was, in the words of her sailing orders, "the protection of our commerce from the piratical depradations of vessels fitted out by those in rebellion against the United States. The principal one of these vessels, the *Sumter*, which has so far eluded our cruisers, when last heard from was in the vicinity of Gibraltar. . . ." The irony lay in the fact that the *Sumter* was a steamship; setting a sailing ship like the *Constellation* to catch her was like sicking a codfish on a shark. The old frigate was reduced to pathetic and useless cruises about the Mediterranean while her captain understandably hoped he would *not* see the quarry which could so easily gobble him up.

The *Constellation* was through. She came home from the Mediterranean to live out the rest of the nineteenth century as a training ship, a receiving ship and a gunnery practice ship. In 1893 she was towed to Newport, made fast to a wharf and left to die.

Somehow she held together, and by 1914 historians began to talk about preserving a ship that was 117 years old. She was refitted. But three years later she even lost her name, temporarily. A new World War I cruiser was to be called the *Constellation*, so the wooden ship was renamed the *Old Constellation*. By 1925, however, she had outlived the cruiser and got her proper name back. She was kept in fair condition at Newport until 1940, when she caught the eye of Franklin D. Roosevelt. He had her put back in full commission, just in time for her to serve in World War II—as "flagship" for Chief of Naval Operations Ernest King, a man with precious little time to spend traveling up to Newport to visit her.

The *Constellation* had not been to sea in fifty-two years when, on a chilly October day in 1946, she moved out of Newport Harbor and once more began to rise and fall to the swells of the open sea. She had no masts. Her deck was housed over. Her hull was bolstered by massive

timbers that took the strain of the steel cable running to the tug. She
was bound for Boston Navy Yard and its dry dock.

A squall came up. Whitecapped seas crashed across her huddled
form. Her weak old hull groaned, and a foot and a half of water sloshed
from side to side in her hold. A desperate bucket brigade kept her
afloat until she could reach the smoother waters of Boston Harbor.
Creaking up to wharfside at last, she settled in the stillness of what
appeared to be her final resting place.

But the cost of her upkeep mounted every year, and the Navy Department, hard-pressed to keep its fighting ships in trim without
worrying about its relics, could no longer finance the battle against
rot. In 1948 Congress passed a bill authorizing enough money to pay
25 per cent of the restoration of the old ship if the public would put
up the rest. The Navy estimated that it would cost $3,500,000 to re-
store the *Constellation* to the condition she was in when she was originally built for $314,000. A public subscription drive was launched.

It netted $93.85.

The old hulk lay at the wharf and started to fall apart. As if by
calculated insult, she lay next to the spanking clean frigate *Constitution*, restored by a public subscription that *had* been successful.

Finally the Navy asked for Congressional permission to break up
the frigate. She was getting to be an eyesore in Boston Navy Yard.
That was when a civic group in Baltimore stepped in. The *Constellation* had been built in Baltimore, and Baltimore wanted her back. By
act of Congress, the Navy encased her in a floating dry dock and towed
her to Baltimore, running before the onrushing gales of a hurricane.
There the *Constellation* was left to the people of Baltimore.

Thus the *Constellation* almost achieved her long-deserved shrine
—almost but not quite. For the old girl's luck is still with her, after a
century and a half. And this last blow is probably the cruelest of
all. Evidence has been presented to indicate that the venerable hulk
on which the Marylanders are doting is the wrong ship.

It appears that, far from being America's oldest warship, this one
is comparatively new as relics go; that she is not the ship that fought
the *Insurgente* and the *Vengeance*, not the ship that stumbled about
the Mediterranean after the Barbary pirates, not the ship that helped

teach John Rodgers and David Porter the art of naval warfare by testing them with every kind of ill fortune imaginable.

Near Baltimore lives a marine architect named Howard I. Chapelle. He is an expert on sailing ships, their designs and their histories. His two most ambitious books, *The History of American Sailing Ships* and *The History of the American Sailing Navy*, are classic reference works for anyone studying United States maritime history. Mr. Chapelle has been looking into the *Constellation* with special attention to his particular interest: her design and its changes over the years. On the basis of this study he states that when the old *Constellation* was supposedly "rebuilt" in 1853-54, she was actually surveyed, found to be thoroughly rotten, and condemned and broken up. A few pieces of her may or may not have been used in the new ship that was then built, but the new vessel was not the *Constellation* any more. She was built as a modern sailing warship of her day. She was not even a frigate, but a corvette. Her new length, for example, was 176 feet (as opposed to her former length of 164 feet); her new beam was 46 feet (instead of 40 feet 6 inches). And while the old frigate carried 36-38 guns, the new corvette carried 24.

Why the fiction of "rebuilding" the old *Constellation?* Simply, says Chapelle, because by this administrative device the Navy could have a new warship without going to Congress for authority and funds. Maintenance and repair money was thereby used to build a new ship. Hence, although the new vessel had to be named the *Constellation*, the old frigate from Baltimore no longer existed.

Mr. Chapelle's reputation in the field is such that when a U.S. Navy officer was first presented with the claim his immediate answer was, "Well, if Chapelle says so, it must be true." But since then the Navy has conducted an investigation and concluded officially that the present ship is simply the old one rebuilt—that the *Constellation* may be running on her patches, so to speak, but she is still the *Constellation*. So has the *Constellation* Committee of Maryland, which holds that the "principle of continuous existence" makes the *Constellation* as much the original as the *Constitution* is. Chapelle's rebuttal is simply that the vessel should then be a frigate and not a corvette.

If Chapelle's view is correct, the old lady now suffers her final degradation. She has been cheated out of all there was left to her, a clear name and a bit of respect at the end. There are those who believe ships really do have personalities of their own. If that is so, there must be a stirring in the sludge at the bottom of Norfolk Harbor these days, as the twisted bones of the real *Constellation* churn in their century-old grave.

VII

Privateer: The PRINCE DE NEUFCHÂTEL

The islanders' dilemma . . . Skeleton crew . . . Thump of a muffled oar . . . Demons run amuck . . . Escape, for a time

She first came into view off the island's south shore. From Mill Hill, the highest spot on Nantucket Island, they could see her as a speck, then slowly taking shape as the fading winds eased her toward the point. As she approached, the watchers on the hill could also make out the ship she had in tow. A little later they saw that she and her companion were being pursued.

The thing about her that most struck the watchers on the hill was the angle of her masts, raked back at almost seventy-five degrees. With these masts and her lean hull, low in the water, she looked fast. But she was not at the moment; with what must have been every sail in her locker, she was straining to make headway in the fleeting airs. She was what was called a hermaphrodite schooner—not quite a schooner but almost. Like a schooner she carried fore-and-aft sails on both main and fore masts. Like a brig she carried square sails on both masts too, the square topsails towering above the fore-and-aft sails below. She was very much like a brigantine as well; only the schooner's foresail made her different. On a curious little royal pole atop her mainmast and on her elongated bowsprit she carried clouds of canvas, conveying an impression of the speed she would have under ordinary winds. Even now, with scarcely a ripple on the waters off Nantucket's south shore, she moved slowly ahead. Her lines, the American flag at her masthead, the thin line of gun ports along her sides all identified her as a U.S. privateer. That meant that the second vessel, a small, square-rigged ship, under full sail but keeping pace only with the aid of the towline, was the privateer's prize. And it meant that the third vessel, off to the south, was a British frigate.

The pursuer was half a dozen miles away, but her bulk loomed on the horizon as she came down on her prey. The breezes that only flickered along the island's shore still held a bit more strongly farther out at sea. The frigate crowded on all sail while they lasted, and before darkness gave the privateer a chance to escape.

On the hill the windmills had ceased creaking as the wind dropped. Across the moors between Mill Hill and the south shore the colors changed as the sun settled off to the right. Few, probably none, of the islanders who stood and watched the slow-motion chase knew the name of the privateer or her prize. Some, though, were no doubt able to identify the frigate. She was H.M.S. *Endymion,* on patrol duty off the Atlantic coast. She had been sent from her station off New York to Halifax for repairs, and on her return she had sighted the privateer and her prize. The *Endymion* had been in these waters before. The frigate's assignment was to patrol the coast, awe the "colonists," blockade their seaborne commerce and destroy privateers. This was her intent as she came ponderously down toward the schooner.

Presumably, in light airs, the privateer could get away, if the frigate did not catch a strong slant of wind first. But the privateer was working in toward the shifting sand bars where the water shoaled off to a few feet. If the privateer captain caught a breeze and tried to cut across the tip of the island, especially in the dark, he could get trapped in the narrow channel between Old Man Shoal and Miacomet Rip. It was partly to warn the privateer captain and partly to find out what ship she was, that one islander decided to launch a boat from the south shore and go out to her.

He was Charles Hilburn, a pilot who knew all the shoals and rip tides around the island. When Hilburn announced that he was going out to the schooner, three or four Nantucketers said they would join him. This was not an easy decision to make on Nantucket Island during the War of 1812.

Nantucket lies thirty miles out at sea, off the tip of the Massachusetts coast. Exposed, isolated, out of sight of the nearest land, the island's location helped mold the individualistic, independent character of its inhabitants. But in wartime Nantucket was defenseless. During the Revolution the islanders had been visited by British raiding parties and had asked the new U.S. government for protection, in vain. In the War of 1812 the pattern was repeated. The American

Navy could not spare a patrol for one island, and Nantucket could hardly arm a navy of her own. So her people had accepted the hard alternative; they had declared themselves neutral. The British admiral in command in the area, Sir Alexander Cochrane, had exacted a high price. On September, 1814, after nearly two years of delaying, Nantucket's selectmen had agreed to pay no taxes to the U.S. government, and the admiral had agreed to let the islanders go unhindered to the mainland for wood and to the Grand Banks for fish. That was one month before the sails of the privateer, her prize and her British pursuer appeared off Nantucket's south shore.

So the islanders faced a dilemma. Most of them were Quakers. It was a violation of their religious principles to take part in the war. Those who did not agree on religious grounds felt that it was a breach of their neutrality agreement to go to the aid of an American privateer in the face of a British frigate. Even putting principles aside, what would the British retaliation be? This situation was not the same as a vessel in distress because of a storm or shipwreck. The privateer had made her own captures and in fact had one under tow. Capture by the British, in turn, was the chance her captain had accepted when he had first set out. And if the frigate did overhaul the privateer, what could the islanders do to help?

But there were others who took a less logical, more emotional attitude. Those were fellow Americans out there, and if they were not already in distress, they soon would be. If, as it appeared in the gathering dusk, a flat calm were settling on the sea for the next hour or so, an islander who knew the waters and the currents could help the captain keep off the hidden shoals. And to some there must have been the furtive anticipation of striking a blow against the fleet that had harassed them for two years. So, despite the objections of some of the Quakers, Hilburn and the three or four other islanders determined to go out to the privateer and lend whatever aid they could through the coming night. Climbing into their little horse-drawn carts, they bumped across the rutted road to the south shore.

By the time a boat was hauled down to the water from one of the fishing shacks along the shore, the sun was nearly down. A small crowd had tramped across the wide sand beach to watch. The privateer lay about half a mile out, her yellow sides turning reddish in the sunset. The last breeze had gone. The schooner's anchor was down. She rolled to the swells coming in off the Atlantic. The prize had been cast loose and had anchored as well. To the south the frigate *Endymion* was barely moving. The cold dampness of the October evening seeped in off the sea. There was no demonstration from the huddled band on the beach as the boat crunched over the last bit of sand and slapped against the waves. There must, however, have been a few murmured good-bys from the wives and mothers who realized what the night had in store.

To the rhythmic slap-slap of bow against water and the thump of oars against tholepins, the islanders worked their way out to the schooner. She rose suddenly out of the dusk ahead of them, the current chirping around her anchor chain and bow, her raked masts lifting into the sky, her yellow hull splotched with powder stains at the gun ports. Because of her long, low design, her bulwarks were almost near enough to the water for the men to climb aboard from their boat. But first, softly in the quiet night, there was the hail and reply, and the islanders learned her identity.

She was the privateer *Prince de Neufchâtel;* John Ordronoux, master. Captain Ordronoux happily accepted the offer of Hilburn and his companions. The Nantucketers climbed aboard. When they looked around her disordered deck and saw what they had let themselves in for, some of them must have wished that they had stayed on shore.

The brutal wear and tear of many battles showed everywhere—in the chipped masts and spars, the patched sails, the spliced halyards. Out of an original crew that should have numbered 150, the *Prince de Neufchâtel* had fewer than forty men; the rest had gone to man prizes that Ordronoux had sent into American or neutral ports. But a more ominous price of the privateer's victories was evident in the sounds that came from below: the rumbling of thirty-seven prisoners who were confined in her hold and were growing restless at the preparations for battle.

Captain Ordronoux had no time for amenities at the moment. His reinforcements were quickly put to work readying the *Prince* for defense. The calm, if it held, meant that there would be no ship-to-ship engagement. That was just as well, since the *Endymion* mounted forty guns and the *Prince* eighteen. But the alternative prospect was little better: a battle that could be murderous under such conditions. The decision to launch this kind of battle was up to the captain of the *Endymion*. If there were no breeze, he could not come up close enough for the classic exchange of broadsides. He could, however, try an attack with his boats.

Nearly everything favored the attacker in such a maneuver. The privateer could be expected to have a skeleton crew. Even from a distance her shape would indicate her low bulwarks, making her easy to board. The *Endymion*'s captain could fill four or five boats with marines and send them down to slip alongside the schooner, swarm onto her decks and overpower her defenses. All this was as obvious to Captain Ordronoux as it was to the British captain, and the privateer skipper hurried his defenses.

Every weapon that could be armed was readied. The gun ports were swung open. The guns were double-shotted and tilted to aim downward at approaching boats. Muskets by the dozens were loaded and stacked along the bulwarks. Baskets filled with loaded pistols were placed within quick reach. The schooner's sides were slushed down with grease, to make it more difficult for attackers to climb aboard. Hammocks of netting were fashioned above the bulwarks, and cannon balls were suspended in them. One swipe of a cutlass would drop them into the boats when they came alongside. More cannon balls were piled on deck, to be thrown over the side into any boats that those in the netting missed. Stations were allotted along the rail. Captain Ordronoux went about explaining each man's mission. By now all light had gone. In the hushed blackness of the night everyone took his station and waited.

The scene can be imagined. The dead calm lay heavy on the sea. Beyond the narrow, visible rim of water the island was lost, its presence revealed only by an occasional flickering light. The swells were slow and smooth, rocking the schooner gently at her anchor. Now and then there would be the creak of a mast as the schooner rolled,

or the slap of a sail which had been brailed up out of the way of action but ready to be loosed at the first wisp of breeze. From the island's shore would come the mew of a gull, the squawk of a fish hawk.
All other sounds would be hushed—the men on the deck of the
privateer treading quietly on their toes, conversing in whispers so as
not to reveal the schooner's presence to the attackers they knew must
come. And now, as they waited, the men from the island had time to
hear the story of the *Prince de Neufchâtel*.

Part of her story could be guessed from her rakish rig. A privateer
born and bred, she could not have been a practical merchantman or
ship-of-the-line. Where a merchantman had a deep hold for cargo,
the *Prince* was slim and sleek, 107 feet long at the water line and less
than 26 feet in breadth. Where a naval vessel was armed and bul-
warked for broadside-to-broadside battles, the *Prince* was lightly
armed. She was pierced with eleven ports on each side but only
carried eighteen guns, probably twelve-pound carronades with two
long eighteen-pounders as chase guns. Everything, even including
fire power, was sacrificed for speed. Her job was not to slug it out
with enemy ships-of-the-line, but to slip away from them. Her prey
was not the enemy's frigates but his lightly armed merchantmen. The
mission of the privateer dictated her special design.

In the War of 1812, as in the Revolution, the naval war had two
aspects. And in both wars the first aspect was at the outset an in-
significant one. There was scarcely a Continental naval vessel worthy
of her name at the start of the Revolution, and the situation was not a
great deal better, comparatively, when war was declared again in 1812.
Some cheering headlines were made by frigate victories of the U.S.
Navy in the early months of the War of 1812—the *Constitution* over
the *Guerrière*, the *United States* over the *Macedonian*, the *Hornet*
over the *Peacock*; few U.S. frigates had the bad luck of the *Constellation*, bottled up in the James River throughout the war. But while most
of the dramatic battles were fought by frigates, the steady, day-by-day
attrition of the war was wrought by the privateers.

The American privateers were a superb expression of the revolution
in ship design being accomplished by the American naval architects
and shipbuilders. No longer was the stately, ponderous, ship-to-ship

line of battle the only method of naval warfare. The privateer was
designed from keel to mast truck for speed and maneuverability,
just as the cruder pirate vessel *Revenge* had concentrated on speed
more than a century earlier. So the spry 107-foot-long *Prince de Neufchâtel* was as different from the powerful, 226-foot-long *Victory* as
a rapier from a broadsword. And the frigates, such vessels as the *Constellation* and the *Endymion*, were somewhere in between.

The difference of course lay not only in design. The naval vessels
were designed and dispatched to battle each other. The privateer
preyed on merchant ships, fighting naval vessels only when necessary
—as it appeared the *Prince de Neufchâtel* would have to do now
if the breeze failed her.

While the *Prince*'s tactics resembled those of the *Revenge*, the
privateer was not a pirate. The privateer was licensed by the government, given a "letter of marque" entitling her captain to capture any
vessel registered under the flag of the enemy. The ship was bonded to
the government, as protection against violations of the letter of
marque restrictions. But in practice the government played little
further part in the activities of the privateer. Whatever she captured
was hers. The financial possibilities were enormous.

All up and down the Atlantic coast merchants rushed to take advantage of these possibilities. In the first months of the War of 1812
nearly any ship that could be put to sea was registered as a privateer
and sent out after British merchantmen. And in those first few
months, before the British Navy could organize convoys or cross the
Atlantic and swing into position for defense, the privateers made rich
hauls. By the end of 1812, however, British frigates were convoying
merchantmen and cruising the entire coast. The slower, less maneuverable privateers, those that had been converted from lumber schooners
or merchantmen or whalers, were quickly swept from the sea. Now
the rewards went to the really swift privateers, the ones that could
outfoot the fastest British frigates. The Americans set about building
just such ships.

There were dozens of them before the war was over—the *Grand
Turk*, the *Rattlesnake* and the *Comet*, for some famous examples.
Some were brigs, carrying square sails so they could run like dolphins

before the wind. Gradually, however, the schooner became the most popular privateer because her fore-and-aft rig made her much more maneuverable than the square-rigged ships; she would work to windward far more efficiently. The *Prince de Neufchâtel* combined some good features of both the fore-and-aft and the square-rigged ships.

She was apparently built in 1813 by Christian Bergh, a shipbuilder in New York City. Her owner was Mme. Flory Charretton, an American citizen with an inherited French fervor for battling the British and a Yankee eye on the most profitable way to do it. Mme. Charretton's spirit was shared by her French son-in-law, John Ordronoux, already a veteran privateer captain of the War of 1812. He had, in fact, been in these same waters before. More than two years earlier, as master of the French privateer *Marengo*, he had captured the British ship *Lady Sherlock* off Nantucket. Then, in the fall of 1813, he eased the *Marengo* past the blockading British frigates and into New York. Mme. Charretton made him captain of her new privateer. The letter of marque was issued for the *Prince* on October 28, and Ordronoux took her racing out into the Atlantic. Across the ocean she went to Cherbourg for fitting out. This took most of the winter, but by spring the fully armed *Prince* was ready.

Setting sail into the English Channel, she ran down and captured nine prizes in quick succession. Her crew depleted to man the prizes and her hold jammed with captured merchandise, she returned to Cherbourg. In June she set forth again. This time her record was even more startling. Between June 4 and 10 she took six prizes—a ship a day; and throughout the British fleet, especially in the Channel, the word spread to be on the lookout for a long, yellow-sided schooner with raked masts and the speed of lightning. Still the *Prince* went uncaught.

She ran up into the Irish Channel and added to her record: eight more brigs; two sloops; a cutter; a transport; two more brigs; a British privateer. She was leading the privateer as a prize when a fast ship of the British Navy hove into view and took off after her. She had to leave the prize behind, but she got away. She was chased seventeen times, and she always got away. One of her pursuers estimated that she must have reached twelve knots, a speed for her size comparable to the fastest of the clipper ships that were developed half a century later, or the fleetest of today's racing yachts. By the time the *Prince* left British waters and headed back across the Atlantic, she had earned almost three million dollars.

Her original owner, Mme. Charretton, had died. But her skipper was still John Ordronoux. It was Captain Ordronoux who brought her, under the noses of the British blockaders, into Boston for a refit. It was Ordronoux who took her out after the British merchant shipping along the American coast. It was Ordronoux who came upon the *Douglass*, a British merchantman bound out for Liverpool, and pounced on her and captured her off Nantucket. It was Ordronoux who now sat off Nantucket's south shore, telling the story of the *Prince* to the newcomers from the island, when the signal sounded softly down the deck. The boats were coming.

At sea at night there is nearly always the sensation that the visibility is better than on land. There is always the contrast between the blackness along the water's surface and the lighter tone of the sky. The lookout at sea makes the most of this contrast. It was what the men aboard the privateer were doing that night. But apparently the first warning came to the ear rather than the eye, as someone heard the thump of a muffled oar.

God only knew how many boats were out there. But gradually the dark, low shapes became visible on the water, moving silently and swiftly, bow-on to present the smallest target, straight for the sides of the *Prince de Neufchâtel.*

It was a few moments before everyone could hear the rubbing of the oars and the drip-drip of water as the boats were stroked toward the target. Their outlines could be made out plainly by now. Five boats were coming in at different angles, toward bow and stern quarters. The attackers themselves were huddled in poised tenseness. Waiting just as tensely at the rail of the *Prince,* the defenders studied the overwhelming numbers of marines and strained to catch the sound of the first boat thumping against the schooner's side, when the night exploded.

At Captain Ordronoux's orders a battery of the *Prince*'s guns had opened fire on the boats. Evidently he had waited too long, and the boats had crept in under the guns' angle of fire, because the broadside missed. But Ordronoux had had the guns loaded with langrage too— iron bars, chain, spikes and other murderous short-range junk. The crashing explosions of the guns were followed by the shrill screams of the attackers as whistling shards of metal cut them up and whirring lengths of chain garroted them. Their cries were taken up in the other boats as they launched the attack.

From the deck of the *Prince* it looked like fireworks as the British muskets went off, and the toughest privateersmen must have been chilled by the battle cries of so many men. The boats now came thumping alongside the *Prince* and the marines made their first attempt to swarm aboard. But the defenders along the rail, not three feet away from the men reaching up from the boats, fought them off with desperation. Some who had waited, cradling heavy cannon balls in their aching arms, hefted them high and sent them hurtling into the boats below. There were crunching sounds of splintering wood, thundering splashes as the balls caromed off into the water, shrieks as skulls were fractured. Other defenders peered over the rail, gingerly to avoid getting pinked in the eye by a rapier, and fired their pistols into the milling mass below. In the flashes of gunfire the faces of the marines stood out, the whites of their teeth and eyes in contrast to their blackened faces. Other privateersmen swung their cutlasses in shimmering arcs, thwacking against the sides of the schooner as they chopped at reaching arms and sliced off grasping fingers. The ship and the boats became a tangled pandemonium of cursing, shouting and screaming as the attack reached battle pitch. And so far the privateersmen were beating off the first wave.

As the pulse of the battle mounted, so did the din. The shouting of the men along the rail was answered by the moans and yells coming up from the attackers in the boats. On deck there was the constant rattle of gunfire, the clatter of empty pistols and muskets being tossed aside and the scramble of powder boys reloading them. And from belowdecks came the echoing and re-echoing yells of the prisoners. As the battle churned above them, they stormed against the barred companionway and the hatch grating, trying to take advantage of the opportunity to break free. So the *Prince de Neufchâtel* was beset from all sides and from within as well. Straining at her anchor as the strong currents rushed past, rocking under the weight of men surging from side to side, her sails lit by the flashes of gunfire, her yards wreathed in smoke, she appeared like a hell ship on which hundreds of demons had run amuck.

Actually her decks were defended by less than forty men, some American, some French like her skipper, some Swedish like her first mate. Still they managed to keep 111 British marines from coming aboard. But they could not hold out much longer. They were firing the pistols and muskets faster than the boys could reload them. Most of the cannon balls on deck had been dropped into the boats below, and apparently had sunk only one. The balls in the netting had mostly been cut away, with little more effect. The defenders at the rail were slipping in smears of blood. The rail itself was a jagged chunk of splinters where knives and cutlasses had chopped at the hands of marines trying to pull themselves aboard. One by one the privateersmen were dropping on the deck or toppling over the side. Captain Ordronoux, counting the forces and assessing the tide of battle, could see that it was finally going against him. In fact, at this point he could not count more than twenty privateersmen fighting. The rest were sprawled on deck, or gone. Below him the uproar of the prisoners indicated that they were on the verge of smashing their way out. Then the marines from the boats under the bow came climbing over the rail and onto the forecastle deck.

Ordronoux was waiting for them with his last defense, a deck gun loaded and aimed toward the bow. He gave the prearranged signal for his men to scramble aft out of the line of fire, but he could not wait for them all. The British marines were already swarming down the deck toward him. Ordronoux fired.

The gun was loaded with canister shot and bags of musket balls. Like a huge spray of buckshot it swept the deck. The marines went down like mowed grass.

But so did most of Ordronoux's crew. Now all the remaining marines had to do was launch one more attack, from the waist or stern of the schooner. There were not enough privateersmen left to hold them off, even for a few moments while Ordronoux swung his deck gun into position. The next attack would be the last.

It never came. In the boats below, the plunging cannon balls, the musketry and the pistol fire had done their work, and the carnage on deck had finished the job. Not only were there no more boarding attempts, but faintly above the din came the cry of a boat commander: "Quarter! Quarter! Quarter!"

A few more shots and it was over. Looking about his deck, Ordronoux discovered that he had exactly eight crew members left. Peering over the bulwarks, he could make out only one of the five British boats; three (it turned out) had drifted away with not enough able-bodied men to propel them. The other had sunk. In the boat still alongside, only here and there did a man move. At least ninety British had been killed, and at least thirty privateersmen. The battle had lasted twenty minutes.

The contrast between the din of battle and the hush that followed was enough to make Ordronoux's ears ring. Now the only sounds were the moans from the deck and from alongside, the thumping of the boat still made fast to the *Prince*'s side, the whimpering of a dying powder boy. Even the howling of the prisoners below had suddenly ceased, as they listened for a sign that would tell them who had won. The acrid smoke of gunpowder hung heavily in the air. And off to the south, the *Endymion* sent up rockets, signaling in vain for her boats to return.

Captain Ordronoux, alone on his quarterdeck binding his wounds, realized that in fact the battle was not yet won. Few British marines in the boat alongside were able to move about, but there were more able-bodied men than he had left. His first mate was wounded. The pilot, Charles Hilburn, who had come out to offer his services, had kept his station at the schooner's helm despite several wounds; finally he had been killed. The *Prince*'s surgeon was injured. Ahead of Ordronoux and his eight remaining able-bodied men lay the job of tending the wounded and preparing the dead for later burial at sea. More important, it would not be long before the British survivors realized that they could still take the *Prince*.

Summoning his eight men, Ordronoux got the British boat hauled toward the bow of the schooner and tied up there. The boat's commander called up to him asking for help; some of his wounded men would not live until morning if they did not get medical help. Ordronoux replied that his surgeon was wounded and that he could not help. He was sorry, but the commander would have to make do with the dressings which Ordronoux would pass down. Ordronoux then set about making his own men as comfortable as he could until morning.

It was a long night. Men cried out as they were moved onto pallets. Others sobbed unceasingly. Once in a while the night was split by the scream of a man gone into delirium. Little by little the sounds tapered off, as some became unconscious and others died. When light blue dawn first streaked the sky out toward the Grand Banks, Ordronoux put into effect what he had planned through the night.

Just aft of the mainmast he had a sail strung across most of the schooner's deck. From his cabin he brought out a fife, and he put two of his remaining men into service. In time with the fife the two men pranced back and forth across the deck, stamping as heavily as they could. Ordronoux hoped that in the boat tied near the bow the British survivors would think that the privateer captain ran a taut ship, and still had enough men for morning muster.

Off to the north the dim shape of the island slowly revealed the green hills, the brightly colored October moors, the south shore and a knot of people who stood at the water's edge as if they had waited there all night. Astern, dangerously near the shore the *Prince*'s prize lay at anchor. Out toward Old Man Shoal, Ordronoux could make out three British boats drifting helplessly, the arms of wounded or dead marines hanging over the side. And off toward the south, her acres of canvas still hanging in the windless air, sat the *Endymion*.

Ordronoux went forward and told the boat commander, a lieutenant named Ormond, that he could go ashore to get help for his wounded. He expected a truce while some of his own wounded were sent to the island for treatment. Ormond agreed. Slowly the barge went off, rowed by a couple of men each, to pick up the three drifting boats and head toward the island. They were followed shortly by a boat from the *Prince*, carrying her most seriously wounded and taking the one or two Nantucket survivors home. By the time they reached the shore, the little group of islanders had increased to a crowd, and men waded into the waves to help unload the sprawled bodies, of attacker and defender alike.

All that day the British frigate and American privateer sat within sight of each other. Though an occasional breeze ruffled her sails, the *Endymion* made no move toward her quarry. Aboard the *Prince* Captain Ordronoux worked to be ready to flee as soon as his boat returned. Aboard the *Endymion* Captain Henry Hope wrote his account of the battle, adding that he had apparently lost more men in this action against a schooner than he would have lost in action against another frigate. He did not so record, but Nantucketers claimed that he did not even make the gesture of a chase when on the next morning the privateer's boat returned, sail was loosed to a light breeze and the *Prince de Neufchâtel* moved off, setting her course northeast to round the tip of Cape Cod.

The *Prince*'s prize, the *Douglass*, did not have such good fortune. On the night after the battle she was betrayed. At the very time when the Nantucketers on the other side of the island were converting the tavern on North Wharf into a hospital and tending the wounded, British and American, some of their neighbors on the south shore sent a message out to the *Douglass'* prize crew: another British ship had been seen from Mill Hill. She was headed for the island. If they wanted to save the *Douglass'* cargo, they had better run the ship aground and unload her. The *Douglass'* prize master did just that. Dozens of Nantucketers, rigging a pulley to the bluff over the beach, helped unload her cotton, sugar, coffee and rum.

The *Douglass'* crew realized the hoax too late. By that time most of the cargo had been hidden by the islanders. Blockaded, starved Nantucket had not seen so much coffee, sugar and rum in more than two years. Some of the looters, however, drank so much of the rum that night that in the morning they could not remember where they had hidden the rest of their spoils. Digging for treasures of coffee and sugar went on in some parts of the island for many years thereafter.

And what of the sturdy schooner that survived one of the bloodiest battles of the war? She sailed triumphantly into Boston to unload her own cargo and the prisoners. Since the custom was to keep the most valuable items of prize cargoes aboard the privateer, Captain Ordronoux evidently realized a fortune large enough to retire. In fact, he was able to pay his share (presumably one-third) of the $21,000 which a new syndicate composed of Ordronoux and two other men paid to purchase the schooner. On December 12 a new letter of marque was issued for her. Nine days later she put to sea on another cruise, this time commanded by one Nicholas Millin, with a crew of 120 men.

She was in the open Atlantic on the day after Christmas when a gale swept down on her. She weathered the gale, only to be sighted by three British frigates. They gave chase. Two of them, the *Leander* and the *Newcastle*, were new and very fast. All day they raced after the *Prince*, in heavy weather that made the going even more difficult for her. Running before the wind, a much more efficient point of sailing for a square-rigged frigate than a schooner, the *Newcastle* logged thirteen knots for hour after hour. Yet the flying *Prince de Neufchâtel* widened her lead.

A superstitious sailor might blame it on the change of captains; she had had such good luck under Ordronoux. Perhaps Captain Millin simply did not yet know—as Captain Ordronoux had so well—how much sail the schooner would take, to the last square inch. Whatever the reason, one of the *Prince*'s spars suddenly cracked. Then another went, and the chase was over. The three frigates were soon sweeping down on the limping schooner like retrievers on a crippled bird. After eighteen escapes from British pursuers, the *Prince de Neufchâtel* had finally been brought down.

She never fought again. Sir George Collier, commanding the British squadron in the area, was so impressed by her that he refused to let her be sent to Halifax to be condemned in the normal manner. Instead he sent her racing across the Atlantic with his dispatches. The Admiralty officers took one look at her and sent her into dry dock to have her lines copied. Then she was scheduled to go to sea as a British warship. But when she was being floated out of the dry dock she hung on the sill of the dock gates and broke her back. She was cashiered into the merchant service. Thereafter she disappears from record. All that remain are her lines and her story— a heroic and typical example of the fast and beautiful American privateer.

VIII

Slaver: The AMISTAD

"Middle Passage" . . . Havana barracoon . . . Threat from below . . . "Kill the white man!" . . . North by night . . . Surrender off Long Island

From a distance the vessel looked like one of the many fast schooners that cruised among the West Indies. Like the privateer *Prince de Neufchâtel*, she was lean and sharp. Her low freeboard gave her hull a long, slim look. Her two masts were raked, and she carried a square yard on her foremast. She was small, about 120 tons. She did indeed look like a trader from the distance; but not close up. Within a hundred yards or more, particularly downwind, one could detect the unmistakable smell of her cargo of human bodies. Her name, the *Amistad* (Friendship) was an ironic one. She was a slaver.

On this voyage her course was a short and easy one, from Havana to Puerto Príncipe, only three hundred miles down the Cuban coast. Under normal circumstances the voyage should have taken no more than two days. On this occasion the *Amistad*'s odyssey was to take a great deal longer, and she was never to reach her intended port.

Her story rightfully begins with her cargo of humans; and their story begins with another vessel. In February of 1839 the slaver *Tecora* slipped into the mouth of Sierra Leone's Gallinas River and dropped anchor near Don Pedro Blanco's barracoons. The deal was closed quickly and the slaves were hurried aboard ship. These were the days when British slave-chasers were patrolling the entire coast. Although slaving had been outlawed by both England and the U.S. early in the nineteenth century, rigid enforcement of the laws had to wait first during the War of 1812 and then for campaigns against pirates like those described in Chapter IV. But even by 1839 American slave-chasers were scarce along the African coast, largely because powerful Southern forces in Washington crippled most attempts at an all-out campaign. The American lack was more than made up for, however, by the energetic activities of the many British patrols. So

the *Tecora* loaded her human cargo as fast as possible, while her captain kept an eye peeled for any sign of a sail on the horizon.

It was an age when slaving ships had to be designed for the job.
Slaving as a business was as old as shipping. But not until the past
few years had determined efforts been made to put an end to the
dirty commerce of "blackbirding." So by the 1830's most successful
slavers—those that had not been captured—were designed for the
special conditions of their trade. Few slavers were large; they had
to work their way up shallow rivers along the Slave Coast, where
every patrolling skipper knew that no large ships had any legitimate
business. Large ships required large crews, which were difficult to re-
cruit for slavers. And it did not pay to invest any more money than
could be helped in building a slaver, since so many were captured.
So the slavers averaged sixty to a hundred feet in length, no more.

The size of the vessel did not mean that she could carry only a few
slaves. For the slaver's interior design was perfectly adapted to
carrying the greatest number of human bodies. Row on row, thigh to
thigh, on decks built so close together that there was scarcely sitting
headroom, the Africans were jammed into the vessel until not a
square foot of space was wasted. Down the length of these decks
went the iron rods, to which the ankle chains were fastened. On most
slavers the men were packed in the forward sections, the women
generally chained in the aft section, with the children amidships. All
were stripped naked, mainly because it was easier to keep them clean
and spot any developing sores that might cripple a slave and lower
his value.

On deck there was rarely more than one weapon, a carronade or a
long gun on a pivot. It was there only to fight off raiders along the
African coast. No slaver captain could expect to shoot it out with a
cruiser. The slaver's real defense was aloft.

Usually she carried the two masts of a schooner or brig. The
schooner rig was most practical along the African coast, but nearly
every slaver carried square sails to help make time crossing the Atlantic. And when a cruiser hove into view, the combination of square
and fore-and-aft sails helped the slaver outmaneuver her pursuer
and escape downwind. In rig and hull design the slaver of the early

and mid-nineteenth century was nearly indistinguishable from the privateer of the War of 1812. The slavers *Amistad* and *Tecora*, the privateer *Prince de Neufchâtel*—all three varied scarcely at all except in size. All were designed for speed and maneuverability, and in fact many a privateer later served as a slaver or a slave-chaser.

So the *Tecora*'s men watched for a rig like their own, which could mean a patrolling cruiser, as the slaver dropped the African shoreline astern. Her course lay straight across the Atlantic—the "Middle Passage"—and then up the South American coast to Havana, where her cargo would be unloaded. With sails set, course laid out and slaves stowed neatly in rows, the *Tecora* ran easily before the trades. She was a Portuguese vessel, with a Spanish crew and commanded by an American; thus her nationality was purposely confused. But the success of her voyage depended mainly upon her speed—not only in outracing any possible pursuers but also in crossing the Atlantic before too many slaves sickened and died.

There were as many packed below as the decks would hold, leaving just enough room for rice for two meals a day. Every day or so a few at a time were unchained and allowed on deck for exercise and fresh air to keep them healthy. Nothing could be more sickening than the decks below. The stench through the narrow gratings pervaded the entire ship and wafted off to leeward. Most of the slaves had been seasick. Some, weakened and emaciated, succumbed to all sorts of germs and spread them through the hold. The rocking of the ship against their chained bodies rubbed sores which swelled and festered. Storms knocked the captives about and broke their bones. One by one they began to die; and as their bodies were slipped overboard, a train of sharks gathered in the slaver's wake.

Occasionally a strong wind could be diverted into the hold by rigging a sail over one of the hatchways. But not even that could clear the pestilential atmosphere below. Twice a day the Spaniards came below with the rice boilers, which the slaves dug into before they were given tin cups of water to wash it down. The crew members also tried to carry away wastes, but emptying buckets had little effect on the stench.

Most of the time the huddled bodies remained quiet. But often there

was a low murmuring or groaning, and a crescendo of outcries meant
that another dead body had been discovered. Only sullen silence
greeted the periodic and painful application of vinegar and powder to
the open sores of the worst cases. Some of the women or children
winced or tried to pull away, but a sailor always stood by with a lash
to make them behave. And so the *Tecora*'s crew kept as many of the
captives alive as they could—not out of humanity but because each
black body was an investment—while the slave ship ran before the
trades across the Atlantic and up the coast to the Caribbean. Finally,
after an eternity of suffering, the survivors were permitted more exercise, were given all the rice they could eat, and were issued cups of
fish oil to rub on their sores and the rest of their bodies. They were
nearing Havana, where the traders preferred the slaves with the
shiniest black skins.

Despite the lackadaisical American efforts to patrol the African
coast and the Middle Passage, it was too risky to take big shiploads
of slaves straight into a U.S. port. So Havana became the clearing-
house—Havana because it was near the American mainland and because the U.S. consul there, Nicholas P. Trist, was proslavery and
could be counted on not to put any obstacles in the way of slaving
transactions. Soon the *Tecora* was beating her way into Havana
Harbor, while her captives, chained by the neck in groups of five,
were led on deck and readied for swift debarkation. The vessel swung
up to a dock. A crude gangplank went out. The long file of black
bodies shuffled onto the dock and off down a waterfront street. That
was the last they saw of the captain and crew of the *Tecora*, who
were paid off at the then lavish amounts ranging from five thousand
dollars for the captain to fifteen hundred dollars for a seaman. After
a short and riotous shore leave, they would run back to the African
coast, making as many as half a dozen round trips a year.

At the end of Havana's waterfront street the Africans found something that reminded them of home: more barracoons. Here their neck
irons were taken off and they were permitted to flop on the soft
ground where they liked, restrained only by chain hobbles on their
ankles. Here too, in the next few days, they were helped to re-

cuperate from their ordeal at sea. They were given nearly as much food as they could eat, and within a day or two the emaciated bodies began to fill out. They were given water to wash with and oil to rub on their clean bodies. Quickly they began to feel fit. With merciful swiftness they forgot the seasickness, the rolling, bruising deck, the stench, the bloody flux, the lashes and the searing pain of vinegar and gunpowder. What the future held for them they did not know. Their past occasionally swept over them in waves of homesickness. But the present was far better than what they had just endured in the barracoons of Sierra Leone and the Middle Passage. Little by little the human spirit reasserted itself, and the captives began to sing together and dance and even laugh.

Then an immaculately dressed Spaniard was shown into the barracoon. Walking among the black bodies, he appraised them carefully and ordered sixty of them to stand in line. From the sixty he chose forty-nine. With no further ado his selection was formed into another line at the door of the barracoon. A few papers were signed, payment of $450 per slave was made, and neck irons were clamped onto the forty-nine. They were now the property of a slave dealer, Don José Ruiz.

Down the streets of Havana they marched again, to the docks and onto the deck of a long, slim schooner. They were to go to sea again; this time their destination was one of the ports of the U.S. South. The schooner was the *Amistad*.

Don José Ruiz was joined by another slave dealer, Don Pedro Montez, with four black children he had purchased. All the slaves were quickly herded below, where their chains were locked to ringbolts in the deck. The oppressiveness of the slave ship settled on them again. The rocking of the schooner at her wharf made some of their stomachs queasy. The almost palpable stench crept over them. As darkness came and the slave deck turned pitch black, the children began to cry. A few of the older slaves groaned. But from some of them came a sound that was new, increasing and ominous. It was the murmuring threat of revolt.

The schooner *Amistad* was commanded by Captain Ramon Ferrer. Ruiz and Montez were listed as passengers. Counting captain, passen-

gers and a crew of four, there were seven whites aboard the *Amistad*
—seven whites and forty-nine strong, well-fed adult blacks.

Smaller than the *Tecora*, the *Amistad* was about seventy-five feet
long. Her black sides and green bottom were divided by a white water
line, and she carried a golden eagle figurehead. Her masts were slim
and raked, with a square topsail on her foremast. Her hold was cut
up into slave decks, with a minimum of space aft for captain, passengers and crew. All available space was utilized to transport slaves.
Little wonder—the bodies that cost $450 apiece in the Havana barra-
coon would bring at least a thousand dollars in Florida, Georgia or
the Carolinas. The *Amistad* could carry many more than the forty-
nine adults now chained in her hold; but this was a large enough number to make a handsome profit. It is possible also that Captain Ferrer
intended to pick up more slaves at his next call, Puerto Príncipe. The
schooner's papers mentioned a cargo of goods and fifty-three Negroes
(including the children) bound for Puerto Príncipe, but the *Amistad*
may well have been scheduled to increase the slave cargo there. Whatever the plan, on the morning of June 27, 1839, the schooner *Amistad*
weighed anchor and sailed out of Havana Harbor into history.

Ordinarily the voyage to Puerto Príncipe, only three hundred
miles along the Cuban coast, took a fast schooner like the *Amistad*
about two days and nights. But as the schooner rounded the last
Havana promontory and the captain set her course, the wind blew
into their teeth. The schooner would have been able to point up
close to the wind if she had not carried a square foretopsail. As it
was, Captain Ferrer had to wear off at about seventy degrees and
run down his true course on a gradual slant, hoping as he set the new
course that the wind would haul about and that they would not have
to beat against it all the way to Puerto Príncipe. But the wind stayed
in this quarter and the *Amistad* plunged into the nearly head-on sea
hour after hour all through the first day and night. Again seasickness
turned the slave decks into a stinking hell, and again the pounding
ship and the chafing irons rubbed raw sores on the captives' necks,
wrists and ankles.

Next day the slaves were brought onto the schooner's narrow open deck, a few at a time, and marched back and forth for exercise. It was hot work under the tropical sun, and the water ration was meager; but the captain refused to issue any more. By next day, with the wind still unfavorable and the *Amistad* pounding into a quartering sea, the slaves were frantic with thirst. As they were being exercised, one of them snatched a cupful from the water cask on deck. He was immediately grabbed and held while one of the crew lashed him with the "cat." Still sobbing from the pain of the vinegar and gunpowder rubbed into the gashes across his back, he was chained below. And that night the slaves began plotting among themselves, reminding each other over and over again that the count was forty-nine to seven.

Next day the wind was still against them. The food and water were getting dangerously low, and rations were cut even more. The strain began to tell on the crew, and more of the slaves were lashed, for no apparent reason. But on the next morning came the break the slaves had been watching for.

The wind, still from the same quarter, had increased. Short, spitting squalls kept every crew member busy trimming sail. When the slaves were brought on deck, they milled about more freely than before. And one of them found a loose nail in the deck planking.

His name was Cinque. He was a strong, young man, the son of an African chief and the most intelligent of the group. He it was who had led the plotting in the conversations below. Now he quickly tucked the nail in his armpit and waited until he and his companions were locked in their chains again.

By nightfall the *Amistad* had worked to within a couple miles of the Cuban shore. The sea slowly subsided. The clouds parted and the moon peeped through. The exhausted captain ordered mattresses brought on deck. With only the man at the helm on duty, captain and crew flopped down on the mattresses to recover from their battle with the head winds and squalls. As they slept, the captives below were quietly working on their locks with the nail Cinque had found on deck that morning.

It took many hours of patient flexing and picking at the locks, but the nail worked. One by one most of the chains were cast off, and by two hours after midnight the last of the slaves had broken free. But before they went on deck, Cinque led them into the cargo hold, where they found a case of sugar cane knives. Then, with each African wielding one of the flat-bladed, sharply honed machetes, Cinque led them up the hatchway and onto the quiet deck.

The moon was still out, with only a few ragged clouds sweeping off astern. The deck was bathed by the soft light, the only other illumination coming from the compass binnacle, which cast a yellow gleam on the face of the man nodding at the helm. There was no sound save the sloshing of the sea at the bow and the slow creak of a mast. Along the deck were scattered the mattresses, on which were sprawled the sleeping bodies of the crew. And nearest to the hatch was the form of Captain Ferrer.

With Cinque in the lead, the Africans padded softly across the deck toward the sleeping captain. But evidently, quiet as they were now, their ransacking of the cargo hold had awakened Don José Ruiz. For at this moment he came on deck from the after cabin.

For a moment he looked about the deck. Then he saw the dark movement of the approaching slaves and the flicker of the moonlight on the blade of a machete. By this time Cinque had reached the sleeping Captain Ferrer and raised his machete for the kill. The two cries, one from Ruiz and one from Cinque, came almost simultaneously.

"No! No!!"

"Kill the white man!"

And the night came alive with the shouts of the Africans, the screams of the sailors and the whack of the machete blade.

Taken completely by surprise, still half asleep and nearly paralyzed by terror, the sailors were quickly overcome. The *Amistad*'s cook had tortured the captives by telling them they were to be eaten; now he was one of the first to die. Captain Ferrer, wounded but not killed by Cinque's misdirected machete blow, got to his feet and fought off a dozen blacks with his rapier. But he was quickly overwhelmed, in time for Cinque to step in again, this time connecting with one whistling swing that split open the captain's head like a pumpkin. Don José Ruiz, beaten into unconsciousness, lay on the deck. Two or three of the crew plunged over the side, preferring to take their chances with the sharks. Don Pedro Montez ran for the cargo hold to hide among the bales and barrels. But his trail of blood was easily followed. Cinque dragged him out of the hold and brought him on deck. Only he, Ruiz and Antonio, the cabin boy, remained, and Ruiz was still recovering consciousness. Cinque had them shackled together, with the chains that had been used on the Africans. In a matter of minutes the situation aboard the *Amistad* had been exactly reversed.

And now came the aftermath. For the rest of the night, while the schooner wallowed about with scarcely a hand on the helm, the freed captives ran riot through the ship. Not a cask or chest in the hold went unopened. Crockery, yards of cloth, crates, everything was scattered through the hold and on deck as if a hurricane had gone through the schooner. The Africans concentrated on the food, strewing cases of beef and biscuit and fruits through the vessel as they gorged themselves. Digging into cases of wine and a shipment of medicine, they drank both wine and medicine, and this is what finally put an end to the orgy of looting and gorging, as the medicines made them sick to their stomachs and the wines put them to sleep. By morning the *Amistad* was like a shipwreck. But she was still afloat, and she was headed away from the coast of Cuba.

Cinque and his followers knew what they wanted to do with the schooner, but they did not know how. Their plan was to sail east. All Cinque knew was that east was the opposite of the direction the *Tecora* had come. So if he now took the *Amistad* east, he should eventually reach the coast of Africa and home. But how to make the ship sail in the direction they wanted? How to keep those yards of canvas from flapping about? How to make sense out of the maze of ropes running from the deck to the tops of the masts?

That was why Cinque had let Ruiz, Montez and Antonio live. He had seen Montez sail the ship when Captain Ferrer had tired after the long battle against the head winds. Presumably Ruiz could sail the schooner also. And Antonio spoke Mendi, Cinque's tongue, so he could serve as interpreter when Cinque's new English failed him, which it did most of the time.

For days after the mutiny Ruiz was only semiconscious. But Mon-

tez quickly recovered from his flesh wounds, and Cinque put him to
work navigating the schooner. His orders were to keep her headed
east day and night, and Cinque's threats of what would happen if he
failed were enough to resign him to his humiliating new role. Montez
had another reason for accepting the *Amistad*'s helm. By day, and
whenever at night Cinque could see the moon, Montez kept the
schooner on her easterly course. But on cloudy nights, and whenever
Cinque was asleep, Montez gradually eased the schooner over onto a
northerly course—north for Florida, the Carolinas, New York or New
England. Whichever landfall they made, this would be his only salvation.

So the *Amistad* worked her way through the waters south of the
Florida Keys, running east by day and north by night. Somehow
she avoided the shoal areas of the Great Bahama Bank. They touched
at Andros Island for wood and water, but broke and ran when they
were spotted by some of the island's few inhabitants. They rounded
the island and anchored off Green Cay, east of Andros, and filled
the water casks. Cinque went below for a good sleep. A few hours
later he was brought on deck by the shouts of the Africans; they
had sighted an island with houses. Montez was racing to take the
Amistad into New Providence, the central island of the Bahamas,
before Cinque awoke. Cinque grabbed the helm and headed her
south and east. Then he had Montez thrashed with the "cat." Howling at the taste of his own medicine, Montez refused to navigate the
schooner any longer. Cinque replied that in that case there was no
further use for him, and drew his rapier. Montez changed his mind.

Next day the schooner anchored off Cape Sainte Maria, the
northern tip of the Bahamas' Long Island. For three days they loaded
the hold with water, fruit and wild vegetables. Then they hauled
anchor. Montez guided the schooner eastward past Rum Cay, Conception Island and San Salvador—the island that nearly three centuries
earlier had signified to Christopher Columbus that his westward
voyage had ended (Chapter II). Beyond here was the open Atlantic,
and Africa.

Don Pedro Montez, hanging on the helm and still recovering from
his lashing, knew that his only chance lay in somehow working the

schooner toward the American coast. So that night he took another chance, this time swinging the *Amistad* not to north but all the way around the west. Before dawn, when Cinque came on deck, Montez had the vessel back on her easterly course. The Spaniard calculated that on this zigzag course he could fetch up near New England, if only the winds did not favor the daytime leg over the nighttime one.

The winds not only did not betray him, but favored him. For the next few days there were light breezes and they came out of the east. Montez had tried to teach the Africans how to handle the sails, but with no success. So the schooner made little headway, and the night-time legs brought them closer to the mainland. For more than a week this went on. Cinque knew that they were not heading east, but he knew that they could not sail into the wind, so he was helpless to do anything but watch the *Amistad* tack north and south. And he was not surprised when, in mid-August, they sighted land.

It was a low-lying land, with wide strips of white sand at the water's edge and green fringes of trees beyond. There was little sign of habitation along the part of the coast they could see. The still, moist heat of the August day was reminiscent of Africa. But this obviously was not Africa. It had been more than a month since they had taken the ship; but Cinque knew that that was not enough time to reach Africa and home.

Slowly the schooner worked her way along the coast, which seemed to stretch interminably to the east. At the helm Montez watched and prayed for the ship he hoped would rescue him and Ruiz, and perhaps even restore their slaves to' them. Soon one vessel, then another and then another appeared, far off on the horizon. But they were too far away to hail, even if Montez had taken the chance. In an agony of frustration he watched them sail away—when suddenly another came into view, headed straight across the course of the *Amistad*.

She was the schooner *Eveline*, Captain Sears, bound from New Bedford to Philadelphia. Studying the *Amistad*'s tattered, flapping sails and her erratic course, Captain Sears decided to investigate.

Aboard the *Amistad* Montez could scarcely contain himself. The schooner came closer and swung out a boat. Then Cinque ordered

Montez dragged below. He and Ruiz were quickly locked in the
main cabin, with a huge African wielding a machete. Cinque made it
clear that one shout from either man would be his last.

The *Eveline*'s boat rowed across to the *Amistad*. Cinque greeted
Captain Sears as he climbed aboard. Through Antonio Cinque announced that the captain of the *Amistad* was too sick to talk. They
needed food and water, for which they could pay with doubloons.
Sears tried to go below, but his way was blocked by stout blacks
with machetes. He returned to the *Eveline* and sent over a keg of
water and a message that food was on the way. Cinque decided not
to take the chance of waiting. When the *Eveline*'s sailors returned,
they were met by musket fire as the *Amistad* moved off east, still
following the long coastline on the port side.

Next day came a repeat of the *Eveline* meeting. A boat sent across
from the pilot boat *Blossom* traded some bread and water for doubloons. But when a sailor tried to climb aboard and discover the reason
for the odd-appearing schooner and her black crew, more musket fire
drove him off. The *Blossom* was joined by another pilot boat, but
both fled to escape the musketry from the *Amistad*. Next day another
approaching vessel was scared away. Then the *Amistad* reached the
point of the long coastline running east.

They were at Montauk Point, at the end of Long Island, New
York. Montez was at the helm again, and he brought the schooner
around the tip of the island and into calm water off Culloden Point.
Cinque decided that they would anchor and go ashore for water and
whatever food they could find. There were two or three houses
visible from the water, but he felt it was worth taking a chance.
In fact, emboldened by his recent transactions at sea, he considered
buying some food. In a money belt around his middle he carried
more of the doubloons which he had found below. He ordered the
boat lowered and climbed into it himself, taking along six of the
Africans and Antonio to serve as interpreter.

The foraging expedition had been ashore only a short while, and
Cinque was trying in vain to buy food from two hunters he had encountered near a marsh, when one of his men called the alarm from
his lookout post down on the beach. Cinque ran to the beach in

time to see a brig of war come sailing down on the *Amistad*, swing into the wind and drop anchor. Before he could even collect his men, a boat from the brig had swung down and, with military precision, was gliding swiftly across the water to the *Amistad*.

Lieutenant Meade of the U.S. surveying brig *Washington* led his men aboard the battered schooner, to be greeted by an onrush of blacks carrying machetes. Clubbing them off with his pistol, Meade advanced down the deck. His sailors, close behind him, aimed their pistols at the blacks as they bunched at one end of the schooner.

And, without a shot, they surrendered. Cinque was still halfway to the schooner, his excited men thrashing the water with their oars. But without him on hand, the *Amistad* Africans capitulated easily. Lieutenant Meade had just started to disarm them when Montez and Ruiz came running on deck. Cinque watched the scene and realized that his only hope was flight. He ordered his men to row for shore, but they were too slow for the brig's boat, which caught up with them quickly.

The triumphant expressions of Ruiz and Montez were too much for Cinque to bear as he was led aboard the *Amistad*. He avoided them, trying to grasp what the naval officer was saying. Then, suddenly, he made one more dash for freedom. Breaking loose, he ran the width of the *Amistad*'s deck, dived over the rail and started swimming underwater toward shore. Surfacing for a gulp of air, he went under again. But when he came up for air again the *Washington*'s boat was almost upon him. Within a few more yards he was captured. Sitting in the stern of the boat, held firmly by two sailors, Cinque studied the long, low silhouette of the disheveled schooner that might have been his deliverance, as he was brought back alongside her familiar hull for the last time.

The *Amistad*'s mutineers became a nationwide *cause célèbre* before their story was done. In the battle that developed over their trial, abolitionists were pitted against powerful proslavery forces and most of America was divided into antagonistic camps before the mutineers were finally freed. Many of them eventually made it back to Africa, under the protection of church organizations. But the trial and other delays kept them in America two years, and most of them, including Cinque, never found their families again. Cinque returned to his village as a missionary, but soon slipped back into his tribal ways.

As for the *Amistad*, she was sold by the District Court in New London, Connecticut. Her name was changed and she entered the busy stream of maritime commerce along the American coast. Still sharp and rakish, she probably made a fast and successful trading schooner. Whether she returned to her nefarious trade again, no one knows. Certainly she was well adapted to it. Whether she did or not, never again did she experience a slaving voyage like the one that ended that moonlit night off the coast of Cuba and made the *Amistad* the most infamous slaver in history.

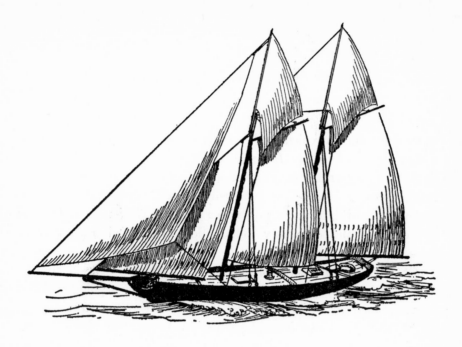

IX

Racing Yacht: The AMERICA

Transatlantic challenge . . . "How in Hell do you stand?"
. . . Cargo of rum . . . The fluke that won the Cup . . .
Twenty million dollars for revenge

No one seems to remember his name, but he was a British business-man with a keen eye for publicity. Sometime in 1850 he wrote a letter to an American businessman (no one knows *his* name either) and dropped a remark that eventually made a racing yacht famous around the world, turned a sport into a great international competition and cost the British twenty million dollars. And all because of a fluke.

For what the British businessman happened to mention to the American businessman was a reminder that 1851 was going to be a British festival year. Given the fact that most Britons, even including Queen Victoria, were devoted yachtsmen, it was natural that there would be a number of yacht races to celebrate the occasion. It is safe to assume that in a polite way the Englishman hinted that he realized there was no one yachtsman in the U.S. who was a match for British yachtsmen. But why didn't a group of Americans get together and put up enough money to build a new yacht that might give the British yachts a run for it? However insulting or polite the hint may have been, the American regarded it as a bald challenge. So began preparations for the most famous yacht race in history.

One of the American businessman's friends was John C. Stevens, a wealthy and famous New York yachtsman. With half a dozen other wealthy yachtsmen, Stevens formed a syndicate and set out to build a yacht and take up the challenge.

For a designer they turned to George Steers. One of thirteen children of a British shipwright who had moved to the U.S., George Steers was designing fast pilot schooners when he was twenty-one and would later build one clipper ship, the *Sunny South*, at the age of thirty-four. Now thirty, he had designed a boat for yachtsman Stevens—the *Gimcrack*, a fifty-one-foot schooner that had the distinction of providing the cabin in which the New York Yacht Club was founded in 1844. Steers went to work on a bigger yacht for Stevens, this one all of a hundred feet long. He designed her along much the same lines as his fast pilot boats, with a sharp entrance, comparatively slim lines and raking masts. He served as foreman while she was being built, in the yard of William Brown, one of the best shipbuilders of the time. The designing and building took nearly a year, as Steers painstakingly formed his model, laid out her lines on the mold-loft floor, changing a curve here and a bulge there. And while the schooner was on the stocks it is said that Steers often went to Brown's shipyard at night when the workmen were gone, to shave a plank a bit more or just run his hand along the smooth sides. She was finally launched on May 1, 1851, and given her name: *America*.

Because of the alterations as she was being designed and built, her dimensions are not certain. But the best guess is that she was 101 feet 9 inches long over-all, 90 feet 3 inches at waterline, with a 23-foot beam and a draught of 11 feet. Her displacement was 146 tons. Her sails were different from those of her British competitors-to-be, which were made of flax, cut full and loose. The *America*'s sails were made of machine-woven cotton and cut to set flat against her boom. She could spread 5,263 square feet of these sails, on masts which raked back five degrees. A good contemporary description of her was in *Bell's Life*, by a writer who studied her as she rode at anchor in English waters:

> She has a low, black hull, two noble sticks of extreme rake. . . . When close to her you see that her bow is as sharp as a knife blade, scooped away as it were, outwards, till it swells toward the front, the sides gradu-ally springing outwards as round as an apple, till a little forward of the mainsail, where she has her greatest helm. . . . Her stern is remarkably broad, wide and full, affording a great accommodation on deck as well as below. She has no bulwarks—at least they are not above 9 or 10 inches high.

Here was a logical development of the earlier privateer-slaver and the contemporary pilot schooner into a pleasure craft. Sharp at the bow like her utilitarian predecessors, she was relatively wider amidships, to provide for the accommodations to which a yachtsman was accustomed. She was designed for comfort, for speed and also for seaworthiness.

But was she fast? Her builder had guaranteed: "If she is not faster than any vessel in the United States, it shall not be binding on you to accept and pay for her at all." The syndicate members had only a few weeks before the *America* would have to leave for England, so they put her through some trial races immediately. Commodore Stevens owned a fast schooner named the *Maria*, and the *America* was tested against her. Stevens and his fellow syndicate members were taken aback when the *Maria* won most of the races. They were non-plused when in one race she sailed circles around the *America*, three times. But one of the conditions the U.S. contender had to face was a transatlantic crossing in order to race, and the *America* seemed a stouter ship for the ocean voyage. So the *America* was paid for ($20,000) and readied to sail to England to uphold the yachting honor of the U.S.

On June 21, 1851, she was towed out of the East River and, to the accompaniment of nine cheers and two guns from a passing steamer, hoisted her pilot sails for the voyage across the ocean (her light cotton racing sails were snugly stowed below). Commodore Stevens, who was to command the *America* when she got to England, was not aboard; he booked passage on a steamer. In command of the *America* was Captain Richard Brown (no relation to Shipbuilder William Brown), a tough, profane old salt who was to be skipper in the race under Stevens' command. At the start of the voyage he summoned all hands aft and bellowed at them: "If there's a damned white-livered dog amongst you wants to stay behind, now is the time for him to bark. How in Hell do you stand? . . . Do you stand by the ship?" Listening to these well-chosen words were designer George Steers, his brother and fellow worker James and James's son Henry. They—and the crew—were not frightened back to land by Dick Brown. But there were to be moments when James, at least, wished he had stayed ashore. James kept a log of the *America*'s crossing; the log was later presented to the New York Yacht Club, and it rests in the club's vault today. From this log we learn why Dick Brown felt some anxiety about how his crew and passengers would enjoy the crossing.

The *America* set off at a good clip, even though she at once began to roll. She had hardly passed Nantucket before the second mate began to feel squeamish and went below. Ten minutes later the first mate, carpenter and even the captain were taking "a little brandy and water, say about 10 drops" to settle their churning stomachs. By 4 A.M. all three were taking Seidlitz powders to keep from being actively sick. All the second day, through a wet, smoky fog, the *America* tossed and rolled. Some of the crew, especially the weak-stomached second mate, were still seasick. But the Steers brothers, and evidently young Henry as well, were healthy, if damp, and quite able to put away a dinner of "veal potpie and Indian fritters with sauce."

By the ninth day, however, when the crew members were getting their sea legs, the constant rolling began to tell on the two boat-builders. The *America* had slatted about in a calm for one day and had wallowed through a storm that moved James to note, "I don't think it ever rained harder since Noah floated his ark." The wind came up so strong that it split one of the sails; then, almost immediately afterward, the wind died again and there was hardly enough breeze to keep her moving ahead. The Steers brothers began to miss New York Harbor. Designer George felt the unmistakable symptoms himself. Brother James was still sound of stomach, but his disgust with the whole undertaking poured out in his entry for June 30: "Light wind and foggy, mixed at times with hard rain. All sail set . . . Brother George seasick, could eat no dinner. Should I live to get home, this will be my last sea trip. All my clothes are wet. It has rained every day since we left."

Young Henry followed his uncle's example, but he quickly recovered. Uncle George, however, got worse. He managed to get up and about to help those aboard celebrate the Fourth of July, which the captain used as an occasion to issue a bottle of gin to the crew. Fortunately the ship's liquor cabinet was well stocked; otherwise George, homesick and disgusted, might well have thrown himself over the side.

However, by the eighteenth day out, the liquor cabinet was empty.

They knew that there was a cargo of rum in the hold, so they calmly broke into it and replenished the cabinet. "George had the bellyache," wrote James, adding laconically, "We were not going to starve in a market place."

By now they were only two days from Havre, where they planned to haul the *America* out and refit her for the race. So, fortified with the new supply of rum, the wet, tired, dejected Steers brothers sat it out until the *America* glided smoothly into the harbor at Havre, twenty days and six hours out of New York Harbor.

It is easy to imagine the consternation of Commodore Stevens when he arrived and made his first check into the liquor supply. And since the Steers brothers continued to dip into the cargo of rum at the rate of two bottles a day, the commodore began to get angry. He locked up the liquor cabinet and kept the key with him, not realizing that the Steerses had foresightedly provided themselves with an extra key for use in case of just such an emergency. Every night Commodore Stevens sat on the cabin deck in his shirt tail, counted his bottles and bellowed at the steward, "Where the hell does my liquor go to?"

"He has not," wrote James thoughtfully, "even asked us to take a drink since he came on board." A result of this war of nerves was that James grew "much dissatisfied myself with 'Old Stevens.' He is a damned old hog, bristles and all."

Not that Commodore Stevens was having the time of his life either. He made a serious mistake on the day he took the *America* up from Havre to Cowes. When the *America* got to within six miles of Cowes, Stevens found the crack British cutter *Laverock* hanging around, obviously spoiling for an impromptu race. Stevens may well have considered the possibility that if he let the *Laverock* beat him, the chances would be greater that the owners of other British yachts would be eager to race the *America* too. But after the lengthy, extensive preparations and the bickering at Havre, Stevens could not resist the temptation to show off the *America*'s stuff. Standing in the yacht's round cockpit, he shouted the order, "Let her go!" Go she did, all the way up to Cowes. She worked to windward much better than the *Laverock*, and beat her handily. It took no time at all for word to get around. When Stevens issued his challenge—to race for any amount from five thousand to fifty thousand dollars—there were no takers.

British yachtsmen, it appeared, were too canny—or careful—to race the yacht that had beaten the *Laverock*. There was also a feeling among the British that a syndicate of owners for a racing yacht was not quite sporting. As the days went by and Stevens waited, he tried to enter the *America* in the race for the Queen's Cup, one of the biggest of the season. He was told flatly that the rules required each entry to belong to a single individual. Wrote James Steers: "Old Pig got mad and went ashore." At the clubhouse of the Royal Yacht Squadron the commodore evidently made quite a scene, informing the British yachtsmen that he would wait only three more days for an answer to his challenge. After that he would take the *America* back to America. To hell with them.

Meanwhile, just to add to his frustration, the *America* seemed to be outsailing every yacht in the area. During one or two races Stevens sailed alongside and, although he could not be sure that the test was on equal terms, the *America* always appeared to outdistance, or at least keep up with, the leader in each race. She looked faster too, with her sleeker lines and flatter sails. In England even racing yachts of the 1850's were still generally "apple-cheeked," with rounded hulls that rode well in storms but did not cut through the water the way the *America* did. So it was more and more galling to Stevens as it became more and more evident that the *America* was not going to get a chance to race the British yachts.

All this was finally too much for the Steers brothers. Angry at Commodore Stevens over the battle of the liquor cabinet, disgusted with the nobility who were constantly coming aboard and sometimes even requesting trial spins ("our freight," James called them), bored with the inactivity while Stevens made his challenges and nobody paid any attention to them, the Steers brothers quit and prepared to return to New York.

At this point, just as Commodore Stevens was also getting ready to go home, he heard from the Royal Yacht Squadron. The club would, he was politely informed, welcome the *America* in an open regatta for a new cup. No size, sail area or tonnage was barred from this race. In other words, if the *America* could sail in it, any boat could. Stevens quickly tried to get the Steers brothers to change their minds. But they had had enough. Nothing could induce them to stay—not even the big test for which they had originally been commissioned the year before. So they sailed from Liverpool August 20, and missed the greatest yacht race in history.

On Friday, August 22, fifteen yachts set out early from the starting line. The early morning mist had scudded away before a light breeze, and it was a clear day. But there was not enough wind to suit Commodore Stevens. The *America* was heavier than most of the British yachts, and the stronger the wind, the better her chances. By 9:30 A.M., however, the breeze freshened, and Stevens made his last-minute study of the rules for the race, which had been passed out to each skipper by the Royal Yacht Squadron. It was at this point, before the starting gun was fired, that the race was decided. By some error two conflicting sets of sailing instructions had been distributed. Whether Stevens studied both and made a shrewd decision or whether he only studied one, no one knows. In any case it was this discrepancy in sailing instructions that settled the race.

By nine-forty-five it was quite a scene off Cowes. A long line of huge white sails stood out against the blue sky as the yachts waited at anchor for the starting gun, fifteen minutes away. Then the *America* got into trouble. She started to run over her anchor, which pulled her about and headed her in the wrong direction. Her sails had to be lowered, where they stayed as Stevens literally listened to the minutes go by: they were called out, minute by minute, by a member of the crew.

Nine-fifty-eight; nine-fifty-nine; nine-fifty-nine-and-a-half; ten seconds; nine; eight; seven; six; five; four; three; two; one—the starting cannon boomed, anchors were weighed and the fleet bore away. Astern of them all was the *America;* her crew had to raise sails as well as anchor.

It was a twelve-mile run out to "the Nab," a lightship anchored off a point known as the Nab. This was the first mark on the fifty-three-mile course. As the *America* belatedly set out after the rest of the fleet, the wind Stevens had been praying for began to come up strong. One by one the *America* began overhauling the slower boats in the race, but by the time she reached the Nab, four British yachts were firmly holding the lead. Also, they clung together in a little knot, like race horses on the inside of a turn, and the *America* could not get through. Then came the break.

Commodore Stevens may have been astonished—or he may simply have been pleased—when the yachts ahead of him kept going straight out past the Nab, in order to round the mark on the outside. That was indeed the rule on one set of sailing instructions. But the conflicting set did not so rule, and Stevens preferred to follow that set. So he simply came about and passed the Nab on the inside of the course. The British skippers wasted precious minutes, and lost all the advantage they had gained by "bunching up," while the *America* set out on the next leg of the race like a barracuda. The wind held strong and Stevens made the most of his advantage, soon leaving the fleet astern.

Aboard the royal steam yacht *Victoria and Albert*, anchored alongside the last leg of the course, stood Queen Victoria. Peering across the tossing water, the queen asked who was in the lead. Someone with binoculars had just made out the *America* and told her. "Who is second?" she asked. The answer, according to legend, was, "Ah, Your Majesty, there is no second."

But the race was far from over. The wind started to die. The *America* got into an unfavorable tide and began to lose her speed. For about an hour the wind continued to diminish, while one British boat after another closed the huge gap. Yachtsmen being what they are, and Stevens evidently being more excitable than most, these must have been apoplectic moments aboard the *America*.

Stevens then had one more break. Three of the British competitors put themselves out of the race. The *Volante* lost her bowsprit. The *Arrow* went aground on the rocks, and the *Alarm* immediately left the race to go to the aid of the *Arrow*. As the wind kept dying, one last possible contender, the *Aurora*, tried desperately to catch the *America*. But the wind held just enough, and in the gathering dusk, ten hours and thirty-seven minutes after the starting cannon had sounded, another went off as the *America* slid past the finish line. Eight minutes and about one mile behind came the *Aurora*.

One can imagine the chilly session at the Royal Yacht Squadron's clubhouse shortly thereafter, as the matter of Nab light was discussed. But partly because of the conflicting sets of sailing directions, and partly because the British, sportsmen all, decided not to make a scene, the *America* was not disqualified. Indeed the argument that went on in the clubhouse has continued to this day, with many U.S. yachtsmen insisting that the *America* would have won anyway (granting that in later years British yachts beat her more than half the time) and with many British yachtsmen insisting that the Nab light incident was what did it. All of this did not seem so important to the British yachtsmen then, crestfallen as they might have been. After all, some of them must have thought, these Americans had stirred up enough of a fuss already. So the trophy that became known as the *America*'s Cup was presented to Commodore Stevens, and the British promptly began making plans to get it back.

The actual value of the cup was about five hundred dollars. But in their attempts over the years to get it back British yachtsmen have spent more than twenty million dollars. Challengers from Britain and Canada have tried seventeen separate times, most recently in the summer of 1958, to repeat the *America*'s performance—so far without success.

And what of the *America* during the years while millions of people all over the world followed the international competition for her cup? After her victory Lord John de Balquiere, one of Britain's wealthiest yachtsmen, made such a good offer ($25,000) that the syndicate sold her to him. He sailed her in many of the races where she had not been able to sail the year before, whereupon many of the yachts the *America* had beaten got their revenge. By the time of the U.S. Civil War she was sold to the Confederate Navy, which used her to run the Union blockade. In March of 1862 she was chased up Saint Johns River, in Florida, by a ship of the Union Navy. Rather than add one more ship to the Northern forces, her skipper scuttled her, and he and the crew slipped ashore in the dusk. His plot failed, however, because the Union Navy was able to raise her and repair her, and the *America* served for the rest of the war on the Union side. After the war she served as a Navy training ship, and in 1870 she was one of the twenty-three U.S. yachts defending the cup against the Britons' first attempt to get it back. She came in fourth.

A few years later General Benjamin Butler bought the *America* for a pleasure yacht. He sailed her for a while, but by the turn of the century she was virtually a derelict. In 1917 a sportsman named Charles Foster purchased her from Butler's heirs. Four years later a group of nostalgic yachtsmen arranged for her return to the Navy. She was towed to Annapolis, where the Navy planned to rehabilitate her and make her a member of its fleet of sailing craft. But World War II came before restoration had begun, and there was neither the manpower nor the money to be spent on an old sailing schooner everyone had forgotten. She was hauled out and stored in a shed.

In 1942 the roof of the shed collapsed on the *America*'s rotting hull. Now she was too far gone—a restoration job would have to be so complete that little if anything of the original ship would remain. On a wet, cold winter's day early in 1947 the workmen went at her with mallets and crowbars and broke her up. It was only four years before the centennial of her great—if controversial—victory.

X

Whaler: The POCAHONTAS

the clock . . . A birthday present on Christmas
chance . . . Slow-motion race with death . . . Pumps around
"She blooooows!" . . . The "young captain" takes a

On December 7, 1850, off the south coast of Brazil, the whaleship *Pocahontas* was having her usual bad luck. She was in company with another fat, stubby whaler, the *Ann Alexander;* both were from New England and both were on their way down around Cape Horn to the rich whaling grounds of the Pacific. But December 7 was a beautiful South Atlantic summer day, so the two whalers were interrupting their run to the Horn for a short cruise on the "Brazil Grounds."

This day's work started at dawn. For the whalemen's hours were dictated by the whale. Sometimes they could sail for days or weeks, crisscrossing and searching the seas without once spotting the misty spouts or the surging black shapes that meant their quarry was near. The round-bowed, wide-girthed ships covered the whaling grounds slowly. The whaler was an offshoot in the development of ship design, in some ways a throwback to the fat merchantmen of earlier centuries. She was not made for speed—her little fleet of whaleboats were designed for that. She was the mother ship and the floating factory where the huge catch was rendered, on the spot, into oil and bone. The *Pocahontas* had none of the rakish look of the privateer, the yacht or the clipper. Her masts were stubby because she was in no hurry and also because they served to haul the huge hides out of the water where the whalemen could get at them and cut them up. Her hull was fat and capacious, for the hundreds of barrels that would have to be filled with oil before she returned home, even if it took four or five years.

While the newly developed Baltimore clippers were the race horses of the American merchant marine, the whalers were the work horses. And the *Pocahontas* looked her part, lumbering through the Brazil Grounds that December morning. The men off watch were still

asleep, wedged in their tiny bunks in the forecastle at the *Pocahontas'*
round bow, when one of the lookouts swinging in circles high atop
a mast gave his ringing call: "Bloooows! Thar she blooooooooooows!"
Within minutes the lumbering ship had come alive, her men pulling
on jackets as they ran to their places. The davits along the ship's sides
creaked as the whaleboats alongside were swung down into the water.
A few minutes later, from the deck of the *Pocahontas*, those who
stayed on the ship could watch the whaleboats set out, their little sails
already catching the wind as the boatsteerers aimed them for the
patch of sea about a mile off, where the surface broke now and then
with the spout or the tail-waving dive of a pod of whales. And those
aboard the *Pocahontas* could see the boats from the *Ann Alexander*
setting out after the same whales.

It took more than two hours of sailing before the *Pocahontas'*
boats were near the whales. Then the sails came down and the oars
came out. Slowly the boats crept up on the quarry. The unsuspecting
whales still plunged about a few hundred yards away, their tails
pounding the water with smacking booms that rolled across the sea.
In the boats no one spoke. The men were trained to keep quiet and
not even turn to look; only the boatsteerer at the big stern oar
directed their course. But as they drew nearer everyone could hear
the whales breaching and plunging, exhaling vaporous gusts as they
rose and pounding the water as they sounded again. Now the boats
rocked in the waves made by the playing whales, and now the boatsteerer of one of the *Pocahontas'* whaleboats ordered the harpooner
to his place.

The man at the forward oar shipped it, turned quickly and knelt
on the little platform at the bow of the whaleboat. At his side was
the harpoon, its long wooden stock made fast to a heavy line that ran
all the way aft, around a loggerhead in the stern and into one of the
tubs where it was neatly coiled, yard on yard, for a hundred yards or
more. The harpoon's barbed point was kept razor sharp to penetrate
the whale's thick layers of blubber. At the boatsteerer's command
the harpooner lifted his weapon and balanced it like a javelin. The
boatsteerer had picked out his whale now, and they were within a
few yards of the huge beast. A few more strokes at the oars, while

the men listened to the water slapping at the whale's sides, and the boatsteerer softly called the order: give him the iron.

With a *whirrup* as the line streaked out of the tub, the harpooner pitchpolled the heavy weapon at the black floating mountain in front of him. There was a *whoosh* as the whale felt the sharp sting, and then the line went taut. The whaleboat lurched ahead and rapidly picked up speed, bouncing over the waves. The men were now on what was known as a "Nantucket sleighride," a fast race across the water pulled by an infuriated whale. At this perilous point the harpooner and the boatsteerer changed places, ducking past each other as the whaleboat plunged and rocked under their feet. At the stern the harpooner now took up the steering oar, first looping another turn or two of the line around the loggerhead. If the whale should suddenly plunge for the bottom, as many did, he would flip off a few turns and let the line run out, giving the beast as much as it wanted, while the line smoked around the loggerhead and the men splashed water on it. The dash across the sea could take an hour or more, until the whale finally tired. Then the line would slowly be hauled in and the boatsteerer would stand ready with his lance; to him went the honor of the kill—a few quick, deep jabs just behind the head into the animal's vital spot. For the moment, however, the *Pocahontas'* men could only hang on and race grimly where the whale took them.

They had just settled their weight in proper balance when there was a ripping, crunching sound and the man at the steering oar almost toppled over the side as the boat swerved. The chocks at the whaleboat's bow, where the line ran forward and out across the water to the whale, had ripped loose. The line surged down along the side of the boat and started to spin them about. One man made a grab at it but only burned his hands. They had no choice. At the boatsteerer's order the harpooner grabbed an ax and chopped the line. It twanged away, and the boat slowed and settled back in the water. Ahead of them the whale, suddenly relieved of the drag, slowed and tried to shake the iron loose.

This was the chance for the second boat from the *Pocahontas*. None of the others had "got on" to a whale, perhaps because the first strike had scared off the rest. But this second whaleboat had just started out to follow the first, in case help were needed at the kill, when the line was cut loose. Now the second boatsteerer guided his oarsmen up behind the rolling, shaking whale. The second harpooner rose, hefted his iron and heaved it.

The harpoon sank into the blubbery mass of the whale's head. This time the whale sounded, while the line smoked out and the men sat anxiously waiting and wondering where the big beast would come up.

It came up right under them, and in a splintering, splashing melee boat and men were sent flying through the air and into the water. Shaking two harpoons and trailing two lines, the whale raced off.

The other whaleboats came alongside and helped the victims right and bail their boat and collect whatever gear was floating. Then they all made their way back to the *Pocahontas*. The whales were gone, and all the *Pocahontas'* men had to show for their morning's work were some minor injuries and the loss of two harpoons and four hundred fathoms of line. In the distance the *Ann Alexander's* men were returning empty-handed too.

The tired oarsmen had scarcely caught their breaths before the call went out from the masthead again: "Bloooows! She bloooows! She blooooows!!" Down creaked the boats again. Into them clambered the weary whalemen. And off across the water they went for another battle.

This time two of the *Pocahontas'* boatsteerers tried working together on one whale. They got up to it and, with perfect timing and co-ordination, both got their irons into the whale. Off over the horizon they went, tied to the racing whale.

It was now five in the afternoon; reaching the whale and getting fast to it had taken three hours. Darkness was falling, and the whale showed no sign of tiring. On and on it went, pulling the two boats miles farther away from the Pocahontas. Then sun went down and night fell on them. But still the whale surged ahead and still the two whaleboats hung on. Against the blackening night the whale spouted jets of blood. Still it did not slow down. The other boats, the ship, everything had long since been left behind the horizon. The two boats, the men—and the whale—were in a watery world of their own.

After their bad luck in the morning the *Pocahontas'* men had been determined not to lose this catch. They now hung on in desperation. But hour after hour the whale showed no sign of quitting. Attempts to shorten line and get within range for the lance or even the harpoon only made the beast rush on faster. For an incredible four hours this kept up, until the exhausted whalemen could continue the battle no longer. Yelling at each other in the dark across the rushing water, the two boatsteerers agreed: they would have to cut line. A few hacks with the hatchet and they were free. The rushing whale surged off into the night. The whaleboat crews rested for a few minutes and then hoisted sail to return to the ship.

Partly by design and partly by providence, they found her. A fair wind had held, and the *Pocahontas* had been able to follow the whaleboats on their chase. So when the boatsteerers cut loose it was only an hour or so before the men spotted the lights of the ship, sailed across her course and hailed her as the squat, stubby-masted shape loomed over them. It was all the worn-out men could do to climb on deck and stagger to their bunks in the forecastle. As they straggled aboard, it did not help their morale to hear that the *Ann Alexander's* men had taken a whale. And the late watch of the *Pocahontas* could see the red glow against the sky as the tryworks of the *Ann Alexander*, just over the horizon, rendered her catch into oil for the casks in her hold. This day seemed to them another indication that the *Pocahontas* was an unlucky ship and the *Ann Alexander* was a lucky one. They did not, of course, know how the next few weeks would confirm this belief.

The *Ann Alexander* was out of sight next day, and the *Pocahontas* continued on her course down toward Cape Horn, bound for the Pacific. For four days there were no whales to halt her steady "southing." Her lookouts, perched in their iron hoops atop the masts, burned under the tropical sun and saw spots before their eyes from their ceaseless searching across the blinding glare of the sea. But the *Pocahontas'* bad luck held. The bluff-bowed whaler rolled slowly south, her boats still idle on their davits, her tryworks on deck cold for want of whales to feed the ovens and render more blubber into oil for her casks. And then, on December 12, the cry from the mast-head came once more. It was a big pod of whales. Now, the *Pocahontas'* men hoped, her luck at last had changed.

The weather that morning was clear and bright. The moderate breeze out of the north was carrying the whaler comfortably down the coast toward the Horn. Only two boats were lowered at first. It took a little more than an hour to sail down on the whales and row quietly near the biggest one. A well-aimed heave of the harpoon, a short wait while the beast sounded, and it was all over, or so it seemed. The whale, a big one that ought to fill dozens of barrels, breached and lay quietly on the surface, apparently spent. The boat moved up to it and the boatsteerer raised his lance for the final, gouging thrust into the lungs and arteries behind the whale's head.

The lance was never thrust. At the moment before the boatsteerer's lunge, the whale gave a sudden roll and made for the boat. Opening its long, jagged jaw, it caught the boat amidships before anyone could move to maneuver out of the way. The crackling, sloshing sounds of the attack were mixed with the yells of the men caught in the gnashing jaws. Two were badly maimed, but they were still conscious and able to hang onto pieces of wreckage and wait for help.

That was not so easy. Whales had wrecked whaleboats and had even broken them in their jaws many times before. But normally, as soon as the boat was sent flying and the drag was off the harpoon line, the whale would run off. Not this one. As the men in the other whaleboat tried to rescue their companions, they found the whale still there, butting and bashing away at what was left of the boat it had smashed. The uninjured men swam and paddled away from the wreckage, dragging the wounded with them. While the whale continued to pound the pieces of the boat with its head and tail, the men were hauled aboard the other whaleboat and taken back to the *Pocahontas*. For more than an hour the *Pocahontas'* captain was below, helping dress his men's wounds. And when he came on deck, he was astonished to see that the big whale was still bashing away at the wreckage.

Captain Joseph Diaz, Jr., was twenty-eight years old, one of the youngest skippers out of New England. He was old enough, though, to know about malevolent whales like this one. In the South Pacific a decade earlier a fierce whale had charged the boats of the English whaler *Desmond* and killed two men. Off the coast of Japan a similar whale, eight years before, had plowed into a group of whaleboats and gnashed two men to pulp. Captain Diaz probably knew of these incidents or ones like them—they were forecastle talk everywhere— and that may be why he made the decision he did. He could not bear to sail off and leave all that potential whale oil. If it was too dangerous to go after the beast in the boats, he would try it in the ship itself.

Usually a maneuver like this would be useless; any whale would hear or see a big whaleship coming down on it and could swing out of the way with great ease. But this whale showed no intention of fleeing, and there was a good chance of getting within harpoon range while it defiantly stood its ground. The puzzling thing about this decision by Captain Diaz is that he must have known about the *Essex*.

She had gone out from Nantucket in 1819. In the vast area of the Pacific south of the Hawaiian Islands a huge whale smashed into the *Essex* head on. She sank in ten minutes, and her men rode across the Pacific in open boats for three months before the survivors were finally sighted and rescued. The story of the *Essex* was known to all whalemen. In fact, at this time, thirty years later, as young Captain Diaz watched the whale chomp at his boat, another Massachusetts whaleman, Herman Melville, was at home converting the story of the *Essex* into the great novel *Moby Dick*. Captain Diaz certainly knew what had happened to the *Essex*. But he also knew that such examples of whales attacking whaleships were extremely rare. Perhaps that is why he gave the order. The startled helmsman altered course, and the *Pocahontas* bore down on the big whale.

Captain Diaz lined the bow and the open bulwarks with men armed with harpoons and lances. Some straddled the rail, others hung onto the ship's side. The line tubs were set up on deck. The breeze was light and the ship slowly gathered way as she moved forward on the new slant. As they approached, the whale slewed around, gave a flap of its tail and slid off a few yards, out of the path of the oncoming ship.

Captain Diaz was about to give up, when he saw the whale swing right back to the wreckage of the boat. The young captain decided to have one more try.

Laboriously the whaler's wide yards were brought about. The *Pocahontas* fell off on a new tack. The men returned to their unaccustomed stations along the bow and bulwarks. The whaleship slowly picked up speed, to a little more than two knots. As they came nearer, the whale did not move. Captain Diaz ordered the head yards backed to slow the ship. The yards had just swung round, when the whale did move.

Turning in a surprising fast arc, it came straight at the ship, aiming for the bow. The *Pocahontas* had only started to lose way; Captain Diaz estimated that she was going about one and a half knots. But he estimated the whale's speed at three to four knots. The gap closed too fast and the whaleship was going through the water too slowly to answer the helm in time. In the ensuing seconds men scrambled back over the bulwarks and away from the rail. Then came the crash.

It was as if the big whaleship had run into an underwater concrete wall. The wide head of the whale struck just below the water line; perhaps at the last moment the whale tried to go under the ship. It then rolled off to one side and plunged away, this time not to be seen again. Aboard the *Pocahontas* there was little time to spend looking for the whale. Many in the crew had been knocked flat. The boats crashed about on their davits. The deck was littered with harpoons, lances, cutting spades, tubs and miscellaneous gear. But the real damage, the wound that could kill the ship, was below.

While the men pushed to get out of his way, Captain Diaz raced the length of the deck and plunged down the narrow ladder into the forecastle. Water was already deepening around the chests and the lower bunks. The whaler's huge stem timber, as thick as the base of the mainmast, had escaped damage. But to starboard of the stem the timbers and planks bulged into the forecastle, their wet surfaces glinting as the captain held an oil lantern up to inspect the damage.

Three of the bow timbers and most of the planking around them were broken and forced inward. The timbers were made of the hardest oak, a foot thick, but they were snapped like kindling. They and the planking were now only jagged edges jutting into the forecastle, rimmed by the inner planking which was also broken and heaved inward. Through this jumbled wreckage flowed a steady stream of water—but not the torrent that Captain Diaz had feared. The only thing that kept the sea from rushing in and filling the ship in minutes was her copper sheathing. Fastened to the hull in overlapping patterns to ward off barnacles and the wood-boring teredo worm, the copper sheathing had now helped absorb the blow. It had bent inward with the impact, but it had held.

How long would it hold? Captain Diaz knew that the first big wave they hit might break this thin layer between them and the sea. Certainly any rough weather would force the thin plates apart, now that the wood to which they had been nailed was broken away. All that could be done was to stuff the huge gap with everything they could (being careful not to burst the sheathing), seal it in place with some new planking and hope it would keep out the sea until they could reach port.

But port was 750 miles away, and at the moment the water had flooded the forecastle so that the ship had started to settle by the bow. At Captain Diaz' order the broken wood was ripped away and the gaping hole was stuffed with canvas and hemp, held in place by new planking. The steady flood dropped to a trickle, but Diaz knew that the leak would increase again as soon as the patching became thoroughly soaked.

The patching job was finished just in time, though. At least now the thin copper sheathing was supported against the force of heavier seas, which rose by next morning. They came with a strong breeze out of the southwest, which permitted the captain to set his course directly north northeast for the nearest port, Rio de Janeiro. All that day and the next the crippled *Pocahontas* plowed along toward her destination while, watch on watch, the men kept the pumps going. At first it took about eight thousand strokes every twenty-four hours to keep ahead of the water pushing through the patched-up hole; this slowly increased to ten thousand strokes. Everyone prayed that they would not run into a real storm. By the second day, December 14, the breezes were accompanied by rain and a few squalls. But the squalls passed before any seas piled up, and the patches held. The wind increased next day, so much that the topgallants had to be furled. The leak increased a little more, but the weather soon moderated. By the seventeenth there was little wind, and the whaler carried full sail. And with more moderate weather the flooding diminished slightly.

But the breezes died to almost nothing. On the eighteenth, after nearly a week of nursing his wounded ship toward port and safety, Captain Diaz began to show the strain. The calm made everything more frustrating. It was a hopeless feeling to pace the broad deck of the whaleship from side to side, waiting for a breeze and seeing no sign of one, watching the empty sails slat and listening to the yards creak back and forth—all to the ceaseless accompaniment of the wheezing pumps. In a way this was worse than fighting through heavy weather, pumping for everyone's life but at least making progress toward a safe port. Captain Diaz wrote in the log as part of his entry for December 18: "I take a book and try to read, but I can't keep my mind on the subject more than a minute at a time. . . ." The man everyone called "the young captain" was growing up fast.

Late that day a light breeze came from the east. But just as the *Pocahontas* started to make time again, the increasing wind hauled around to the north. The bluff-bowed, stubby-rigged whaleship could not sail efficiently much closer than ninety degrees, particularly since Captain Diaz did not dare let his patched bow take the increasingly heavy seas head on. So the ship had to wear off to the west, then come about and sail east, making practically no progress toward Rio. For three days this kept up. On the fourth day of head winds the seas grew higher and the leak increased. Captain Diaz wrote in the log: "Took in topgallantsails and single-reefed the topsails. Ship heading E by S. If this is not enough to make a man curse, I don't know what is. . . ."

By next day, December 22, the wind had died a bit. But by that evening it was gone altogether. Again the whaler wallowed back and forth, her sails slatting hopelessly. Next morning the sun rose orange-red over a glassy sea. Everywhere men grumbled; a few were sick. All were exhausted from the long hours at the pumps. But still the pumps were the only signs of life on the ship. And much as every man hated his turn at them, every man grew nervous when they paused for too long at a changing of the watch. The rhythmic wheezing of the pumps, almost like the human heart, made the difference between life and death for the ship and for her crew. And so the immobile whaleship with her sucking pumps sat off the coast of Brazil while her helpless captain hoped for the breath of breeze that could save them all.

In twelve days, with the nights as bad as days, they had come only two-thirds of the way—five hundred miles, a good three-day run by a merchant ship. And Captain Diaz well knew that the makeshift patch in his ship's bow could not hold out much longer. Under the pressure of the steady stream of water the canvas and hemp were rotting and wearing away. The heavy seas of the past few days must have weakened the copper sheathing, if it had not already broken through. And how long could the pumps work before some part broke? Then would they be able to make repairs fast enough, or would the water finally get ahead of them? As he pondered these possibilities, Captain Diaz had reason to conclude that the *Pocahontas* was indeed an unlucky ship.

But if the *Pocahontas* was unlucky, her captain was not. There were those aboard the whaler superstitious enough to believe that it was Captain Diaz' luck that did it—because it happened that he had been born on Christmas Day. And now, on Christmas Eve, at 6 P.M., as the captain noted in the log, a breeze at last came up. It was fresh out of the southwest, exactly what the *Pocahontas* needed for a straight run to Rio.

The wind held fair, and at 10 A.M. on Christmas Day Captain Joseph Diaz, Jr., celebrated his twenty-ninth birthday by sighting land. Now the *Pocahontas* raced forward. The winds grew stronger and the rain came in squalls. But no one minded the discomfort as the whaleship closed the last miles to her port.

There remained a final frustration. At the very entrance to Rio's harbor the winds, still mixed with squalls, swung around and blew into the *Pocahontas'* path. All the day of the twenty-sixth the weary whalemen tacked the ship back and forth without making the harbor. By late afternoon the winds died; now they sat outside the harbor, as helpless as they had been while trying to fight their way in against the wind. When a breeze did come up, from the southwest for a fine run into the harbor, it was too late and dark to risk the entrance.

But the night of the twenty-sixth was the last test of the *Pocahontas'* and her crew's endurance. By eleven-thirty the next morning the fat, weather-beaten whaler, now leaking nearly five hundred strokes an hour, came creaking safely to rest at anchor in six fathoms of water in Rio Harbor.

Little is known about the career of the *Pocahontas* after her encounter with the big whale and her trying run for safety. Within five months she had been repaired and had rounded Cape Horn. In the Pacific, off the coast of Chile, she rejoined the *Ann Alexander*. For nearly a week they cruised together; the *Ann Alexander* had most of the luck. On May 2, 1851, they parted, and the *Pocahontas* sailed off into obscurity. Not the *Ann Alexander:* she is remembered because four months later her crew was rescued after she had been rammed by a whale and sent to the bottom of the Pacific.

XI

Clipper Ship: The FLYING CLOUD

The port and the shipbuilder . . . Golden decade . . . "Blood boats" . . . Lane for Cape Horn . . . "Set all possible sails" . . . "Ship very wet fore and aft" . . . The still unbeaten record . . . The age of sail ends

Built for freight, and yet for speed,
A beautiful and gallant craft;
Broad in the beam, that the stress of the blast,
Pressing down upon sail and mast,
Might not the sharp bows overwhelm;
Broad in the beam, but sloping aft
With graceful curve and slow degrees,
That she might be docile to the helm,
And that the currents of parted seas,
Closing behind, with mighty force,
Might aid and not impede her course.

In the shipyard stood the Master,
With the model of the vessel,
That should laugh at all disaster,
And with wave and whirlwind wrestle!

A frequent visitor to the shipyard of Donald McKay in East Boston, Massachusetts, in the 1850's was Henry Wadsworth Longfellow. Often the poet came to the yard to relax, to talk with his friend McKay and to watch the construction of McKay's clipper ships. It was after one of his visits that Longfellow started to write these lines, as part of his famous poem "The Building of the Ship."

Because his poem was also a comment on the ship of state and the storms it faced, Longfellow gave the ship in his poem the symbolic name of *Union*. But, as we know from the owner of the ship McKay was building at the time, Longfellow was celebrating the construction of a particular clipper. Perhaps with his poet's eye for beauty he could see that the lines of this clipper ship would make her one of the most famous in history. She was to be the *Flying Cloud*.

Indeed her name might have come from Longfellow. But it did not;

it evidently came from George Francis Train, junior partner of
Enoch Train & Company, who commissioned her. Other sources indicate that McKay himself said, "We will call her the *Flying Cloud*."
Whether Train or McKay named her, it was Train who made a decision he was to regret for the rest of his life. The clipper was still
on the stocks in the East Boston yard when some New York shipping
representatives dropped by to see her. Even on the stocks she was an
impressive sight. Made of the finest oak and pine, she was 208 feet
long at the keel, 235 feet over-all; only a few years previously anything 130 feet long had been regarded as a big ship. The *Flying
Cloud*'s beam was only 41 feet, narrow for a ship so long. The depth
of her hold was 21½ feet, and she was planned to register at 1,793
tons. Perhaps at this point in her construction her figurehead—a
winged angel blowing a trumpet—had not been completed, and certainly her towering masts had not yet been stepped. But to the
practical eyes of the scouts from New York, this was a ship with great
potential, and so they reported to their bosses in New York.

Their bosses were the partners in the big shipping firm of Grinnell-
Minturn & Company. Robert B. Minturn was wealthy and public-
spirited; he served as New York's Commissioner of Emigration, and
his wife is credited with originating the idea of establishing Central
Park. Minturn's partner, Moses H. Grinnell, was a canny business
gambler, as indicated by how he acted on his scouts' report. He went
straight to the East Boston yard, studied the sleek, fast lines of the
new ship and asked Enoch Train & Company how much they wanted
for her. The answer was ninety thousand dollars. Grinnell replied,
"We will take her." This was a 100 per cent profit for Enoch Train
& Company. It was a considerable gamble for Grinnell-Minturn &
Company. Until recently no ship over a thousand tons had been
built, and most shipbuilders were convinced that this was as far as
they could go with wood; anything larger would weaken under the
stresses of a long, pounding sea voyage. But this 1,793-ton gamble
more than paid off for Grinnell-Minturn & Company, as we shall see.

The *Flying Cloud* was built for challenging times. American shipping, which had been growing and prospering ever since the War
of 1812, was now entering its golden age. The centuries-long history

of sailing ship design, not only in America but in all the world, reached its culmination in these clippers. Such ships had not been dreamed of by naval architects from the time of the Vikings to the yacht, *America*. Such ships would never be seen again. And of all the great clippers built during this brief decade, none surpassed the *Flying Cloud*.

The challenge came from around Cape Horn. When gold was discovered in California in 1848, the fever rapidly spread east. Immediately there was a huge demand for ships; the voyage around Cape Horn was arduous enough, but it was better, at least faster, than the grueling trek overland or even the trip across the Isthmus of Panama. Still the voyage from New York to San Francisco took an average of 150 days—almost half a year. But the tales of fabulous wealth discovered in the gold fields of California made it worth the voyage for the ever-increasing hordes of Easterners. The demand for ships was tremendous, and the faster the ship, the greater the demand.

The *Flying Cloud* was not the first ship to fill this demand. First came the famous clipper *Rainbow*, built by Designer John Griffiths for the Howland and Aspinwall firm for the China run. When the experts first saw her on the stocks and studied her sharp bows, so different from the bluff lines of contemporary merchant ships, they predicted that the *Rainbow* would plunge into the first big wave and never come up. Even her owners delayed her completion for a year while they fussed over the tall masts and great spreads of canvas planned for her. But on her first voyage, to China on February 1, 1845, less than two weeks after her launching, she sailed so fast and well that her captain, John Land, announced, "The ship couldn't be built to beat her." This boast led to the second famous clipper. Another skipper in the Howland and Aspinwall stable was the colorful Robert Waterman, and "Bully" Waterman, as he was known because of the way he handled his crews, asked Howland and Aspinwall to build him a clipper too. Waterman was a "driver," and even in 1845 it was obvious that speed was becoming more and more important. So Howland and Aspinwall commissioned the *Sea Witch*, another Griffiths-designed clipper which was launched in 1846. Bully Waterman brought her back from Canton in seventy-seven days, a

record that has never been equaled under sail. The premium the shippers were able to charge for delivering the season's first cargo of
perishable tea so quickly indicated that the *Sea Witch* would shortly
prove an extremely profitable investment.

Donald McKay promptly proved that point when he decided to
follow Griffiths' lead. McKay designed and built the *Stag Hound*,
his first clipper. She was long and lean and spread more than eight
thousand yards of canvas. The marine underwriters charged extra
premiums to insure her; and in fact her main topmast and all three
topgallant masts were blown down by a gale when she was only six
days out. But she raced on to California, making the run from New
York to San Francisco in 113 days, an impressive record alongside
the average 150-day voyages. From California she sped on to Manila
and Canton to load tea, and then she came winging home to New
York. There she demonstrated that speed paid off. After this one
voyage of less than eleven months, her owners paid for her and split
eight thousand dollars' profit.

No wonder then that McKay was busily building another clipper
even before the *Stag Hound* set sail. But it was this second clipper
that was to be his greatest. This one was the *Flying Cloud*.

> Choose the timbers with greatest care;
> Of all that is unsound beware;
> For only what is sound and strong
> To this vessel shall belong.
> Cedar of Maine and Georgia pine
> Here together shall combine.

The best materials went into the new clipper—but it was another
element that made her symbolize all the finest clippers of the golden
age. This element was the genius of Donald McKay. Normally it is
the skipper who is most credited with a great ship's performance—
Columbus aboard the *Niña*, Nelson aboard the *Victory*. And Captain
Josiah Perkins Cressy had much to do with the *Flying Cloud*'s record
speeds. But Cressy is no longer remembered as McKay is, and McKay
it is who deserves most of the credit.

He was born in Shelburne, Nova Scotia, on September 4, 1810. His grandfather, a British Army officer, came from Ross County, Scotland, and emigrated to Nova Scotia after the American Revolution. Donald's father was a farmer, and Donald was one of eighteen children. As a boy he showed little interest in the farm, and spent most of his time on Shelburne's Jordan Bay with his younger brother Lauchlan. When Donald was in his early teens the two brothers built their own fishing boat. And Donald was only sixteen when he left Nova Scotia to travel a thousand miles through stormy seas on a Halifax coaster to New York, there to search for a job in a shipyard.

He quickly found work in the yard of Isaac Webb, who later became known as the "Father of Shipbuilders" because so many famous designers started their careers working for him. By 1827 McKay had signed an indenture as an apprentice to Webb, for four and a half years at forty dollars a year. By the time he was twenty-one he was a qualified shipwright and could command $1.25 for a fifteen-hour day, starting at 4:30 A.M. and running to 7:30 P.M. (with an hour off for breakfast and two hours off for dinner at noon). In 1832 McKay married Albenia Boole, daughter of a well-to-do shipbuilder and an expert ship draftsman herself. McKay's rise in the profession was marred only temporarily, when he was employed as a foreman at the Brooklyn Navy Yard and the native Americans under him bullied him out of the yard because he was a "foreigner." Partly because of this the McKay family, now including a five-year-old son, moved to Maine, where McKay promptly introduced New York modernization to the yards of Wiscasset. By 1840 McKay had saved enough money to buy a partnership in a firm in Newburyport, Massachusetts, and within a year the performance of the vessels from the firm of Currier & McKay was the talk of shipping circles. Within five years McKay had his own shipyard in East Boston. He was thirty-four years old. And he was about to prove himself the master builder of America's greatest ships during America's greatest shipbuilding age.

When Donald McKay's *Flying Cloud* sailed into New York Harbor, the signs of that golden age were already apparent everywhere. Rows of tall masts lined every pier. South Street, along the waterfront, was an arch of bowsprits, under which wagons rumbled over the cobbles, rushing cargoes to big ships from whose foreyards hung banners proclaiming "FOR CALIFORNIA." In 1847 no more than thirteen vessels had sailed to San Francisco from all Atlantic ports; and nine of these were whalers. But in 1849 New York alone sent 214 vessels out to San Francisco. By the following year, when the *Flying Cloud* loaded for California, the rush was even greater. Only a very few were clippers like her, and they could be picked out instantly—long, slim-waisted and towering above the pierside warehouses and all the ships around them. This was a new type of ship altogether, a far cry from the fat East Indiamen that carried one-sixth the amount of sail and furled that sail every night at sea. The clippers were the new aristocrats. Already a few of them dominated New York Harbor, just as a few dozen of them would dominate the oceans of the world in the next decade, a short, dramatic period of history that would henceforth be known as the "clipper ship era." The *Flying Cloud* was the apotheosis of a new fleet of ships that were to alter the course of U.S. maritime history. The fast, stable clippers affected passenger traffic not only to California but also to Australia, to the Orient and the packet lines of the "railroad route to Europe." The clippers changed the seagoing freight rates of the world by providing such fast passages that they could carry less than half the cargo of their predecessors and charge far more than twice as much in premiums. The clippers, by their sheer beauty, transformed ship design throughout the world. But the clippers also provided a paradox: they were known as the "queens of the sea"; they were also known as the "blood boats."

The reason was that they came on the scene about a generation too late. Perhaps if Donald McKay and Isaac Webb and John Griffiths and the other master builders had been born thirty years earlier, the world would not have waited for clippers until nearly 1850. Perhaps if gold had been discovered in California right after the War of 1812 instead of in 1849, other men would have filled the shipping vacuum as McKay and his colleagues did at mid-century. But the times and the men coincided at a point when every element was right except one. And that element was a vital one: the crew.

Until the 1820's the forecastles of American ships were inhabited by some of the best youth of America. To go to sea, especially in the footsteps of a father or uncle, was a highly honorable career throughout New England and much of the rest of the U.S. Most ship captains of these days were men who had "come in at the hawse-hole" (started as ordinary seamen) and not "through the cabin window" (appointed to the office). They worked hard and obeyed orders for little pay because they knew they stood a good chance of rising rapidly to command. Many of the best captains were in their thirties, and a few were in their twenties; most of them had started as cabin boys or foremast hands in their early teens. But as the opening of the West offered more tempting opportunities, more of the best young men forsook the sea. As America looked west and inland, the ship-owners made the mistake of not trying to compete; wages stayed the same, or even fell lower. The forecastles filled with larger percent-ages of waterfront scum, men who could not hold jobs anywhere else. Confronted with loafers and rebellious crewmen, the skippers adopted harsher discipline. So the vicious circle completed itself, until by the mid-nineteenth century the situation was beyond remedy.

In 1803 the average foremast hand's wage was ten dollars a month. This was low enough to precipitate a badly organized sailors' strike in New York, which did little more than erupt into a bloody riot be-tween marching strikers and city police. By the 1850's, with the big clippers requiring many more hands, the wage was down to eight dollars. And by that time the clipper ship era was producing so many good jobs ashore that even fewer men wanted to go to sea.

They went, though—mainly because of the "agent," who dealt with the boardinghouse crimps and the whores and asked no questions about the drunken or drugged bodies that were produced at sailing time. Many a seaman, and many a young man who had never been to sea, awoke after a New York binge to find himself in the forecastle of a clipper. He had no money, and in fact his first three months' wages had gone to the agent. After he had recovered from hangover and seasickness, he was forced further in debt by having to purchase his jumper, sea boots and sou'wester at an outrageous markup from the ship's "slop chest." No wonder that he was in a mutinous mood, and no wonder that the skipper turned, reluctantly or not, to the "bucko mate" to beat the new men into submission. The "cat," the iron belaying pin, the "persuader" (a stick with a nail projecting from its tip) were the normal methods employed. So it was always a taut ship, and often a near-mutinous one, that sailed down to the screaming gales off Cape Horn and up to San Francisco in the clipper ship era.

The same "Shanghai method" was usually employed at San Francisco, since most of a clipper's crew disappeared ashore and dashed for the gold fields. And those who returned to New York were met, even before the ship reached dock, by the agents who swarmed aboard the clipper from their own boats. Seizing what luggage the sailor had, they led him to another "boardinghouse," featuring the usual bar, dance hall, and "hostesses" who could tear a man limb from limb. Some clipper ship captains fought off these agents, occasionally having to shoot them off the ship's rails. Once the shipowners banded together to try to stop the practice and refused to sign on any man provided by the agents. For two weeks the ships sat at the piers, unable to sail because not enough hands could be found to work ship. Then the shipowners gave in and the agents and their crimps became even more entrenched.

Another factor, of course, was the tide of immigration. Here was a vast supply of cheap foreign labor. While the young Americans whose fathers had once gone to sea now went west, the clipper ship forecastles filled with the worst elements from abroad, the wharf rats, the bums and the criminals who could not even get jobs in New England and New York factories. Congress tried to cope with the phenomenon by passing a law requiring two-thirds of an American ship's crew to be American citizens. But few shipowners paid any attention to the law. (Captain Arthur H. Clark, the famous clipper captain who later wrote *The Clipper Ship Era*, says that he had a Chinese cook who signed on as "George Harrison of Charlestown, Mass.")

It was because of crews like this that the most successful clipper ship captains became known as bullies as well as drivers. Captain "Bully" Waterman had earned his nickname on earlier voyages aboard such clippers as the *Sea Witch*, before he took the clipper ship *Challenge* out of New York in 1851. But he had reason to show how tough he could be before he reached San Francisco on the quarterdeck of the *Challenge*. His crew consisted of fifty-six men and eight boys, only two of whom were Americans. A search of the forecastle produced so many pistols, bowie knives, knuckle-dusters and bottles of rum that Waterman seriously considered returning to New York. But the prospect of facing the shipowners after forcing them to lose three months' wages on an entire crew was enough to make Waterman decide to continue on around Cape Horn. Only six of the crew could handle the helm. Half of the men had had no sailing experience whatever, and had enlisted only to get to the gold fields. At one point seventeen of the crew were incapacitated by venereal disease in its late stages; five died of it. Four of the crew attacked the first mate with knives and cut him up badly before Waterman came to the rescue. He laid about them with an iron belaying pin, with such effect that two of the attackers died. Waterman sent the "free passengers" out onto the yards with the others, and three of them fell to their deaths off Cape Horn. As usual, Waterman kept padlocks on the main sheets, to make sure no fainthearted landlubber would cast loose because he thought the ship was carrying too much canvas. When the *Challenge* reached San Francisco on October 29, 108 days from New York, the surviving crew members rounded up an extemporaneous "Vigilance Committee" which went looking for Waterman with the announced purpose of lynching him. Waterman demanded a formal investigation and was exonerated and commended for bringing the mutinous ship in safely.

Nearly as well known as "Bully" Waterman was "Joe" Cressy, Josiah Perkins Cressy (sometimes spelled "Creesy" because his name was pronounced that way). Where Waterman was handsome and flamboyant, Cressy was plain and taciturn. And while Cressy never earned the nickname "Bully," he was not regarded as a soft touch. He had come up the hard way; after learning to sail on the waters off Marblehead, his birthplace, he shipped out on an East Indiaman and worked his way up through the ranks until he was a captain at twenty-three and was given command of the China tea clipper *Oneida*. He drove her so hard that he made her famous. Now he was rewarded with the *Flying Cloud*, at the age of thirty-seven.

Not a great deal of attention was paid to the *Flying Cloud* as she
set sail after sail and picked up speed down New York Harbor on
June 3, 1851. She was a beautiful sight, with studding sails, royals
and skysails set as she flashed past Sandy Hook. But the few watchers
on shore who saw her off never expected that she would make the
record she did on this maiden voyage.

The breeze was westerly and the sea an early summer blue as the
Flying Cloud reached the open ocean. Captain Cressy set her course,
on a sweeping arc from Cape Horn. The best sailing route was not due
south; this had been discovered by the researches of Lieutenant
Matthew Fontaine Maury, who was known as the "Pathfinder of the
Seas." For years Maury had studied the logs of sailing vessels, and
by comparing their best passages had compiled what he called "lanes"
—the fastest routes across the oceans of the world. Captain Cressy
now set his course on the "lane" for Cape Horn. Or perhaps Mrs.
Cressy did this; she always accompanied her husband on his voyages,
and was herself a skilled navigator.

Before the day was out the westerly had freshened to near gale
force. But Captain Cressy kept all except the studding sails and skysails set. The *Flying Cloud* dipped her lee rail under. White foam
raced across her port deck. Her masts began to creak with the strain.
But her beautiful hull sliced through the seas and slid straight down
her course. Then came trouble.

She was three days out when the squall suddenly caught her. Here
was one of the major dangers to these lofty ships. Because of their
sleek hulls and soaring masts, the conservatives expected the clippers
to be driven right under the waves. Like the other clippers, the
Flying Cloud drove through instead of up and over the heavy seas.
But she did not go under. Her vulnerability, as with the other clippers, was in her top hamper. Because Cressy was a driver and kept
her plunging along on the very edge of trouble, she could not absorb
the sudden slam of the squall.

Before sail could be shortened, there was a crackling smash as the
Flying Cloud lost her maintopsail yard and her main and mizzen topgallant masts. While Captain Cressy and the first mate bellowed above
the howl of the wind, all hands swarmed on deck and into the rigging

to chop away the tangle of shrouds before the big spars plunging alongside could punch a hole in the *Flying Cloud*'s side. But Cressy would not permit any slackening of the sail that remained. As the masts, two of them broken off at the top, groaned under the strain, the *Flying Cloud* flew on, toward Cape Horn and California. And immediately Cressy set the men to work fashioning new topgallant masts and yards. While the clipper roared down her course, her sails still pulling strongly, the new spars were hoisted and fitted in place. Captain Cressy laconically noted in the log: "June 6—Lost maintopsail-yard and main and mizzen topgallant masts. June 7—Sent up topgallant masts and yards. June 8—Sent up maintopsail yard, and set all possible sails." Within forty-eight hours the *Flying Cloud* was repaired and racing along faster than ever.

But other troubles arose. On June 14, eleven days out, Cressy discovered that the squall had also sprung the mainmast; he quickly had it repaired. Then came near-calms. The *Flying Cloud* seemed to do well in light airs too; with virtually no wind she ghosted along, crossing the Equator only twenty-one days out.

The squall, the frightening work atop the masts at breakneck speed, and then the nerve-racking calm began to tell on the *Flying Cloud*'s crew. A mutiny nearly erupted. But it never got started; Cressy promptly clapped the leaders in irons.

The *Flying Cloud*'s real test was yet to come. Would her lean hull cut through or plunge too deeply under the huge seas off Cape Horn? Would the repaired spars stand up under the squalls off the Cape? Would the sails hold out against the sleet-laden winds that lashed this forbidding area near the bottom of the world? Many a ship bound for California was never reported on the other side of Cape Horn. And the new, radically designed, untried *Flying Cloud*, with an unseamanlike crew and many of them in irons, might well become another entry on the missing list.

The battle started with thunder and lightning storms on July 11, as the *Flying Cloud* raced along the Argentine coast. Captain Cressy was impressed enough by the storm to douse the royals and topgallants. Soon the clipper was dipping and plunging along under close-reefed topsails. The roaring winds split two staysails. The sea piled higher, sending green mountains the length of the *Flying Cloud*'s deck. The gale screamed at the ship and sent her reeling from side to side. Then, at 1 P.M., a crewman reported to Captain Cressy that the mainmast had sprung again.

Cressy shortened no more sail. Instead he ordered the yards and booms lowered from atop the sprung mainmast, to relieve the pressure on it until it could be repaired in calmer waters.

Next day the *Flying Cloud* battled gales out of the southwest, right in her teeth, and made only forty miles in twenty-four hours. By the thirteenth, officers and men were so weary and storm-battered that Cressy ordered the mutinous crewmen released from their irons. Summoning them aft, he tersely told them: work or drown. They worked, especially a few hours later when the gales swept away more gear and the sailors had to go aloft to make more repairs. By the nineteenth, as the *Flying Cloud* reached 50 degrees South Latitude, the wind direction had changed; but its force was undiminished, and the clipper raced along under single-reefed topsails. By July 20 the gales brought thick snow. By 8 A.M. on the twenty-third the clipper soared past Cape Horn, which Cressy could see only five miles away; the black rock stood out starkly against the coastline back of it, which was blanketed with snow. And by July 26 the *Flying Cloud* went running north past 50 degrees again—she had rounded Cape Horn in only seven days.

A week later Captain Cressy was writing in the log: "Fresh breezes and fine weather. All sail set." But by six that evening another squall had struck. The lower and topgallant studding sails were quickly taken in, and no harm was done. The winds increased hour by hour. By 7 P.M. Cressy had to order the royals furled. By 2 A.M. the foretopmast studding sails had to come down. Still the wind came on stronger and the *Flying Cloud* ran faster. Cressy noted: ". . . strong gales and high sea running, ship very wet fore and aft." During some of the squalls the line measuring the clipper's speed registered its full limit of eighteen knots. And when the distance for the twenty-four-hour period was calculated, even Cressy found it hard to believe.

They had raced 374 miles—an *average* of more than fifteen knots. It would be twenty-three years before an oceangoing steamship achieved this speed. Few freighters can do it even today; and the *Flying Cloud* was a freighter.

The wind moderated only slightly, but enough for Cressy to order topgallants set. Next day more gales forced the *Flying Cloud* down to double-reefed fore and mizzen topsails. That day she ran 334 miles. Up the west coast she went, every spar straining and every sail thundering. Then, on August 29, the foretopgallant mast went crashing over the side. Captain Cressy knew that they were only two or three days away from San Francisco; but still he ordered a new foretopgallant mast stepped, the sailors fighting to secure it atop the foremast while the ship bucked and plunged under them and the spray reached up toward them. By next day the job was done. And by eleven-thirty that morning the *Flying Cloud* went flying through the Golden Gate—*eighty-nine days and twenty-one hours from New York.*

This was about two-thirds the time that most ships had taken for the sixteen-thousand-mile voyage which Pathfinder Maury called "the longest and most tedious within the domains of commerce . . . It tries the patience of the navigator, and taxes his energies to the very utmost. . . . It is a great race-course, upon which some of the most beautiful trials of speed the world ever saw have come off." During the next decade hundreds of fast clippers would try to beat the *Flying Cloud*'s mark, some of them half again as big as she, and many of them designed by Donald McKay. But none ever matched it. The record remained to be broken by the *Flying Cloud* herself when, in 1854, she cut it down by half a day: eighty-nine days, eight hours. On this voyage she left nine days after the fast clipper ship *Archer*, caught up with her off Cape Horn, where Cressy passed on the latest news, rapidly left her astern and went on to reach California nine days ahead of her. The only challenge to the *Flying Cloud*'s record was made by the clipper *Andrew Jackson*, which made the voyage in ninety days, twelve hours. (The *Andrew Jackson*'s owners claimed a record of eighty-nine days, four hours; but the correct time, anchor to anchor, was ninety days, twelve hours. From pilot to pilot, the *Andrew Jackson*'s time was eighty-nine days, twenty hours, but this time did not match the *Flying Cloud*'s even on her first voyage, since she picked up her pilot a few hours before dropping anchor, and her anchor-to-anchor time was eighty-nine days, twenty-one hours.)

> Removed beyond the evening chill,
> The father sat and told them tales
> Of wrecks in the great September gales,
> Of pirates coasting the Spanish Main,
> And ships that never came back again,
> The chance and change of a sailor's life,
> Want and plenty, rest and strife,
> His roving fancy, like the wind,
> That nothing can stay and nothing can bind,
> And the magic charm of foreign lands,
> With shadows of palms, and shining sands,
> Where the tumbling surf,
> O'er the coral reefs of Madagascar,
> Washes the feet of the swarthy Lascar,
> As he lies alone and asleep on the turf.

On across the Pacific went the *Flying Cloud* after her first run to California. This time she went to Canton to load tea. Though she was left short-handed by crew members who deserted her for the gold mines, she posted another 374-mile day's run the first day out of San Francisco. At Canton she loaded her tea and set out for home, making the run to Java Head in six days, half the previous record time. She came slicing through the waters of Sandy Hook on April 10, 1852, only ninety-four days from Canton.

New York went wild. The *Flying Cloud*'s wrecked top hamper was taken in triumph to the Astor House and put on exhibit. Captain Cressy became a national hero. The *Flying Cloud*'s log was printed in gold on silk for distribution to the public. And in the shipyard of Donald McKay, where he was busy on even bigger and sharper clippers, the orders poured in. Every shipper wanted a copy of the *Flying Cloud*.

The clipper ship fever now reached its height. Down the ways they slid—the *Challenge* and the *Comet*, the *Sword-Fish* and the *Flying Dutchman*, the *Young America* and the *Neptune's Car*. Some were fully rigged, even to skysail yards, while still on the stocks, then rushed to the piers in New York Harbor where the premium cargoes waited for them. But the best clippers still were made in East Boston, in the shipyard of Donald McKay. All bore his hallmark of beauty and speed; even their names breathed the element that set them apart—the *Flying Fish*, the *Sovereign of the Seas*, the *Westward Ho*, the *Lightning*, the *Romance of the Seas*. In the entire clipper ship era only twenty-two passages were made around Cape Horn to California in fewer than one hundred days; seven of them were made by McKay ships, two of which, the *Flying Cloud* and the *Flying Fish*, did it twice. The only competitors to come close were Samuel Hall of Boston and Jacob Westervelt of New York, each of whom produced two ships that made this fast a passage.

So the *Flying Cloud* epitomized an era that was as exciting, beautiful—and fleeting—as the ship herself. Like the dozens of racers that followed her, she continued to make breathless passages to California and the Orient. But, as with the other clippers, her time rapidly ran out. Californians began producing their own needs, and the hordes of "Forty-Niners" dwindled as the gold fields were scratched clean. Many of the clipper ships were tried on normal runs, but they were not profitable where speed did not command a huge premium. By the mid-fifties even Donald McKay was building medium clippers— with the same sharp bows but with broader, more capacious beam and less sail area. By the late fifties the racers were racing no more.

Many ran themselves to death; the *Rainbow* dashed into the gales off Cape Horn and never came out; the *Sovereign of the Seas* ran onto Pyramid Shoal in the Straits of Malacca and was wrecked. Others drifted into demeaning, even dishonorable, trade: the *Sea Witch* carried guano, and went aground on the coast of Cuba while transporting a cargo of coolies; the *Nightingale* was captured as a slaver. But the *Flying Cloud* still raced on for a while. Her skipper, Captain Cressy, retired to Salem, returning to service for a while during the

Civil War and to make two more voyages to China in the *Archer*, the clipper he had beaten so handily with the *Flying Cloud*. By the time Cressy died, in 1871 at the age of fifty-seven, the *Flying Cloud* was still fighting the steamers. Now she was running to Australia, under the British flag as a packet ship of James Baine's Black Ball Line. She was bought by Smith Edwards, a British shipowner with a fondness for clippers. In June, 1874, she went aground on the coast of New Brunswick, trying to get into Saint Johns. She was floated easily but while she was on the patent slip for repairs she caught fire. Still the *Flying Cloud* did not die. A Saint Johns merchant used her in the timber trade for a while. Then what were left of her lofty spars were dismasted, and she was used as a lighter in Saint Johns Harbor. Her rotting hulk was last seen in the backwaters of the harbor in the 1920's. Eventually the *Flying Cloud* simply disintegrated. With her death the sailing ship as such died too.

Donald McKay once said, "I never yet built a vessel that came up to my own ideal." But none came closer to the ideal than the *Flying Cloud*. She expressed, in the words of Samuel Eliot Morison, "the long-suppressed artistic impulse of a practical, hard-worked race. . . . The *Flying Cloud* was our Rheims. . . ."

Certainly none of the ships to come out of McKay yard after the fifties could compare with the *Flying Cloud*. Scotsman McKay adapted himself to the changing times. He built medium clippers. He turned out ironclads for the Union Navy. He built a few steamers. His last project was a fitting one: he repaired the racing yacht *America* (Chapter IX) after the Union Navy had saved her from being scuttled by the Confederates. Then, in 1875, the famous shipyard closed its gates. Donald McKay retired to a farm in Hamilton, Massachusetts, one much like the farm he had left behind at sixteen when he came to the United States to make his career as a shipbuilder. But this time too he was not long a farmer. On September 20, 1880, he died of consumption. He was buried atop a rise in Newburyport's Oak Hill Cemetery, in view of the seas off Massachusetts where the *Flying Cloud* had raced over the horizon, bound out for New York, Cape Horn, and history.

Thirty years before Donald McKay's death, his friend Longfellow had written, in the poem celebrating the *Flying Cloud:*

> Like unto ships far off at sea,
> Outward or homeward bound, are we.
> Before, behind, and all around,
> Floats and swings the horizon's bound,
> Seems at its distant rim to rise
> And climb the crystal wall of the skies,
> And then again to turn and sink,
> As if we could slide from its outer brink.
> Ah! It is not the sea,
> It is not the sea that sinks and shelves,
> But ourselves
> That rock and rise
> With endless and uneasy motion,
> Now touching the very skies,
> Now sinking into the depths of ocean.
> Ah! if our souls but poise and swing
> Like the compass in its brazen ring,
> Ever level and ever true
> To the toil and the task we have to do,
> We shall sail securely, and safely reach
> The Fortunate Isles, on whose shining beach
> The sights we see, and the sounds we hear,
> Will be those of joy and not of fear!

XII

"There Is No Frigate Like a Book"

—EMILY DICKINSON

Those of you who are still with me have realized by now that no single volume can do more than recount the highlights of the history of the sailing ship. Nor does this book attempt to satisfy the historian; it is intended for the amateur fan of maritime history (like myself). Both expert and student, however, may want to delve further into the history of the ships whose stories I have told. And for every example included in this book there are many others whose stories supply more detail, more background and more orientation. It is of course impossible to present here a complete bibliography of the sailing ship. But for those who might like to explore a bit more, herewith a listing of the books which I liked best and which I recommend for further reading.

There are countless general histories of the sailing ship. Those I found most interesting were:

Cherish the Sea; a History of Sail—by Jean de la Varende. A fascinating history of sail from earliest times to present, with emphasis on the maritime history of France, and with an intriguing account of the Battle of Trafalgar as seen from the Combined French-Spanish, rather than the British, side.

The Sailing Ship—by Romola and R. C. Anderson. A short but very full history, heavily illustrated.

The Sailing Ship—by Stanley Rogers. The craftsman's point of view, beautifully illustrated by an English marine artist who has been a historical adviser to the Royal Navy.

Oars, Sails and Steam—by Edwin Tunis. A picture history, complete and fascinating, embracing power as well as sail.

The Story of the Ship—by Charles E. Gibson.

The Way of a Ship; The Set of the Sails; By Way of Cape Horn; Falmouth for Orders—all by Alan Villiers. The best general-subject books by this justly famous author-sailor. No one now writing can bring a ship alive on paper as Alan Villiers can.

The best of the books on the Vikings are, in my opinion:
The Swan's Road—by Naomi Mitchison.
The Ultimate Viking—by Eric Linklater.
Leif Eriksson, Discoverer of America—by Edward F. Gray.
The Norsemen's Route from Greenland to Wineland—by H. P. Stunsby.
The Norse Discovery of America; Viking Tales of the North—both by R. B. Anderson.
The Viking Ships—by A. W. Brogger.
Seafaring and Shipping During the Viking Days—by Alexander Bugge.
A very full account of the early days of sail is *The Ancient Mariners*, by Lionel Casson. Other particularly good studies of particular eras:
The China Clippers—by Basil Lubbock.
Tall Ships to Cathay—by Helen Augur.
Yankee Ships in China Seas—by Daniel Henderson.
And of course no general history of sail can beat the famous *Maritime History of Massachusetts*, by Samuel Eliot Morison. Which leads us to:

The *Niña*.
Not only is the same Samuel Eliot Morison's *Admiral of the Ocean Sea* the classic work on Christopher Columbus, but it will undoubtedly remain so for all time. Admiral Morison's researches led him to every known source on Columbus; and not content with that, he formed the Harvard Expedition which actually sailed the course of the *Niña*, the *Pinta* and the *Santa Maria*. There are those who disagree with Morison's contention that Watlings Island was Columbus' New World landfall. Not me; none of the other candidates makes as convincing a claim as Morison, in my opinion.
Try first Morison's short one-volume *Christopher Columbus, Mariner*. This will whet your appetite for his larger one-volume *Admiral of the Ocean Sea*, and you will soon probably find yourself reading as well his definitive two-volume edition of the same book. When you have read Morison on Columbus, you will see how much any writer on the subject is in his debt. Certainly I could not have written my *Niña* chapter without the benefit of Morison's exhaustive studies. Other books helped, particularly the *Writings of Christopher Columbus*, edited by P. L. Ford; *The Great Age of Discovery*, by Paul Herrmann; and Columbus' *Journal of His First Voyage to America* (introduction by Van Wyck Brooks); this last is actually an abstract of the original journal, but much of it is evidently in Columbus' own words. None of these works, however, will give you as complete and authentic a picture of the historic voyage of the *Niña* as will the great works by Admiral Morison.

The *San Martín*.

What Morison has done for Columbus has nearly been matched by a magnificent study of the Spanish Armada. It is *The Armada*, by Garrett Mattingly, and it is an absorbing reconstruction of that little-understood battle. My narrative of the *San Martín* obviously owes much to this work. Another highly readable account is another journal, this one from the *San Martín* and titled *The Spanish Official Journal, Kept on Board the Duke of Medina-Sidonia's Ship*.

Also recommended:

The Spanish War, 1585-1587; Drake and the Tudor Navy—both by J. S. Corbett.

The Spanish Armada (Introduction by Captain Alfred T. Mahan)—by William Frederick Tilton. This detailed account is in *Century* magazine, Volume LVI (June, 1898).

The Age of Drake; Hawkins of Plymouth—both by J. A. Williamson.

And if you'd like a sample of British rejoicing over the defeat of the Armada, try *Eliza; a New Musical Entertainment*, which was performed in the Haymarket in celebration of the great victory; it was written by Richard Rolt.

But as with Morison on Columbus, nothing can compare with Mattingly on the Armada.

The *Revenge*.

The chief source of most pirate history is the famous *General History of . . . Pirates*, by Captain Charles Johnson, written in the eighteenth century. No one knows who Captain Johnson really was, and it was once the custom to accuse him of writing more fiction than history. But a great deal of independent research over the years has tended to confirm much of Johnson's *History*. Among the best of the more modern works are:

Jolly Roger—by Patrick Pringle. No single book on piracy can match this one.

The History of Piracy; The Pirates' Who's Who—by Philip Gosse.

The Great Days of Piracy in the West Indies—by George Woodbury.

The Age of Piracy—by Robert Carse.

Privateering and Piracy in the Colonial Period—by John F. Jameson.

And you might even like my book—*Pirate: Rascals of the Spanish Main*.

For particular detail on the pirates like Stede Bonnet who infested the Southern American coast, I'd recommend:

Our Own Pirates, Blackbeard and Bonnet—by Samuel Asche.

Piracy and the Middle Colonies—by Harriet L. Dallas.

Pirates of Colonial Virginia—by Lloyd H. Williams.

The Carolina Pirates—by S. C. Hughson.

And for a flavorsome book on the lore and the atmosphere of piracy, try the incomparable *On the Spanish Main,* by John Masefield.

The *Victory.*

The best possible source on this famous ship is the ship herself. She still sits at her dock in Portsmouth Harbor, England, and no one can go aboard her without being awed by the almost palpable sense of history all about her. Short of making this pilgrimage, there are some very good substitutes in the form of books on the ship and on her great commander, Lord Nelson. The best, in my opinion, are:

H.M.S. Victory—by Kenneth Fenwick.

The Story of H.M.S. Victory—by Geoffrey Callender.

Nelson's Victory—by Alexander Grant.

The Story of H.M.S. Victory—by F. W. Enghalm.

A Short History of H.M.S. Victory—by W. L. J. Wharton.

The Anatomy of Nelson's Ships—by C. N. Longridge.

The Life of Nelson—by Robert Southey. The early and famous biography, somewhat superseded now by such works as:

Victory, the Life of Lord Nelson—by Oliver Warner.

Nelson—by Carola Oman.

Nelson the Sailor—by Captain Russell Grenfell, R.N.

And for the Battle of Trafalgar, here are some of the best accounts:

Trafalgar—by Oliver Warner.

The Campaign of Trafalgar—by J. S. Corbett.

England Expects—by Dudley Pope.

The Year of Trafalgar—by H. Newbolt.

The Trafalgar Roll—by Col. R. H. MacKenzie.

There is, by the way, an excellent diorama of the Battle of Trafalgar in the Nelson Museum alongside the *Victory* at Portsmouth. And in Monmouth a Nelson fan named Percy Harris has constructed a wonderfully lifelike model of the battle. Mr. Harris built it for the Nelson Museum at Monmouth, where it should be installed by now.

The *Constellation.*

If you want to study the plans of this frigate, and of nearly every other famous American sailing ship, for that matter, don't miss Howard I. Chapelle's two masterpieces: *The History of the American Sailing Navy* and *The History of American Sailing Ships.* No study of American maritime history is complete without a careful reading of these two authoritative, exhaustive works. Nor should you overlook:

The Age of Fighting Sail—by C. S. Forester.

Naval War of 1812—by T. R. Roosevelt.

History of the United States Navy—by James Fenimore Cooper.

And for an excellent account of the *Constellation*'s battles against the *Insurgente* and the *Vengeance*, see Fletcher Pratt's highly readable *The Navy* and *Preble's Boys*.

The *Prince de Neufchâtel*.

Here too Chapelle has the plan of the *Prince*, in his *History of American Sailing Ships*. And the Cooper, Roosevelt, Forester and Pratt books mentioned above also have a lot of good reading on the privateers.

The privateers get the expected thorough coverage in Samuel Eliot Morison's *Maritime History of Massachusetts*. Some other recommended books on these ships, of which the *Prince* was only one of many, are:

History of the American Privateers—by George Coggeshall.

Privateers and Privateering—by Commander E. P. Stratham, R.N.

Colonial Ships and Sailors—by R. D. Paine.

History of American Privateers—by Edgard S. MacLay.

Logs of Baltimore Privateers—by William D. Hoyt.

There is also a novel which brings the *Prince*'s battle to life in an authoritative way; it is *Thread of Scarlet*, by Ben Ames Williams.

The *Amistad*.

One book on this slaver stands out from those I have read. It is *Slave Mutiny*, by William A. Owens. Other good books on the *Amistad* and on slavers in general are:

The Captives of the Amistad—by Simeon Baldwin.

A History of the Amistad Captives—by John Warner Barber.

The American Slave Trade—by John R. Spears.

Slave Ships and Slaving—by George Francis Dow.

Black Ivory—by Norman Collins.

The Navy and the Slave Trade—by Christopher Lloyd.

Rum, Romance and Rebellion—by Charles Taussig.

The Law of the Sea—by William McFee.

Adventures of an African Slaver—by Captain Theo. Canot.

Revelations of a Slave Smuggler—by Captain Richard Drake.

The *America*.

No book that I have seen gives as complete a history of this racing schooner as does *America*, by Herbert Stone. His *America's Cup Races* is also a full and lively account of all the attempts to win back the "mug."

There is a good account of the fluke that helped the *America* win, in

Yachting; a History, by Peter Heaton. And a couple of good books on the whole subject are:
The History of Yachting—by Arthur H. Clark.
Winning the King's Cup—by Helen G. Bell.

The *Pocahontas*.
The best single account of the *Pocahontas'* close call is in *The Long Harpoon*, by Arthur C. Watson. For the best and most thorough history of whaleships and whaling, try *The Sea Hunters*, by Edouard A. Stackpole. And if you are anywhere near Connecticut, go to the Mystic Marine Museum (of which Mr. Stackpole is Curator) and go aboard the *Charles W. Morgan*, the last of the American whaleships; like Nelson's *Victory*, the *Morgan* is moored for all to see, and is an unforgettable sight.
Another particularly good book on whaling is *Thar She Blows*, by Chester Howland. And a fine, highly readable contemporary record is *Whale Hunt*, by Nelson Cole Haley (who, incidentally, served aboard the *Morgan*). For an interesting account of Herman Melville's experiences as a whaleman, read *Melville in the South Seas*, by Charles R. Anderson. And you might try my own *Yankee Whalers in the South Seas;* besides covering the subject generally, it has a much fuller bibliography on whaling than this one can be.

The *Flying Cloud*.
There is no fuller—nor better—account of the great age of clipper ships than the classic *Clipper Ship Era*, by Arthur H. Clark. A close second is *Greyhounds of the Sea*, by Carl Cutler. And a full account of Donald McKay and his clippers, including the *Flying Cloud*, is the book with the resounding title: *Some Famous Sailing Ships and Their Builder Donald McKay*, by Richard C. McKay.
Other recommendations:
Clipper Ship Men—by Alexander Laing.
Yankee Ships—by Reese Wolfe.
The Reign of the Clipper—by Henry C. Brown.
Clipper Ships and Yachts—by Frank G. Griswold.
American Clipper Ships—by O. T. Howe.
Ships and Sailors—by William H. Clark.
And for an excellent chapter on the tea clippers, especially the *Cutty Sark*, try *The Way of a Ship*, by Alan Villiers.

You should enjoy all of these books. I am indebted to all of them, some much more than others. And I happily acknowledge my particular

debts—to Admiral Morison; to Professor Mattingly; to Alan Villiers; to
Patrick Pringle; to Carola Owen; to Oliver Warner; to Howard I.
Chapelle; to William A. Owens; to Hubert Stone; to Edouard A. Stackpole; to Chester Howland; to Carl Cutler; and to this book's illustrator,
Alex Little. But my biggest debt of all is to my wife Jane, who did so
much of the vast research such a book as this requires. Indeed there were
times when I was convinced that the real title of this book should have
been: *Jane's All the World's Sailing Ships.*

Old Greenwich, Conn.
March, 1960

INDEX

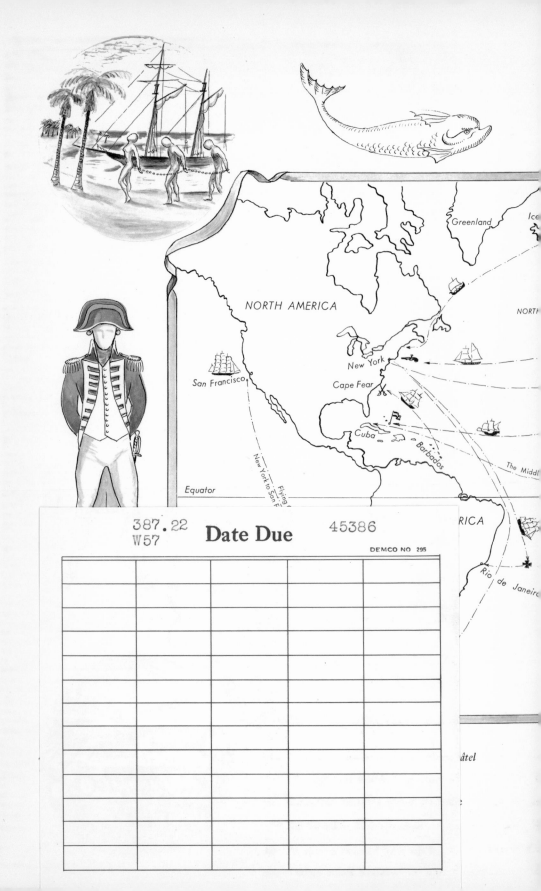

NORTH AMERICA

Greenland

Ice

NORTH

New York

San Francisco

Cape Fear

Cuba

Barbados

The Middl

New York to San F

Flying

Equator

RICA

Rio de Janeiro

âtel